STRATEGIC MARKETING MANAGEMENT

Alexander Chernev

Kellogg School of Management
Northwestern University

Seventh Edition

Strategic Marketing Management

Seventh Edition | August 2012

ISBN: 978-1-936572-15-1 (Paperback)

ISBN: 978-1-936572-16-8 (Hardcover)

TABLE OF CONTENTS

ABOUT THE AUTHOR

Alexander Chernev is a marketing professor at the Kellogg School of Management, Northwestern University. He holds a PhD in Psychology from Sofia University and a PhD in Business Administration from Duke University.

Dr. Chernev's research applies theories and concepts related to consumer behavior and managerial decision making to develop successful marketing strategies. He is an area editor for the *Journal of Marketing* and serves on the editorial boards of top research journals, including the *Journal of Marketing Research, Journal of Consumer Research, Journal of Consumer Psychology, Journal of the Academy of Marketing Science,* and *International Journal of Research in Marketing.* Dr. Chernev's research has been published in the leading marketing journals and has been frequently quoted in the business and popular press, including *Scientific American, Associated Press, Business Week, Forbes, Newsweek, The Wall Street Journal, Financial Times, The New York Times, The Washington Post,* and *Harvard Business Review.* He has written numerous articles focused on corporate planning, marketing strategy, and brand and customer management.

Dr. Chernev teaches marketing management, strategic marketing, marketing research, and behavioral decision theory in MBA, PhD, and executive education programs. In addition to teaching, he advises companies around the world on issues of strategic marketing planning and analysis, business innovation, brand and customer equity, new product development, and customer management.

ACKNOWLEDGMENTS

This book has benefited from the wisdom of many of my current and former colleagues at the Kellogg School of Management at Northwestern University: Nidhi Agrawal, Eric Anderson, Jim Anderson, Robert Blattberg, Ulf Böckenholt, Anand Bodapati, Miguel Brendl, Bobby Calder, Tim Calkins, Gregory Carpenter, Yuxin Chen, Anne Coughlan, Patrick Duparcq, David Gal, Kelly Goldsmith, Kent Grayson, Sachin Gupta, Karsten Hansen, Julie Hennessy, Dawn Iacobucci, Dipak Jain, Robert Kozinets, Lakshman Krishnamurthi, Angela Lee, Sidney Levy, Michal Maimaran, Prashant Malaviya, Eyal Maoz, Blake McShane, Vikas Mittal, Vincent Nijs, Christie Nordhielm, Yi Qian, Neal Roese, Derek Rucker, Mohan Sawhney, John Sherry, Jr., Louis Stern, Brian Sternthal, Alice Tybout, Song Yao, Philip Zerrillo, Florian Zettelmeyer, and Andris Zoltners.

I would like to thank Andrea Bonezzi (New York University), Aaron Brough (Pepperdine University), Pierre Chandon (INSEAD), Akif Irfan (Goldman Sachs), Mathew Isaac (University of Seattle), Ryan Hamilton (Emory University), and Ajay Kohli (Georgia Institute of Technology) for their valuable comments.

I owe a considerable debt of gratitude to Philip Kotler, one of the leading thinkers in the field of marketing, who through his insightful writings sparked my interest in marketing. I am also indebted to Jim Bettman, Julie Edell Britton, Joel Huber, John Lynch, John Payne, and Rick Staelin at the Fuqua School of Business at Duke University for their advice and support at the outset of my academic career.

FOREWORD

Marketing is both an art and a science. Many of its practitioners view marketing as an art, in which both intuition and creativity play a major role—a popular view, particularly in the advertising and sales spheres. Yet, if marketing plans were to be based primarily on intuition and creativity, they would be less effective and less credible to senior management and the company's stakeholders and collaborators. What gives marketing its growing respect and impact is the development and use of a broad range of scientific and analytic tools.

Over the past decades, the field of marketing has accumulated numerous tools. They help define goals and target markets, and facilitate positioning, differentiation, and branding. These tools, however, are usually scattered within marketing textbooks and fail to come together in a clear framework. Here lies the unique contribution of *Strategic Marketing Management*. This concise book presents the major tools and decision processes involved in planning and controlling marketing.

The theory presented in this book is based on three cornerstone ideas:

The first idea is that an offering's ultimate success is determined by the soundness of the five key components of its business model: goal, strategy, tactics, implementation, and control, or the G-STIC framework. This framework is used to streamline a company's marketing analyses and deliver an integrative approach to marketing planning.

The second idea is that when developing its offerings, a company should strive to create value for three key market entities: target customers, the company, and its collaborators. An offering's value proposition, therefore, should be optimized to deliver superior value to target customers in a way that enables the company and its collaborators to reach their strategic goals. These three types of value—customer value, collaborator value, and company value—comprise the 3-V framework, which is the foundation of strategic marketing analysis.

The third idea is that a company's marketing activities can be represented through the process of designing, communicating, and delivering value to its key constituencies, or the D-C-D framework. This framework offers a novel interpretation of the traditional 4-P approach to capture the dynamic nature of the value management process.

The second part of the book applies these ideas to common business problems, such as increasing profits and sales revenues, developing new products, extending product lines, and managing product portfolios. By linking the theory to practical applications, this book offers a structured approach to analyzing and solving business problems and delineates a set of methodologies to ensure a company's success in the market.

Student testimonies are evidence that this book is very helpful for analyzing marketing cases in the classroom. This book is also very helpful to managers involved in the development and implementation of marketing plans. I further recommend it to senior executives to improve their understanding of what constitutes great marketing analysis and planning.

A company's main focus should be on maximizing value for the customer, the company, and its collaborators. This can be achieved by applying the strategic marketing framework outlined in this book.

Philip Kotler
S. C. Johnson Distinguished Professor of International Marketing
Kellogg School of Management
Northwestern University

PART ONE

THE BIG PICTURE

Chapter One

Marketing as a Business Discipline

*Marketing is the whole business seen from the point of view of
its final result, that is, from the customer's point of view.*

Peter Drucker

A great deal of confusion exists about the nature of marketing. This confusion stems from a more general misunderstanding of marketing as a business discipline. Managers often think of marketing in terms of tactical activities such as sales, advertising, and promotion. In fact, within many organizations marketing is thought of as an activity designed to support sales by helping managers sell more of the company's products and services.

The view of marketing as an activity designed to support selling is particularly common among sales-oriented organizations whose primary activity is selling large inventories of warehoused products. These companies often view the goal of marketing as "selling more things, to more people, more often, for more money." While marketing certainly can facilitate selling, it is not limited to supporting sales. The goal of marketing is to create a product that sells, not to sell a product. "Marketing is not only much broader than selling, it is not a specialized activity at all," writes Peter Drucker. "It encompasses the entire business. The aim of marketing is to make selling superfluous."

In the same vein, many organizations equate marketing with advertising and sales promotion. These organizations view marketing as an activity that helps bring products to market, oblivious to marketing's role in creating the very products that need to be promoted. This myopic view of marketing as a tactical tool limited to creating awareness and incentivizing customers to make a purchase precludes companies from harnessing marketing's full potential to develop a comprehensive business strategy.

Marketing is far more than tactics. In addition to specialized tactical activities that include sales and promotion, marketing also involves strategic analysis and planning, which provide the foundation for the success of its tactical elements. This view of marketing as a central business function that permeates all areas of an enterprise is the basis of the strategic marketing theory outlined in this book.

Marketing as a Value-Management Process

There are many definitions of marketing, each reflecting a different understanding of its role as a business discipline. Some define marketing as a functional area that—similar to finance, accounting, and operations—captures a unique aspect of a company's business activities. Others view marketing as a customer-centric philosophy of business. Some define it as a process of moving products and services from a concept to the customer. Yet others view marketing as a set of specific activities that marketers are involved in, such as product development, pricing, promotion, and distribution. And for some marketing is simply a department in the company's organizational grid.

The reason for this diverse set of definitions is that marketing serves multiple functions. Marketing is a business discipline, a functional area, a business philosophy, a set of specific business activities, as well as a distinct unit in a company's organizational structure. Although diverse, these views of marketing are conceptually related. Marketing as a business discipline is defined by the view of marketing as a philosophy of business, which in turn defines marketing as a set of processes and activities coordinated by the marketing department. Thus, the key to defining marketing is delineating its core business function, which in turn can help define the specific processes and activities involved in marketing management.

The integrative nature of marketing as a business discipline calls for a definition that captures its essence and can serve as a guiding principle in managerial decision making. Because marketing studies consumer and business markets, the exchange of goods, services, and ideas that takes place in the market is the focal point of marketing. Furthermore, because the driving force for an exchange is the process of creating value, the concept of value is central to marketing. This view of marketing as an exchange that aims to create value for its participants leads to the following definition:

> *Marketing is the art and science of creating value by designing and managing successful exchanges.*

Marketing is an *art* because it is often driven by a manager's creativity and imagination. In addition to being an art, marketing is also a *science* because it represents a body of generalized knowledge about marketing phenomena. The scientific aspect of marketing that distills the logic underlying the processes of creating and managing value is the focus of this book.

Marketing is a science about markets; consequently, its focus is on the *exchange* of goods, services, and ideas—the defining activity of a market. In this context, marketing aims to develop and manage successful exchanges between the participating entities: the company, its customers, and its collaborators.

Because the main function of the marketing exchange is to create *value*, the concept of value is central to marketing. The goal of marketing is to ensure that a company's offerings create superior value for target customers in a way that enables the company and its collaborators to achieve their strategic goals. Optimizing value for target customers, collaborators, and the company is the key principle that guides managerial decision making and serves as the foundation for all marketing activities.

Marketing is not limited to maximizing monetary outcomes; rather, it can be defined in broader terms as *success* that reflects the ability of the marketing exchange to create value for its participants by fulfilling their goals. Thus, in addition to defining value and success using financial benchmarks such as net income, return on investment, and market share, the goal of marketing can be defined by nonmonetary outcomes that include customer satisfaction, technology development, and social welfare.

Value is a strategic concept that captures the utility customers receive from the market exchange. The value of a company's offering is conveyed though its tactics: its product and service attributes, its price and price incentives, its brand image, communication campaigns, and distribution channels. The goal of marketing, therefore, is to ensure that all tactical aspects of a company's offering work together to create customer value in a way that benefits the company and its collaborators.

The view of marketing as a process of creating and managing value has important implications for how managers should think about marketing. Because the role of marketing is to create value for the key participants in the marketing exchange—customers, the company, and its collaborators—marketing plays a pivotal role in any organization. Consequently, marketing is not just an activity managed by a company's marketing department; it spans all departments. As David Packard, the cofounder of Hewlett-Packard, succinctly put it, "Marketing is too important to be left to the marketing department."

The Role of Frameworks in Marketing Management

The rapid growth of technological innovation, ever increasing globalization, and the emergence of new business models have made today's markets exceedingly dynamic, unpredictable, and interdependent. The increasing complexity of the environment in which companies operate underscores the importance of using a systematic approach to market analysis, planning, and management. Such a systematic approach can be achieved by using frameworks.

Frameworks facilitate decisions in several ways. Frameworks help identify alternative approaches to thinking about the decision task, thus providing managers with a better understanding of the problem they are trying to solve. In addition to helping formulate the problem, frameworks typically provide a generalized approach to identifying alternative solutions. Frameworks further enhance decision making by providing a shared vocabulary with which to discuss the issues, streamlining the communication between the entities involved in the marketing process.

Because of their level of generality, frameworks rarely offer answers to specific marketing questions. Instead, they provide a general algorithm that enables managers to identify the optimal solution to a particular problem. Using a framework calls for abstracting the problem at hand to a more general scenario for which the framework offers a predefined solution and then applying this solution to solve the specific problem. By relying on the abstract knowledge captured in frameworks, a manager may effectively sidestep the trial-and-error-based learning process.

The role of frameworks in business management can be illustrated with the following example. Imagine that a client, a cereal manufacturer, asks your advice on how to price its new cereal. After analyzing the industry dynamics, you identify five key factors that need to be considered when deciding on the price of the cereal: customer willingness to pay for the cereal, the availability and pricing of competitive offerings, the cost structure and profit goals of the company, the margins that suppliers and distributors charge, as well as the more general context factors such as the current economic environment, consumption (health and diet) trends, and legal regulations concerning pricing strategies and tactics.

A month later you receive an assignment from a different client, a gas pipeline manufacturer, asking for your help with setting pricing for a new pressure valve. You diligently analyze the industry and end up suggesting the same five factors: customer willingness to pay, competitive pricing, company costs and goals, collaborator (supplier and distributor) margins, and the current context.

The following month you receive another assignment from a telecommunications company, asking for your advice on pricing their new mobile phone. By this time you have realized that the three recent requests are conceptually similar, calling for setting a price for a new product. Moreover, you realize that setting the price in all three tasks calls for analyzing the same five factors: customer willingness to pay, competitor prices, company goals and cost structure, collaborator prices and margins, and the overall economic, regulatory, technological context in which the company operates. (These five factors comprise the 5-C framework, which will be discussed in the following chapter.)

As the above example illustrates, frameworks build on already existing generalized knowledge to facilitate future company-specific decisions. Thus, many of the business problems companies face on a daily basis can be formalized into a more general approach, or framework, that can be applied to solving future problems. The role of frameworks as a problem-solving tool is captured in the words of French philosopher René Descartes: "Each problem that I solved became a rule which served afterwards to solve other problems."

The effective use of frameworks as a problem-solving tool in managerial decision making involves three key steps. First, a manager should be able to generalize the specific problem at hand (e.g., how to price a new mobile phone) to a more abstract problem that can be addressed by a particular framework (e.g., how to price a new product). Second, the manager should be able to identify a framework that will help answer the specific problem (e.g., 5-C framework) and use it to derive a general solution. Finally, the manager needs to be able to apply the generalized solution suggested by the framework to the specific problem at hand. Thus, relying on generalized knowledge captured in frameworks can help managers circumvent the trial-and-error approach to solving business problems (Figure 1).

Figure 1: The Role of Frameworks in Marketing Management

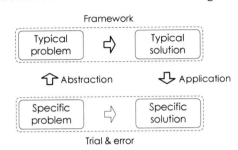

Although most frameworks add value by offering a structured approach to analyzing business problems, some have greater practical implications than others. The practical value of a framework is determined by two key factors: the degree to which it addresses an important problem frequently encountered by managers, and its ability to offer actionable solutions that produce a better outcome than a trial-and-error approach. The greater the ability of a framework to help achieve better outcomes, the greater its practical value to the company.

The frameworks presented in this book include those with the greatest conceptual importance and practical value. In addition to presenting individual frameworks, this book offers an integrative view that combines individual frameworks into a systematic and streamlined approach to marketing analysis, planning, and management. This integrative framework for marketing management is outlined in more detail in the following chapter.

ADDITIONAL READINGS

Drucker, Peter (1954), *The Practice of Management.* New York, NY: HarperCollins.

Kotler, Philip (1999), *Kotler on Marketing: How to Create, Win, and Dominate Markets.* New York, NY: Free Press.

Levitt, Theodore (1975), "Marketing Myopia," *Harvard Business Review* (September–October), 2–14.

CHAPTER TWO

THE FRAMEWORK FOR MARKETING MANAGEMENT

Vision without action is a daydream. Action without vision is a nightmare.

Japanese proverb

The central role of marketing in a company's business activities and the increasing complexity of these activities call for the use of an overarching framework that brings a systematic approach to marketing management. Such a systematic approach to marketing, which is outlined in this chapter, streamlines strategic analysis and planning by promoting the understanding of complex marketing problems and facilitating the development of actionable solutions.

The Key Marketing Principle

A company's goal is to create value for its stakeholders by creating superior value for its target customers and collaborators. Optimizing these three types of value—company, customer, and collaborator value—is the key principle that serves as the foundation for all marketing activities (Figure 1). To succeed, an offering must create superior value for its customers in a way that benefits the company and its collaborators.

Figure 1: The 3-V Principle of Managing Value

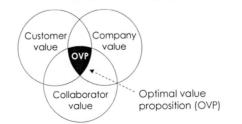

Because value optimization is the fundamental marketing principle, value management permeates all aspects of designing an offering's strategy and tactics. Business success can be achieved only when an offering's value is optimized for the company, its target customers, and its collaborators. Accordingly, to evaluate the market potential of an offering a manager needs to answer three key questions:

- Does the offering create superior value for target customers?
- Does the offering create superior value for the company's collaborators?
- Does the offering create superior value for the company?

The term *superior value* means that the value provided by the offering for target customers, collaborators, and the company is greater than that provided by competitors' offerings and/or by the other offerings in the company's own product line. The ability to create superior value for customers, collaborators, and the company is the ultimate criterion for achieving market success. Failure to create superior value for any one of the relevant market participants inevitably leads to an inefficient marketing exchange and market failure.

Marketing Management: An Overview

Marketing management involves a series of activities that create value for the relevant participants in the marketing exchange: target customers, the company, and its collaborators. The process by which a company creates value is captured by five key activities: setting a *goal*, developing a *strategy*, designing the *tactics*, defining an *implementation* plan, and identifying a set of *control* metrics to measure the success of the proposed action. These five activities comprise the G-STIC framework, which is the cornerstone of marketing analysis and planning (Figure 2).

Figure 2: The G-STIC Framework for Action Planning

The G-STIC approach to marketing management calls for internal consistency of its individual elements. Thus, a company's goals should define its strategy, which in turn should determine its tactics and implementation, while controls should monitor for changes in the environment and ensure adequate goal progress. The individual components of the G-STIC framework are discussed in more detail below.

Setting a Goal

The action plan begins with a goal that guides all of the company's marketing activities. Because of its central role in the strategic planning process, setting a goal is pivotal in determining a company's overall success. Without a well-defined goal, an organization cannot design an effective marketing strategy or evaluate the success of its current activities.

Setting a goal involves two decisions: identifying the focus of the company's actions and defining the specific performance benchmarks to be achieved.

- The **focus** identifies the key criterion for a company's success. Common goal foci include net income, profit margins, sales revenues, and market share. A company's goal is often detailed in a series of more specific objectives delineating specific outcomes to be achieved with respect to target customers (customer objectives), collaborators (collaborator objectives), the company (internal objectives), and competitors (competitive objectives). To illustrate, the company goal of increasing net revenues can be associated with the more specific objective of increasing the frequency with which its customers repurchase the offering (customer objective) and/or increasing the shelf space for its offering in distribution channels (collaborator objective).

- **Benchmarks** define the quantitative and temporal aspects of the goal. Quantitative benchmarks identify the specific milestones to be achieved, whereas temporal benchmarks identify the time frame for achieving a particular benchmark.

To illustrate, a company's ultimate goal may involve generating net income (focus) of $10B (quantitative benchmark) by the end of the fourth quarter (temporal benchmark). A customer-specific objective may involve increasing market share by 10% by the end of the fourth quarter. A collaborator-related objective might involve securing 45% of the distribution outlets by the end of the fourth quarter. An internal objective might involve lowering the cost of goods sold by 25% by the end of the fourth quarter.

Developing a Strategy

Strategy outlines the master plan of action aimed at achieving the company goal. Marketing strategy involves two key decisions: identifying the target market and developing the offering's value proposition.

Identifying Target Markets

The markets in which a company's offerings compete are defined by five key factors: *customers* whose needs the company's offering aims to fulfill, the *company* managing the offering, *collaborators* working with the company on this offering, *competitors* with offerings that target the same customers, and the overall *context* in which the company operates. These five factors are commonly referred to as the "Five Cs" and the resulting framework is referred to as the 5-C framework.

- Target **customers** are the potential buyers whose needs the company aims to fulfill with its offerings. Target customers can be either consumers (in the case of business-to-consumer markets) or businesses (in the case of business-to-business markets). Target customers are typically defined by the needs the company aims to fulfill with its offering(s).

- **Company** is the particular business unit (a department, division, branch, or the entire company) managing the offering. A company's ability to successfully compete in a given market is defined by its resources (core competencies and strategic assets).

- **Collaborators** are entities that work with the company to create value for target customers. Common collaborators include suppliers, manufacturers, distributors (dealers, wholesalers, and retailers), research and development companies, service providers, external sales force, advertising agencies, and marketing research companies.

- **Competitors** are entities with offerings that aim to fulfill the same needs of the same customers as the company's offering.

- **Context** involves the relevant aspects of the environment in which the company operates. The key context factors include the economic, technological, sociocultural, regulatory, and physical environment.

The choice of target customers is fundamental to defining the other aspects of the target market: It determines the scope of the competition, the range of potential collaborators, the core competencies and assets of the company that are necessary to fulfill the needs of target customers, and the specific context factors pertinent to the chosen target segment. Accordingly, different customer segments tend to be served by different competitors, require a different set of collaborators (different suppliers and distribution channels), are managed by different business units of the company, and operate in a different context (Figure 3).

Figure 3: Identifying Target Markets: The 5-C Framework

Identifying target customers typically involves two decisions: selecting which customers to serve and identifying actionable strategies to reach these customers. Selecting which customers to serve, also referred to as *strategic targeting*, is guided by the offering's ability to fulfill customer needs in a way that benefits the company and its collaborators. Because fulfilling customer needs is central to the success of an offering, target customers are typically chosen based on their underlying needs. Selecting target customers based on needs, however, complicates a company's ability to reach these customers in a cost-effective way because customer needs are not readily observable. Therefore, a company must identify a set of observable characteristics that can be used to reach the customers whose needs it aims to serve, a process referred to as *tactical targeting*. Such observable characteristics typically involve demographic (e.g., age, gender, and income), geographic (e.g., country, region, and postal codes), psychographic (e.g., personality traits, values, and lifestyle), and behavioral (e.g., purchase frequency, purchase quantity, and price sensitivity) factors.

Developing a Value Proposition

Developing a value proposition involves defining the value that the offering creates for its target customers, the company, and its collaborators. Because value creation is the ultimate goal of marketing, the selection of target customers is guided by the company's ability to develop an offering that will satisfy a particular need of its target customers better than the competition, and do so in a way that creates value for the company and its collaborators (Figure 4).

Figure 4: Identifying Target Customers and Developing a Value Proposition

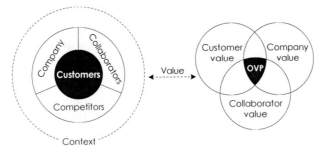

The development of a value proposition is often complemented by the development of a *positioning strategy* that singles out the most important aspect(s) of the offering's value proposition. An offering's positioning strategy builds on its value proposition. However, unlike the value proposition, which reflects *all* of the offering's benefits and costs, an offering's positioning defines only the most important benefit associated with the offering. Thus, positioning aims to create a distinct image of the offering in buyers' minds, providing them with a compelling reason to choose the offering. For example, Volvo's positioning emphasizes safety, Toyota underscores reliability, Rolls-Royce highlights luxury, and BMW focuses on the driving experience.

Designing the Tactics

Tactics outline a set of specific activities employed to execute a given strategy. In marketing, tactics are defined by seven key elements, often referred to as the marketing mix: product, service, brand, price, incentives, communication, and distribution. These marketing tactics represent the key marketing decisions that embody an offering's marketing strategy. The seven marketing mix factors can be summarized as follows:

- The **product** aspect of the offering reflects its key functional characteristics. Products typically change ownership during purchase; once created, they can be physically separated from the manufacturer and distributed to buyers via multiple channels.

- The **service** aspect of the offering also reflects its functional characteristics but, unlike products, services typically do not imply a change in ownership; instead, customers obtain the right to use the service for a period of time. Because they are simultaneously created and consumed, services are inseparable from the service provider and cannot be inventoried.

- The **brand** aims to create a set of unique associations that enrich the offering's value beyond its product and service benefits.

- The **price** refers to the amount of money the company charges its customers and collaborators for the benefits provided by its offering.

- **Incentives** are tools used to selectively enhance the value of the offering for its customers, collaborators, and/or employees. Incentives may be monetary— such as volume discounts, price reductions, coupons, and rebates—and non-monetary, such as premiums, contests, and rewards.

- **Communication** informs current and potential buyers about the offering. Communication may involve each of the other six marketing mix variables: product, service, brand, price, incentives, and distribution. Thus, a company may promote the functionality of a product or service, communicate the meaning of its brand, publicize its price, apprise buyers about current incentives, and inform them about the availability of the offering.

- **Distribution** refers to the channel through which customers receive the offering. Similar to communication, distribution may involve each of the other six marketing mix variables: product, service, brand, price, incentives, and communication. To illustrate, a company's products might be delivered through retailers, its service could be delivered through dedicated service centers, and the brand can be delivered by enabling customers to experience it firsthand (Disney World theme parks and Apple retail stores "deliver" Disney and Apple brands to customers). In the same vein, price delivery includes the channels for collecting customer payments and processing refunds. Finally, incentives and communications may be delivered through various channels, including television, radio, print, point of purchase, personal selling, and online.

The above seven factors are the means that managers have at their disposal to develop an optimal value proposition (Figure 5). These seven factors are the "7 Ts" that define the 7 Tactical aspects of the offering; they are the 7 Tools that managers use to create value for target customers, the company, and its collaborators.

Figure 5: The Seven Marketing Tactics for Creating an Optimal Value Proposition

The seven marketing tactics also can be represented as a process of designing, communicating, and delivering value. Here, product, service, brand, price, and incentives compose the value-design aspect of the offering; communication captures the value-communication aspect; and distribution reflects the value-delivery aspect of the offering. Considering the individual marketing mix decisions as elements of the overarching process of creating customer value helps underscore the relationship between the different aspects of the offering's value proposition. Representation of the seven marketing mix factors as a process of *designing, communicating,* and *delivering* value is also referred to as the D-C-D value-creation framework.

Defining the Implementation Plan

The implementation component of market planning delineates the logistics of executing the offering's strategy and tactics. Implementation involves three key components: defining the business infrastructure, designing business processes, and setting the implementation schedule.

- The **business infrastructure** reflects the organizational structure and the relationship among relevant entities involved in creating and managing the offering. This involves identifying the business unit (or cross-functional team) of the company in charge of the offering, identifying its key personnel and organizational structure, and identifying its relationships with key collaborators (e.g., suppliers, distributors, and co-developers).

- The **business processes** depict the specific activities involved in designing and managing the offering, such as the flow of information, goods, services, and money.

- The **implementation schedule** identifies the sequence and time frame in which individual tasks will be performed to ensure effective and cost-efficient completion of the project.

Identifying Controls

The uncertainty and dynamics associated with most business markets necessitate that companies continuously evaluate their performance and monitor changes in the environment. Accordingly, marketing controls (also referred to as marketing metrics) serve two key functions: to evaluate the company's progress toward its goal and to analyze the changes in the environment in which the company operates.

- **Performance evaluation** involves monitoring the company's progress to ensure that the company is on the right track to reach its goal and adjusting the action plan as necessary to close performance gaps.

- **Environmental analysis** involves monitoring the environment in which the company operates to ensure that the company's action plan remains optimal, and adjusting the action plan as necessary to take advantage of new opportunities (e.g., favorable government regulations, a decrease in competition, or an increase in consumer demand) and counteract potential threats (e.g., unfavorable government regulations, an increase in competition, or a decline in consumer demand).

Marketing Management: The Big Picture

The focus of marketing management is on developing and implementing action plans that create value for target customers, the company, and its collaborators. Most action plans follow the structure delineated by the five components in the G-STIC framework: goal, strategy, tactics, implementation, and control. These key steps and the main decisions underlying each individual step can be presented in the form of a pyramid as shown in Figure 6.

Figure 6. The G-STIC Action Planning Pyramid

The action plan begins with an outline of the goal that identifies the company's focus and the performance benchmarks to be achieved. Setting the goal is followed by the company's strategy, which delineates key aspects of the target market(s) in which the company will compete and outlines the offering's value proposition for target customers, the company, and its collaborators. The strategy outline is followed by an overview of the tactics, which involve decisions concerning the product, service, brand, price, incentives, communication, and distribution. The tactics are followed by an implementation plan that outlines the timeline and the logistics of executing an offering's strategy and tactics. Finally, the control section of the action plan indicates the procedures for evaluating the company's performance and analyzing the environment in which the company operates.

In addition to structuring the managerial decision process, the G-STIC framework also serves as the basis for developing a marketing plan for designing and managing a company's offerings. The typical marketing plan comprises four key components: (1) an executive summary that outlines the highlights of the marketing plan, (2) a situation analysis that reviews the environment in which the company operates and identifies the target market(s) in which it will compete, (3) an action plan that outlines the goal, strategy, tactics, implementation, and control aspects of the offering, and (4) exhibits that provide additional information about specific aspects of the marketing plan. Because the ultimate purpose of the marketing plan is to guide a company's actions, the action plan is the central component that ultimately determines the viability of the marketing plan. The process of writing a marketing plan is discussed in more detail in Chapter 21.

SUMMARY

The goal of marketing is to create value by designing and managing successful exchanges. Consequently, a company's goal is to develop offerings that create value for all relevant participants in the exchange: customers, the company, and its collaborators. Optimizing these three types of value—a process captured in the 3-V framework—is the foundation for all marketing activities.

On the most general level, marketing management involves five main steps: setting a *goal*, developing the *strategy*, designing the *tactics*, defining the *implementation* plan, and identifying the *control* metrics to measure progress toward the set goal. These five steps comprise the G-STIC framework.

Strategy outlines the master plan of activities aimed at achieving a company's goal; it is defined by two decisions: identifying target customers and developing a value proposition. Identifying target customers—a process commonly referred to as *targeting*—is the key to developing a successful marketing strategy. The process of identifying target customers is guided by the company's ability to develop an offering that will satisfy a particular need of these customers better than the competition, and do so in a way that creates superior value for the company and its collaborators. The development of a value proposition involves defining the key benefits and costs associated with the offering for target customers, the company, and its collaborators. The development of a value proposition is complemented by the development of a positioning strategy that singles out the most important aspect(s) of the offering's value proposition to provide customers (as well as collaborators and the company) with a compelling reason to choose the offering.

Tactics reflect the means used to translate the desired strategy into a specific set of actions, commonly referred to as the marketing mix. When designing the marketing mix, the company's goal is to create a superior value proposition that optimizes the value for target customers, the company, and its collaborators. The marketing mix is defined by its seven key components: product, service, brand, price, incentives, communication, and distribution. The seven tactical aspects of the offering (the 7 Ts) can also be represented as a process of designing, communicating, and delivering value (the D-C-D framework), where product, service, brand, price, and incentives compose the value-design aspect of the offering; communication captures the value-communication aspect; and distribution reflects the value-delivery aspect of the offering.

In addition to structuring the managerial decision process, the G-STIC framework also serves as the basis for developing a marketing plan for designing and managing a company's offerings. Thus, most marketing plans are organized in a similar fashion, they start with an executive summary, follow with an overview of the current situation; continue with an outline of the company's action plan (defined by its goal(s), strategy, tactics, implementation, and controls), and conclude with a set of exhibits. Because the ultimate purpose of the marketing plan is to guide a company's actions, the action plan is the central component that determines the viability of the marketing plan.

RELEVANT MARKETING FRAMEWORKS

The G-STIC framework outlined in this chapter builds on several existing frameworks, extending and integrating them into a cohesive approach to marketing analysis, planning, and management. Three of these frameworks—the 3-C, S-T-P, and 4-P frameworks—are discussed below.

The 3-C Framework

The 3-C framework was advanced by Japanese business strategist Kenichi Ohmae, who argued that to achieve a sustainable competitive advantage a manager should evaluate the following three key factors: company, customers, and competition. The 3-C framework suggests that managers need to evaluate the environment in which they operate: the strengths and weaknesses of their own company, the needs of the consumer, and the strengths and weaknesses of their competitors. The 3-C framework is simple, intuitive, and easy to understand and use—factors that have contributed to its popularity.

Despite its popularity, the 3-C framework has a number of important limitations that hinder its applicability to marketing analysis. A key limitation of the 3-C framework is that it overlooks two important factors: the company's *collaborators* and the *context* in which the company operates. The importance of collaborators in today's networked environment can hardly be overstated; virtually all business activities involve some form of collaboration to create the offering, communicate its benefits, and deliver it to consumers. In the same vein, the economic, technological, sociocultural, regulatory, and physical context in which the company operates plays a significant role in formulating its business model and can determine the ultimate success or failure of the company's offerings. Another important limitation of the 3-C framework is that it does not account for the interdependencies among its individual components, and specifically, the central role of customers in defining the other "C"s.

The S-T-P Framework

The Segmentation-Targeting-Positioning (S-T-P) framework describes the process of selecting the "ideal" customers and developing the offering's value proposition for these customers. Specifically, the S-T-P framework highlights three decision steps: (1) dividing customers into groups with similar preferences (segmentation), (2) identifying customer segment(s) that the company will serve with its offering (targeting), and (3) defining the key reason why customers will buy the offering (positioning).

The S-T-P framework offers a relatively simple, common sense approach to describing the process of value creation, which has contributed to its popularity. Despite its intuitive appeal, however, the S-T-P framework has a number of limitations. One such limitation is that the S-T-P framework defines customer value by focusing only on how the offering should be positioned. The problem with this approach is that positioning captures only the most distinct aspect of a company's value proposition and does not take into account the total value of the offering created by *all* relevant benefits and costs. By focusing solely on the most distinct aspect of a given offering while ignoring the offering's entire value proposition, the S-T-P approach offers a rather narrow view of creating and managing customer value. The scope of the S-T-P framework is further limited by its focus only on the customer side of the marketing process, which does not address the processes of creating company and collaborator value.

The 4-P Framework

The 4-P framework identifies four key decisions that managers must make when designing and managing a given offering. These decisions involve (1) the functionality and design of the company's *product*, (2) the *price* at which the product is offered to target customers, (3) the company's *promotion* of the product to target customers, and (4) the retail outlets in which the company will *place* the product.

Despite its popularity, the 4-P framework has a number of important limitations. One significant limitation is the lack of separate *service* and *brand* components. Because it was developed over a half-century ago with a focus on consumer packaged goods, the 4-P framework does not explicitly account for the service element of the offering—a key drawback in today's service-oriented business environment. Furthermore, the brand is not explicitly considered as a separate marketing mix variable and instead is viewed as part of a company's product and promotion decisions—a fact that is difficult to justify given the crucial role brands play in marketing.

Another important limitation of the 4-P framework concerns the term *promotion*. The problem is that promotion is a very broad concept that includes two distinct types of activities: (1) *incentives*, such as price promotions, coupons, and trade promotions, and (2) *communication*, such as advertising, public relations, social media, and personal selling. While considering these two activities jointly is common accounting practice, each has a distinct role in the value-creation process. Incentives aim to enhance the offering's value, whereas communication aims to inform customers about the offering without necessarily enhancing its value. Using a single term to refer to these distinct activities muddles the logic of the marketing analysis.

Another shortcoming of the 4-P framework involves the term *place*. The increased complexity of delivering the company's offering to customers calls for using a more accurate description of the entire process, not just the location at which the company's offering is made available to buyers. Consequently, the term "place" is rarely used in contemporary marketing analysis and is most commonly substituted with the terms *distribution* and/or *channel*.

Some of the limitations of the 4-P framework can be overcome by describing the marketing mix in terms of seven (rather than four) factors: product, service, brand, price, incentives, communication, and distribution. Here, product, service, and brand comprise the first *p*; price is the second *p*, incentives and communication are the third *p*, and distribution is the fourth *p*. Some of the additional limitations of the 4-P framework can be surmounted by considering these seven factors as a process of designing, communicating, and delivering value, as implied in the D-C-D framework discussed earlier in this chapter.

ADDITIONAL READINGS

Aaker, David A. (2009), *Strategic Market Management* (9th ed.). New York, NY: John Wiley & Sons.

Chernev, Alexander (2011), *The Marketing Plan Handbook* (3rd ed.). Chicago, IL: Cerebellum Press.

Kotler, Philip (1999), *Kotler on Marketing: How to Create, Win, and Dominate Markets*. New York, NY: Free Press.

Kotler, Philip and Kevin Lane Keller (2011), *Marketing Management* (14th ed.). Upper Saddle River, NJ: Prentice Hall.

Lehmann, Donald R. and Russell S. Winer (2007), *Analysis for Marketing Planning* (7th ed.). Boston, MA: McGraw-Hill/Irvin.

Ohmae, Kenichi (1982), *The Mind of the Strategist: The Art of Japanese Business*. New York, NY: McGraw-Hill.

PART TWO

MARKETING STRATEGY

INTRODUCTION

All men can see the tactics whereby I conquer, but what none can see is the strategy out of which victory is evolved.

Sun Tzu, Chinese military strategist

The term *strategy* comes from the Greek *stratēgia*—meaning "generalship"—used in reference to maneuvering troops into position before a battle. In marketing, strategy outlines the master plan of actions aimed at achieving the company goal.

The five key aspects of strategic analysis outlined in this book include (1) identifying target customers (2) developing a value proposition to meet the needs of these customers, (3) analyzing a company's ability to create value for target customers as well as its own stakeholders, (4) creating value through collaboration in business markets, and (5) managing the competition. These five topics are briefly summarized below and discussed in greater detail in the following five chapters.

- **Identifying target customers** is the stepping stone for the development of a marketing strategy. Identifying target customers involves grouping customers into segments, selecting which segments to target, and identifying actionable strategies to reach the selected target segments. The key aspects of identifying target customers are discussed in Chapter 3.

- The selection of target customers is guided by a company's ability to create a superior value proposition for these customers. The processes of **developing a value proposition** that articulates the benefits and costs of the company's offering and a **positioning** that formulates the primary reason for customers to choose the offering are discussed in Chapter 4.

- **Company value analysis** focuses on creating stakeholder value by managing revenue, share, and profit growth. The key aspects of company value analysis are discussed in Chapter 5.

- **Collaborator value analysis** aims to identify entities that work with the company to create value for target customers. The key aspects of creating value in business markets are the focus of Chapter 6.

- **Competitive analysis** involves identifying the key current and potential competitors, evaluating the competitive intensity of the selected target market, and developing a sustainable competitive advantage. The key aspects of competitive analysis are discussed in Chapter 7.

CHAPTER THREE

IDENTIFYING TARGET CUSTOMERS: SEGMENTATION AND TARGETING ANALYSIS

I don't know the key to success, but the key to failure is trying to please everybody.

Bill Cosby

U nderstanding customer needs and identifying market opportunities is the starting point in formulating a company's marketing strategy. A key aspect of customer analysis involves identifying groups of customers with similar preferences (segments) and deciding which segment(s) to target. These two strategic decisions—segmentation and targeting—are the focus of this chapter.

Segmentation

Segmentation divides customers into groups with similar characteristics. The process of segmentation is based on the idea that the efficiency of a company's marketing activities can be greatly increased by ignoring the nonessential differences among customers within each segment and treating these customers as a single entity. Segmentation is a tool that focuses marketing analysis on the important aspects of customer needs, enabling managers to group customers into relatively few large segments and, consequently, develop strategies for these segments rather than for each individual customer.

Segmentation serves two main functions. First, it optimizes the *effectiveness* of a company's actions by identifying the key differences among customers to develop a customized offering for each segment. Second, it optimizes the *cost-efficiency* of a company's actions by circumventing the irrelevant differences among customers to create a single offering for all customers within each segment. The key benefit of segmentation is in allowing the company to optimize marketing expenditures by grouping customers who are likely to respond in a similar fashion to the company's offerings. The key disadvantage of segmentation is that grouping customers into segments might not take into account potentially important differences that may exist among customers within each segment.

Segmentation, Mass Marketing, and One-to-One Marketing

The concept of segmentation can be better understood when considered in the context of two alternative marketing approaches: mass marketing and one-to-one marketing (Figure 1). Mass marketing refers to a scenario in which the same product or service is offered to all customers. A classic example is the strategy adopted by Ford's Model T, in which a single type of car was offered to all customers. In contrast, in one-to-one marketing, the company's offering is customized for each individual customer. *Haute couture*—made-to-order high-end clothing—exemplifies the one-to-one marketing strategy.

Figure 1. Segmentation, Mass Marketing, and One-to-One Marketing.

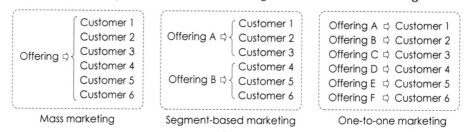

Segmentation represents a compromise between the mass-marketing approach and the one-to-one approach. By recognizing the diversity of customer needs, segmentation allows a company to design offerings that meet the needs of customers more effectively than the mass-marketing approach. The downside of segmentation vis-à-vis mass marketing is that developing different offerings for each segment could potentially lead to higher product development, communication, and distribution costs. In the same vein, in cases when it is not cost efficient to develop an individual offering for each customer (as implied by the one-to-one approach), segmentation enables companies to streamline their product lines by developing offerings for groups of customers with similar needs. However, because grouping customers inevitably ignores the individual differences within each group, segmentation may decrease the attractiveness of the company's offering by not fully customizing the offering to fit the needs of individual customers.

An important issue in segmenting markets is determining the extent to which a market should be segmented and how large each segment should be. Segment size could potentially vary between a single segment encompassing the entire market (as in the case of mass marketing) and multiple segments of one customer each (as in the case of one-to-one marketing). As a general rule, segmentation is beneficial when the incremental value from customizing the offering to the needs of resulting segments outweighs the costs of developing separate offerings for each segment. To illustrate, when the cost of customization is relatively high (as with durable goods such as cars, household appliances, and electronic equipment), companies tend to develop offerings that serve relatively large segments, whereas in industries where the cost of customization is relatively low (as in the case of delivering online information such as news), offerings can be tailored for smaller segments.

The process of segmentation is illustrated in Figure 2. Here, customers are represented by shaded shapes reflecting their underlying needs. For simplicity, let's assume that customer needs vary on two factors (represented by shading and shape) and each of these factors has three levels. In this context, there are three possible segmentation strategies: by shading, by shape, and by shading and shape. The choice of a particular segmentation criterion is a function of the degree to which this criterion captures strategically important aspects of customer reaction to the company's offering. Consequently, the greater the degree of differences (heterogeneity) among potential buyers, the greater the number of resulting customer segments.

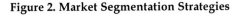

Figure 2. Market Segmentation Strategies

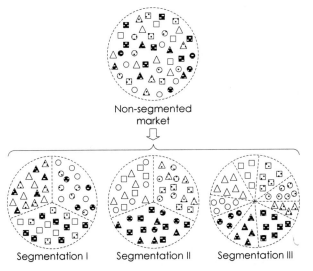

As a general rule, a larger number of segments results in greater similarity between the customers within each segment. Thus, segments resulting from Segmentation III in Figure 2 are most consistent (homogeneous) with respect to underlying customer preferences, whereas Segmentations I and II allow for a greater degree of diversity between the customers in each segment. On the flip side, Segmentation III calls for the development of three times as many customized offerings compared to the first two segmentations—a strategy that can be justified only in cases when the underlying differences between these segments are essential to the company's ability to create customer value.

Criteria for Segmentation

When segmenting the market, a company's goal is to identify segments that are meaningful with respect to its ability to create value for its target customers. Thus, segmentation should yield groups of customers that vary in the way they react to the company's offering, such that customers in the same segment react in a similar fashion to the offering, while customers in different segments react differently.

In general, effective segmentation should yield segments that are mutually exclusive and collectively exhaustive (also referred to as the MECE rule). Segments should be sufficiently different from one another so that they do not overlap (i.e., mutually exclusive); at the same time, identified segments should include *all* customers in a given market (i.e., collectively exhaustive). Such mutually exclusive and collectively exhaustive segmentation can be achieved by using well-defined criteria to segment the market.

At the most general level, there are two types of criteria used to divide customers into segments: criteria reflecting the *value* sought by customers and criteria related to customer *profiles*. Reliance on these criteria leads to two distinct segmentation types: value-based segmentation and profile-based segmentation.

- **Value-based segmentation** groups customers based on their needs and the benefits they seek from the company's offerings. Customer needs can involve *functional* factors such as quality, performance, aesthetics, reliability, durability, and safety; *monetary* factors such as pricing, financing, and promotion preferences; as well as *psychological* factors such as image and social status.

- **Profile-based segmentation** groups customers using their readily observable characteristics. In consumer markets, four types of characteristics, or profiles, are commonly used: demographic, geographic, psychographic, and behavioral:

  - *Demographic profile* includes factors such as age, gender, income, education, social status, and stage in the life cycle.

  - *Geographic profile* includes location identifiers such as country, region, city, postal code, and area code. Geographic profile is not limited to the physical space; it also includes location identifiers in cyberspace such as email, web, and IP addresses.

  - *Psychographic profile* includes relatively stable individual traits such as personality, moral values, and lifestyle.

  - *Behavioral profile* captures the way customers react to the company's offering, including user status (e.g., user vs. nonuser), distribution channel used (e.g., brick-and-mortar vs. online), volume purchased, frequency of repurchase, price sensitivity, promotion sensitivity, and loyalty.

In business markets, profile-based segmentation, referred to as *firmographics*, involves factors such as location, size of company, industry, buying process, growth, and profitability.

Because segmentation aims to facilitate the process of creating customer value, value-based segmentation is almost always the starting point of marketing analysis. Value-based segmentation is complemented by profile-based segmentation, which identifies effective and cost-efficient communication and distribution strategies for the previously created value-based segments (a process referred to as tactical targeting, discussed in the following sections).

Targeting

Targeting is the process of identifying customers for whom the company will develop and optimize its offering. Targeting involves two distinct activities: (1) selecting which customers to serve (referred to as strategic targeting) and (2) identifying the actionable characteristics describing the customers that the company wishes to serve (referred to as tactical targeting).

Strategic Targeting

Strategic targeting involves identifying which customers (segments) to serve and which to ignore (Figure 3). The basic principle underlying the selection of target customers is an offering's ability to deliver superior value to these customers while enabling the company and its collaborators to achieve their strategic goals. Because it is guided by the company's ability to fulfill customer needs better than the competition, strategic targeting is typically derived from value-based segmentation.

Figure 3. Strategic Targeting: Selecting Value-Based Segments

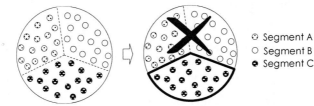

The process of identifying target customers is guided by the company's ability to develop an optimal value proposition by creating an offering that will (1) satisfy a particular customer need better than the competition and (2) do so in a way that creates value for the company and its collaborators. These two criteria—customers' ability to create value for the company and the company's ability to create value for customers—are essential for identifying effective target segments.

- **Segment attractiveness** reflects the ability of a particular segment to deliver value to the company and its collaborators. Customers' ability to create company/collaborator value is a function of two key factors: the company/collaborator goals and the ability of target customers to fulfill these goals.

  - *Company and collaborator goals* identify the criteria used to identify target customers. These goals might involve monetary outcomes such as maximizing net income, earnings per share, and return on investment, and nonmonetary outcomes such as facilitating other strategically important offerings and increasing the overall customer/social welfare. In general, the more aggressive the goals, the higher the bar for choosing target customers.

  - *Customers' ability to fulfill company/collaborator goals.* In the case of monetary goals, customers' ability to create company/collaborator value is a function of the revenue stream from target customers and the cost of acquiring and serving these customers. The revenue potential is typically determined by factors such as the size of the market, its growth potential, buying power, competitive intensity, and inherent loyalty. The cost of acquiring and serving target customers depends on the cost of developing customized offerings for each customer segment, as well as the degree to which each segment can be reached effectively and in a cost-efficient manner through the company's communication and distribution channels.

- **Segment compatibility** reflects the ability of the company and its collaborators to fulfill the needs of the target customers. Segment compatibility is a function of two factors: customer needs and the ability of the company and its collaborators to fulfill these needs better than the competition.

  - *Customer needs* are the key drivers of customer behavior. Needs determine the benefits that customers seek when evaluating market offerings and are the key to defining the company's offering. In general, more complex and/or unique needs require a higher level of resources to fulfill those needs.

  - *Company resources* reflect the company's ability to create superior value for target customers relative to the competition. The company's resources are to a large degree determined by its core competencies and strategic assets that enable it to compete in the chosen market(s).

Successful targeting requires that a segment meet all of the above criteria to create an optimal value proposition for customers, the company, and its collaborators. For example, the fact that a particular segment is inherently attractive is not a sufficient reason to target this segment; it is also important that serving this segment is consistent with the company's goals and that the company has the resources to deliver value to this segment in a way that cannot be matched by competitors.

Tactical Targeting

Deciding which customers to serve and which to ignore is a key step in identifying target customers. This decision is driven by the company's understanding of the needs of its customers and its ability to fulfill these needs better than the competition. Yet, while knowing customer needs is important for identifying target customers, it is not sufficient for reaching these customers. This is because customer needs are not readily observable, which makes reaching these customers difficult and/or costly. Thus, without knowing who target customers are, the company has to promote and make available its offering to *all* customers—an approach that is not cost effective, especially when targeting niche markets.

To address the unobservable nature of needs, companies use customers' readily observable characteristics to identify those customers whose needs fit the value-based target. This is achieved by linking the value-based segments (i.e., customers with a certain need that can be fulfilled by the company's offering) to profile-based segments defined by their demographic, geographic, behavioral, and psychographic characteristics. The process of identifying value-based segments by linking them to corresponding observable and actionable profiles is the essence of tactical targeting (Figure 4).

Figure 4. Tactical Targeting: Linking Value-Based and Profile-Based Segments

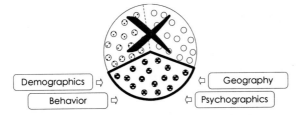

To illustrate, consider a credit card company seeking customers who would like to receive travel rewards for using the card and who are not likely to default on payments. The problem faced by this company is that customer needs are unobservable, meaning that a priori it is difficult to know which consumers have a particular need and are likely to behave in a certain fashion. To solve this problem, the company must link the targeted needs and behaviors with certain observable characteristics that can identify customers with these needs and behaviors. To identify customers with a low likelihood of default, the link between the unobservable (e.g., the likelihood of repaying the loan) and the observable (demographic, geographic, behavioral, and psychographic) factors is provided by the customer's credit score and purchase history, reflecting this customer's buying patterns, purchasing power, and likely future behavior—including the probability that s/he will repay the loan. Furthermore, to identify customers with certain needs (e.g., looking for travel rewards), a company's promotional activities are facilitated by linking these unobservable needs to the observable aspects of customers' behavior, reflected in the magazines they read, the shows they watch, and the information they search for. Thus, by focusing its efforts on customers whose behavior displays certain interests (e.g., travel), a company can maximize the efficiency of its promotional activities.

Tactical targeting is similar to strategic targeting in that both involve identifying target customers. However, unlike strategic targeting, which aims to determine which customers to target and which to ignore, tactical targeting aims to develop an effective and cost-efficient approach to communicate and deliver the offering's value to already selected target customers. The link between strategic and tactical targeting can be further illustrated by viewing marketing as a process of designing, communicating, and delivering value (discussed in Chapter 2). Accordingly, value design involves defining the product and service aspect of the offering, building its brand, and setting its price and incentives; communication involves creating awareness of the offering, and value delivery involves bringing the offering to customers. In this context, strategic targeting, with its focus on customer needs, guides the value-design aspects of the offering, whereas tactical targeting with its focus on communicating and delivering the offering, guides the communication and distribution aspects of the offering.

The efficiency of tactical targeting is determined by the fit between the value-based target segment (customers who share a particular need) and the readily identifiable target segment (customers who share certain identifiable profile characteristics). The efficiency of a company's targeting strategy is represented by the overlap between the value-based target segment and the identifiable profile-based segment. The greater the overlap, the more efficient the company's targeting strategy.

In the ideal scenario, the identifiable segment perfectly fits the value-based segment (also referred to as "sniper targeting"). In reality, however, it is rarely possible to achieve a perfect fit. Specifically, there are three common types of targeting misfits. "Shotgun" targeting is a form of inefficient targeting in which the value-based target segment is identified too broadly. In contrast, "oversegmentation" involves an overly narrow identification of the target segment that excludes some of the "ideal" target customers. Finally, the "shot-in-the-dark" approach involves a scenario in which the company's communication and distribution efforts are completely misaligned and are directed to a segment that might not include its target customers (Figure 5).

Figure 5. Tactical Targeting Scenarios

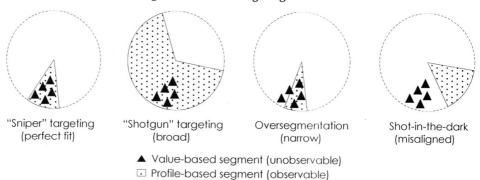

| "Sniper" targeting (perfect fit) | "Shotgun" targeting (broad) | Oversegmentation (narrow) | Shot-in-the-dark (misaligned) |

▲ Value-based segment (unobservable)
⊡ Profile-based segment (observable)

When choosing its tactical targeting approach, the company walks a fine line between defining the market too broadly and defining it too narrowly. Overly broad segmentation is inefficient because it calls for the expenditure of significant resources to reach customers for whom the offering is unlikely to create value. Overly narrow segmentation, on the other hand, is inefficient because it will likely cause the company to overlook customers interested in the offering. The goal, therefore, is to find the optimal link between the need-based target segments and the corresponding profile-based segments.

Targeting Multiple Segments

The discussion so far has focused on a scenario in which a firm identifies and targets a single customer segment. In today's world of customization and one-on-one marketing, single-segment marketing is the exception rather than the rule. Most offerings exist as part of a product line targeting multiple segments.

Because the needs of each customer segment are distinct, the basic principle in targeting multiple segments is that the company develops a unique strategy for each segment it decides to pursue (Figure 6). To accomplish this, a company must evaluate the underlying customer needs of each targeted segment, its own core competencies and strategic assets, the ways it will create value for its collaborators and deal with its competitors, as well as the impact of the relevant context factors.

Figure 6: Targeting Multiple Segments

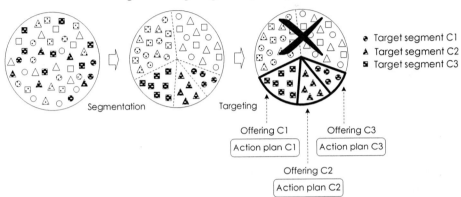

The process of developing offerings that are part of a company's product line is similar to developing freestanding offerings. The main difference in the case of targeting multiple segments is that in addition to developing a strategy for each individual offering, a company needs to develop a product-line strategy that outlines the relationship between the individual offerings in the company's product line. The process of developing and managing product lines is discussed in more detail in Chapter 17.

SUMMARY

Understanding customer needs and identifying market opportunities is the starting point in formulating a company's marketing strategy. A key aspect of customer analysis involves identifying groups of customers with similar preferences (segments) and deciding which segment(s) to target.

Identifying target customers typically involves three key decisions: (1) dividing customers into groups with similar characteristics (also referred to as segmentation), (2) selecting which customers to serve and which to ignore (also referred to as strategic targeting), and (3) creating an effective plan to reach these customers (also referred to as tactical targeting).

Segmentation should yield segments that are both mutually exclusive and collectively exhaustive. Segments should be sufficiently different from one another so that they do not overlap; yet they should include all customers in a given market. Two main criteria are used to divide customers into distinct segments: value and profile. Value-based segmentation groups customers based on their (usually unobserved) needs and the benefits they seek from the company's offerings, whereas profile-based segmentation captures some of the observable customer characteristics (which are often not directly related to the targeted needs).

In consumer markets, four types of profile characteristics are commonly used: demographic (age, gender, income, and education), geographic (country, region, and city), psychographic (personality, moral values, and lifestyle), and behavioral (user status, volume purchased, and price sensitivity). In business markets, profile-based segmentation (firmographics) is usually based on firm-specific factors (location, company size, and industry).

Strategic targeting involves identifying which customers (segments) to serve and which to ignore. Because it aims to optimize value for customers, the company, and its collaborators, strategic targeting is typically derived from value-based segmentation rather than from profile-based segmentation. The targeting decision is guided by two key criteria: segment attractiveness (customers' potential to create value for the company) and segment compatibility (a company's ability to create value for the customers).

Tactical targeting involves developing an effective and cost-efficient plan to communicate and deliver the offering's value to the already selected target customers. Tactical targeting links the (typically unobservable) value-based segments to specific observable and actionable characteristics.

Because the needs of each customer segment are distinct, the basic principle in targeting multiple segments is that the company develops a unique strategy for each segment it decides to pursue. To accomplish this, a company must evaluate the underlying customer needs of each targeted segment, its own core competencies and strategic assets, the ways it will create value for its collaborators and deal with its competitors, as well as the impact of the relevant context factors.

RELEVANT CONCEPTS

Demographics: A set of characteristics used to describe a given population. Demographics commonly used in marketing include factors such as population size and growth, age dispersion, geographic dispersion, ethnic background, income, mobility, education, employment, and household composition.

Firmographics: The key characteristics of an organization, typically used for segmentation purposes. Firmographics include factors such as location, company size, industry, purchasing process, growth, revenues, and profitability.

Heterogeneous Market: Market composed of customers who vary in their response to a company's offering.

Homogeneous Market: Market composed of customers likely to react in a similar manner to the company's offering (e.g., they seek the same benefits, have similar financial resources, can be reached via the same means of communication, and have access to the offering through the same distribution channels).

Niche Strategy: Marketing strategy aimed at a distinct and relatively small customer segment.

Occasion-Based Segmentation: Segmentation strategy that groups customers based on purchase and consumption occasions. Occasion-based segmentation is more useful in cases in which customer needs vary across purchase occasions, and the same customer is likely to fall into different usage-based segments. For example, when buying wine, a customer's preference may vary as a function of the occasion (for cooking, for daily consumption, for a special occasion, or for a gift). By focusing on usage occasions rather than on the individual characteristics of the customer, occasion-based segmentation accounts for the fact that the same customer is likely to display different needs depending on the occasion.

User-Based Segmentation: Segmentation strategy that groups customers based on their relatively stable individual characteristics, which are likely to determine their needs and behavior across different purchase and consumption occasions. User-based segmentation is appropriate in settings in which customers' needs are relatively stable across purchase occasions and, hence, can be used as a reliable predictor of their behavior on any particular purchase occasion. To illustrate, the preference for regular versus light (diet) soft drinks is fairly stable across individuals and calls for user-based segmentation.

ADDITIONAL READINGS

Gordon, Ian H. (2002), *Competitor Targeting: Winning the Battle for Market and Customer Share.* New York, NY: John Wiley & Sons.

McDonald, Malcolm and Ian Dunbar (2004), *Market Segmentation: How to Do It, How to Profit from It.* Amsterdam: Elsevier.

Prahalad, C. K. (2006), *The Fortune at the Bottom of the Pyramid: Eradicating Poverty Through Profits.* Philadelphia, PA: Wharton School Publishing.

Weinstein, Art (2004), *Handbook of Market Segmentation: Strategic Targeting for Business and Technology Firms* (3rd ed.). New York, NY: Haworth Press.

CHAPTER FOUR

CREATING CUSTOMER VALUE: DEVELOPING A VALUE PROPOSITION AND POSITIONING

There is only one boss. The customer. And he can fire everybody in the company from the chairman on down, simply by spending his money somewhere else.

Sam Walton, founder of Walmart

Managing customer value is a pivotal element of a company's strategy. Because customers are the ultimate source of value for the company and its collaborators, managing customer value is essential for a company's success. The two key aspects of managing customer value—developing a value proposition and developing a positioning strategy—are the focus of this chapter.

Developing a Value Proposition

The value proposition reflects an offering's ability to create superior value for target customers relative to competitors' offerings. The processes of creating customer value and achieving a competitive advantage are discussed in the following sections.

Creating Customer Value

An offering's value is determined by the fit between its attributes and the needs of the target customers: The better the offering attributes fit the needs of its target customers, the greater the value created by this offering. This customer-centric nature of an offering's value underscores the importance of understanding customer needs and relating the offering's value proposition to these needs.

Because value depends on customer needs, the same offering can have a different value for different customer segments: offerings that are very appealing to one segment might have little or no value to another. In some cases, the same attributes that are seen as beneficial by one segment can be perceived as drawbacks by another segment. For example, the large display and full-size keyboard of a laptop are viewed as an advantage by customers who seek to maximize performance, and as a liability by those whose primary concern is portability. In the same vein, low price can be seen as an advantage by price-conscious customers and as a disadvantage by those seeking high performance and exclusivity.

Depending on the type of underlying customer needs, an offering can create value in three different domains: functional, monetary, and psychological (Figure 1). These three dimensions of customer value are briefly outlined below.

Figure 1. The Three Dimensions of Customer Value

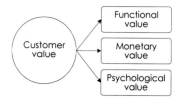

- **Functional value** is defined by the benefits and costs directly related to an offering's performance. Attributes that determine the functional value of an offering include performance, reliability, durability, compatibility, ease of use, design, customization, form, style, and packaging (see Chapter 8 for more details).

- **Monetary value** is defined by the monetary benefits and costs associated with the offering. The monetary value involves the offering's price, fees, discounts, rebates, and the monetary cost of ownership (e.g., repair and maintenance costs). Note that although from a customer's perspective monetary value is typically associated with costs, an offering can also carry monetary benefits, such as cash-back offers, monetary bonuses, prizes, rewards (e.g., cash bonus for opening a bank account), and credit toward the purchase of another offering.

- **Psychological value** is defined by the psychological benefits and costs associated with the offering. For example, customers might value the emotional benefits provided by a car, such as the joy of driving a high-performance vehicle as well as the social status and lifestyle conveyed by the car.

Even though they represent different dimensions of customer value, these domains are not mutually exclusive; an offering can create value in all three domains. At the same time, while these aspects of value define the overall value of the offering, the relative importance of each of the three aspects varies depending on the type of customer need fulfilled by the offering. For offerings that serve primarily utilitarian functions, such as office and industrial equipment, functionality is often the paramount consideration. In commoditized categories with undifferentiated offerings, the monetary aspect of the offerings tends to be the dominant criterion for choice. Finally, in categories such as luxury and fashion, where customers seek symbolic and self-expressive benefits, the psychological value conveyed by the offerings is often of primary concern.

An offering's ability to create value is a function of three key factors: (1) the attributes that are relevant to target customers, (2) the relative importance of these attributes, and (3) the offering's performance on these attributes. In this context, one approach to increasing the value of an offering is to improve its performance on attributes that are most important to target customers. For example, to make a software program more attractive to customers who care most about performance, a company might consider improving its speed. An alternative approach to make an offering more attractive is to change the relative importance of its attributes in a way that bolsters an attribute on which it is superior to other options and devalues the attributes on which the company's offering is inferior. For example, a company with software that is not very fast but is highly compatible with many other existing software products might downplay the importance of software speed and instead promote compatibility. Finally a company can enhance the value of its offering by promoting an attribute that has traditionally not been considered relevant by target customers. For example, a company offering software with a superior user interface might promote the importance of user interface even though this attribute is not one of the factors typically considered by target customers.

When designing an offering, it is important to keep in mind that its value is necessarily subjective, and that objective performance does not directly translate into subjective value. Rather, it is a function of some general principles that influence people's value judgments. One such general principle is that of diminishing marginal value, according to which the subjective value (utility) of increasing an offering's performance on a given attribute tends to decrease as its overall performance increases. For example, once an offering reaches a certain level of performance on a given attribute, further improvements in performance on this attribute tend to be perceived as relatively less valuable. Diminishing marginal values and other properties of the value function are discussed in more detail at the end of this chapter.

Competitive Advantage as a Source of Customer Value

An offering's ability to create value for target customers is necessary but not sufficient to ensure its market success. In addition to fulfilling customer needs, an offering should be able to fulfill these needs better than the competitive offerings. Therefore, an offering's ability to create customer value should always be considered in a competitive context by focusing on the offering's competitive advantage. An offering's competitive advantage is determined by its ability to deliver greater value to target customers than the competition does. It is not just about differentiation; it is about differentiation that creates superior customer value (Figure 2).

Figure 2. Competitive Advantage and Customer Value

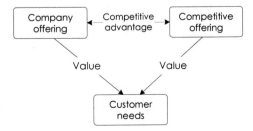

Because competitive advantage is determined by an offering's ability to create superior customer value, only attributes that are relevant to customer needs can create a competitive advantage. Differentiating on attributes that are irrelevant and do not add value for customers does not lead to a competitive advantage. In fact, differentiation on irrelevant attributes might even have the opposite effect and decrease the perceived value of the offering if customers believe that the irrelevant attributes come at the expense of other benefits that they must forgo.

In an ideal world, an offering should aim to dominate the competition on all attributes. In reality, however, this is rarely the case. Because firms vary in their competencies and assets, their offerings vary in the benefits they deliver to target customers. In this context, an offering's competitive advantage is typically defined by two types of factors: points of difference and points of parity.

- **Points of difference** involve attributes that are relevant to target customers and on which the company's offering is perceived to be different from that of its competitors. Depending on whether a given offering is an advantage or disadvantage, there are two types of points of differences: *competitive strengths*, which describe relevant attributes on which an offering dominates competitive offerings, and *competitive weaknesses*, which describe attributes on which an offering is inferior to the competition. Differentiation is not about actual differences; it is about differences that are perceived as such by target customers. Thus, an offering might have a competitive advantage even when its attributes objectively are identical to that of competitive offerings as long as they are differentiated in the mind of the customer. For example, Volvo is commonly believed to be one of the safest cars, even though in reality its safety might be on par with that of competitors.

- **Points of parity** refer to attributes on which an offering's performance matches that of the competition. Offerings need not be identical to be at parity; what is important is that customers perceive them to be indistinguishable. In this context, minor differences that are not noticeable by target customers are considered insignificant and the offerings are considered to be at parity. For example, if target customers cannot tell the difference in the performance of a 250 and a 255 horsepower car or if they find this difference meaningless, these offerings will be considered at competitive parity.

A company's goal is to develop offerings that have multiple strengths on key attributes, are at parity on the other important attributes, and have limited, if any, weaknesses on the less important attributes.

Developing a Positioning Strategy

Positioning reflects the company's view of how its offering should be perceived and remembered by customers; it is the process of creating a distinct image of the company's offering in a customer's mind. For example, Volvo positions its cars as the safest vehicles on the road, Toyota emphasizes reliability, and BMW focuses on the driving experience.

The concept of positioning can be better understood when compared with the concept of the value proposition. Unlike the value proposition, which captures *all* of the benefits and costs of an offering, positioning focuses customers' attention only on the *most important aspect(s)* of the offering's value proposition. Thus, positioning aims to present the advantages of the offering in a way that accentuates its key benefit(s) and provides customers with a compelling reason to choose the company's offering.

The key to positioning is making tradeoffs—deciding not to promote certain benefits to bring the key benefit(s) into focus. To illustrate, the driving experience is one of many aspects of BMW's value proposition, which also includes attributes such as comfort, fuel economy, design, quality, reliability, and safety. Yet, BMW has consciously decided to emphasize performance above and beyond the other attributes to create a distinct image in the minds of its target customers.

An offering's positioning often can be summarized in a single phrase that is commonly used as a tagline in company communications. Here are a few examples: *Fresh, hot pizza delivered in 30 minutes or less, guaranteed* (Domino's); *Better Ingredients. Better Pizza* (Papa John's); *If it's not Peet's, it's not coffee* (Peet's Coffee & Tea); *We try harder* (Avis); *If it's got to be clean...it's got to be Tide* (Tide); and *It's everywhere you want to be* (Visa).

Because positioning involves prioritizing an offering's existing benefits and costs, the same offering can often be positioned in multiple ways. Consider TiVo, the personal digital video recorder. Its multiple benefits include pausing live television, recording every episode of a series through the "season pass," one-step recording, instant replay, ability to record multiple channels simultaneously, and an up-to-date program guide. All of these benefits comprise TiVo's value proposition. Successful positioning requires further ordering these benefits and identifying the single most important benefit that delivers value to the customer and differentiates TiVo from the competition. For example, TiVo could be positioned as a device that allows viewers to pause live television, as a one-step recording device, or as a device that allows viewers to record one channel while watching another.

It is important to note that a company's positioning efforts do not always succeed in establishing the image it intends for its offering. Indeed, despite a company's best efforts to create a certain image in the minds of its target customers, these customers might form a very different perception of the company's offering. In this context, social media, including peer-to-peer communication and product review forums, play an important role in creating an offering's image in customers' minds.

The development of a positioning strategy involves two key decisions: (1) defining the reference point used to position the offering and (2) identifying the primary source of the offering's value.

Defining the Frame of Reference

The frame of reference determines how consumers think about the offering. For example, by naming its multifunction device "iPhone," Apple framed consumer perceptions of the device as a phone with a variety of extra functionality (an alternative positioning would have been as a personal digital assistant with the ability to make phone calls).

Depending on the choice of a reference point, two types of frames of reference can be distinguished: noncomparative and comparative.

- **Noncomparative frames** directly relate the value of the offering to customer needs without explicitly contrasting it to competitors' offerings. Noncomparative framing can involve three types of reference points: customer needs, a particular product category, and the offering's user base.

  - *Need-based framing* directly links the benefits of the offering to an identified customer need. For example, Coca-Cola's positioning as "the pause that refreshes" (1929) appealed directly to customers' need for a refreshment.

  - *Category-based framing* describes the offering by linking it to an already established product category. For example, Coca-Cola's positioning as "The great national temperance beverage" (1906) defined Coke through its membership in a particular product category.

  - *User-based framing* defines the offering by linking it to a particular type of user. For example, brands like Rolls-Royce, Louis Vuitton, and Patek Philippe are often associated with the upper social class and are often used to convey the image of high status and exclusivity.

- **Comparative frames** describe the offering by explicitly contrasting it to other offerings. The referent offering can be explicitly identified, or it can be broadly described without identifying a particular brand ("It's not delivery. It's DiGiorno"). Comparative framing typically involves one of two core positioning strategies: differentiation and similarity.

  - *Differentiation-based positioning* is by far the most prevalent approach, reflecting the belief that differentiation is the key source of an offering's value. Examples of a differentiation-based approach include 7-Up's positioning as the "Uncola" and Porsche's "There is no substitute."

  - *Similarity-based positioning*, also referred to as a "me-too" strategy, aims to show a lack of differentiation between the company's offering and competitors' offerings. The goal here is to establish multiple points of *parity* and steal share from the referent company, typically the market leader, because of customer indifference toward the two products. For example, Unilever's cosmetic brand Suave claims to "work just as hard as expensive brands."

As a general rule, comparative positioning is usually employed by niche offerings trying to steal share from the market leader. Comparative positioning is rarely used by the market leader because by comparing its offering with one with a smaller share, the market leader often ends up implicitly promoting the referent offering. This rule, however, does not hold for offerings in different price tiers that do not directly compete for the same customers; in this case, a larger share brand could actually benefit by comparing itself with a smaller share upscale brand (e.g., Volkswagen comparing itself to Porsche).

Identifying the Primary Reason for Choice

Identifying the primary reason for customers to choose a company's offering involves prioritizing its benefits—a process often referred to as benefit laddering. There are three basic strategies to prioritize the benefits associated with an offering: single-benefit positioning, multi-benefit positioning, and holistic positioning.

- **Single-benefit positioning** involves emphasizing the value delivered by the one (primary) attribute the company believes will most likely provide customers with a compelling reason to choose its offering. To illustrate, safety is the primary attribute for Volvo and performance is the primary attribute for BMW. Single-attribute positioning does not imply that the offering is inferior on its secondary attributes; it simply highlights the importance of a single attribute in order to establish a distinct message in the minds of customers. Depending on the nature of the primary benefit used to position the offering, three types of positioning strategies can be identified: functional, monetary, and psychological.

    - *Positioning on functional benefits* emphasizes a particular aspect of an offering's performance. For example, Toyota emphasizes reliability and Visa emphasizes its worldwide acceptance.

    - *Positioning on monetary benefits* emphasizes the monetary value associated with the offering. To illustrate, Southwest Airlines, Walmart, and Priceline.com emphasize low price as a key aspect of their value proposition, and the Discover credit card emphasizes its cash-back feature as "America's number one cash rewards program."

    - *Positioning on psychological benefits* emphasizes the intangible benefits associated with the offering's image. For instance, offerings such as Montblanc, Rolls-Royce, and Dom Pérignon are positioned to instill feelings of luxury, exclusivity, and prestige. An offering's positioning may also be influenced by the company's positioning as a leader in innovation (Apple, General Electric, and Procter & Gamble) or by its image as a socially responsible organization (Ben and Jerry's, Newman's Own, and Ecolab). Finally, an offering can be positioned by emphasizing risk-related benefits, such as reducing uncertainty and gaining peace of mind—a strategy exemplified by Allstate Insurance's slogan "You're in good hands with Allstate."

- **Multi-benefit positioning** involves emphasizing the benefits delivered by the offering on two or more attributes. To illustrate, a classic dual-benefit positioning is the one utilized by Procter & Gamble's Ivory Soap: "99$\frac{44}{100}$% pure; it floats." The advantage of multi-benefit positioning over single-benefit positioning is that it captures multiple aspects of the offering's value proposition. On the downside, however, multi-benefit positioning runs the risk of diluting the offering's image in the mind of the customer and failing to establish a compelling reason for choice. Consequently, multi-benefit positioning is the exception rather than the norm and is most often limited to two attributes.

- **Holistic positioning** emphasizes overall performance without highlighting individual attributes, enticing customers to choose an offering based on its performance as a whole rather than on particular attributes. For example, Gillette's positioning as "the best a man can get" aims to create a perception of superior overall performance. Colgate Total, as implied by its name, claims to offer the best overall package of category benefits. Similarly, Amoco's positioning as "America's number one premium gasoline," Tylenol's positioning as "the brand most hospitals trust," and Hertz's positioning as the "#1" car rental company in the world emphasize market leadership to signal superior overall performance.

An offering's positioning strategy is outlined in a positioning statement that identifies the offering's target customers and its value proposition for these customers. The key principles of writing a positioning statement are discussed in more detail in Chapter 21.

SUMMARY

Because customers ultimately create value for the company and its collaborators, managing customer value is essential for a company's success. The two key aspects of managing customer value involve developing a value proposition and developing a positioning strategy.

The *value proposition* reflects all benefits and costs associated with a particular offering. Because value is a function of customers' needs, an offering's ability to create value is customer-specific: An offering that creates value for some customers might fail to do so for a different customer segment. The success of an offering is determined by the degree to which it can fulfill customer needs better than the competition on each of the three value dimensions: functional, monetary, and psychological.

Unlike the value proposition, which captures *all* of the benefits and costs of an offering, *positioning* focuses customers' attention only on the most important aspect(s) of the offering's value proposition. Positioning involves two key decisions: identifying the frame of reference and defining the main reason for customers to choose the offering. Depending on the frame of reference, two positioning strategies can be differentiated: noncomparative positioning, which relates the offering's benefits directly to customers' needs and comparative positioning, which contrasts the offering's benefits to those of a competitive offering. Based on the main reason for choice, most positioning strategies involve single-benefit positioning, multi-benefit positioning, or holistic positioning.

RELEVANT CONCEPTS: THE VALUE FUNCTION

People do not evaluate offerings based on their actual attributes but based on the expected subjective value (utility) of these attributes. The translation of attribute performance into subjective value is not direct but is rather represented by an S-shaped curve with three key properties: (1) the value is determined in terms of changes from a reference point, (2) the value diminishes on the margin—the value function is concave for gains and convex for losses, and (3) people are averse to losses, which loom larger than corresponding gains (Figure 3).

Figure 3. The Value Function[1]

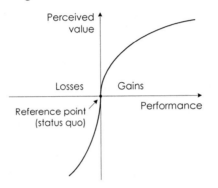

The three key properties of the S-shaped value function—reference dependence, diminishing marginal value, and loss aversion—are outlined in more detail below.

- **Reference-point dependence.** The reference-dependence aspect of the value function reflects the fact that subjective value is not inherent in the offering; rather, it is determined in terms of changes from a reference point (viewed by individuals as the status quo), such that its disadvantages are framed as losses and its advantages as gains. To illustrate, when evaluating the processing power of a computer, people are likely to compare it to a reference point (e.g., the processing power of their current computer). As a result, a 2GHz processor is likely to be evaluated as an improvement (gain) relative to a 1GHz processor and as a downgrade (loss) relative to a 3GHz processor.

- **Diminishing marginal value.** The principle of diminishing marginal value implies that an increase in an offering's performance on a given attribute will yield greater value when the initial level of this attribute's performance is low rather than when it is high (Figure 4A). To illustrate, an increase of 100MHz in computer processing power is likely to have greater subjective value when added to a slower (e.g., 100MHz) than to a faster (e.g., 1GHz) processor.

- **Loss aversion.** The loss-aversion property of the value function is reflected in the asymmetric valuation of the benefits and costs of the offering: The value function is steeper for losses than for gains, meaning that losses are exaggerated relative to corresponding gains (Figure 4B). To illustrate, the subjective value of a 100MHz in processing power will be greater when people consider it as something they need to give up compared to when they consider it as something they stand to gain.

Figure 4. Diminishing Marginal Value and Loss Aversion

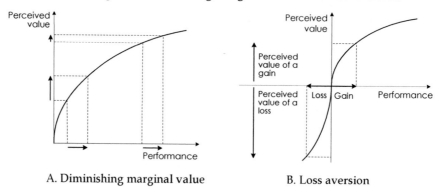

A. Diminishing marginal value   B. Loss aversion

RELEVANT CONCEPTS: POSITIONING MAPS

An offering's value proposition can be visually represented using perceptual maps, which reflect customers' view of how the benefits of the offering relate to their needs vis-à-vis the other offerings in the marketplace. Perceptual mapping offers a unique ability to represent the interrelationships between the various offerings in the marketplace and the factors used by customers to determine the value of these offerings. In general, two types of perceptual maps can be distinguished: value maps and positioning maps.

- **Value maps** (also referred to as value curves) capture customer evaluations of the attribute performance of the offerings in a given market (Figure 5). Higher levels of customer value associated with a particular benefit correspond to higher levels of an offering's performance on that attribute, and the competitive advantage of an offering is defined by the differences in its customer value vis-à-vis that of competitors' offerings. By capturing an offering's performance on all relevant attributes, value maps enable the company to better understand the drivers of its unique value proposition for target customers.

Figure 5. Value Map

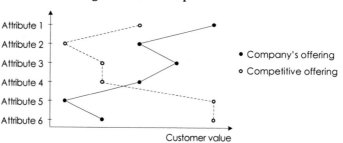

To account for the fact that some attributes are more important than others, individual attributes are ordered in terms of their importance, starting with the most important one. In addition, the relative importance of each attribute (typically given as percentages totaling 100) can be incorporated into value maps.

- **Perceptual maps** reflect buyers' perception of an offering's performance relative to that of the competition. Similar to value maps, positioning maps are derived from customer evaluations of various aspects of the offerings available in a given market. Unlike value maps, which reflect performance on *all* relevant attributes, positioning maps reflect perceived performance only on the *most important factors*. These factors may be individual attributes, such as those used in the value map or, alternatively, they may reflect holistic evaluations of different aspects of the offerings, such as a map of the overall benefits and costs delivered by the offerings. In addition to plotting the available offerings, perceptual maps can also display consumers' ideal points, which reflect their ideal combinations of different aspects of the offering.

Perceptual maps can have any number of dimensions, although two-dimensional maps are the most common because they are the easiest to interpret (Figure 6). To illustrate, in the case of headache remedies, a positioning map can illustrate the relative performance of different drugs on factors such as effectiveness and duration, such that the most effective and longest lasting drugs will occupy the upper right corner of the chart and the least effective and shortest duration drugs will occupy the lower left corner.

Figure 6. Perceptual Map

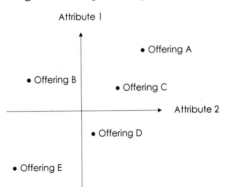

Perceptual maps can be derived by asking respondents to rate an option's performance on a set of predefined attributes (as in deriving a value map) and then aggregating these attribute-based evaluations into a few (usually two) more general factors. Alternatively, perceptual maps can use customers' similarity-based evaluations of the offerings to derive the underlying dimensions and plot the offerings onto a two-dimensional space.

Perceptual maps offer two main advantages over value maps. First, by using only a few composite dimensions instead of many individual attributes, perceptual maps offer a holistic view of an offering as it is perceived by customers. Second, unlike value maps, which typically depict an offering's intrinsic value, perceptual maps illustrate the offering's value relative to the other offerings in the market—an approach that reveals customers' beliefs of an offering's competitive positioning. At the same time, a major shortcoming of perceptual maps is that they do not capture the impact of individual attributes on an offering's overall attractiveness and do not relate the offering's value to that of its competitors.

The complementary nature of the advantages and shortcomings of value and perceptual maps reflects the fact that these two tools focus on different aspects of the value-creation process and, therefore, should be used jointly in marketing analysis.

ADDITIONAL READINGS

Barwise, Patrick and Sean Meehan (2004), *Simply Better: Winning and Keeping Customers by Delivering What Matters Most*. Boston, MA: Harvard Business School Press.

Ries, Al and Jack Trout (2001), *Positioning: The Battle for Your Mind* (20th ed.). New York, NY: McGraw-Hill.

NOTE

[1] Kahneman, Daniel and Amos Tversky (1979), "Prospect Theory: An Analysis of Decision under Risk," *Econometrica*, 47 (March), 263-91.

CHAPTER FIVE

CREATING COMPANY VALUE: MANAGING SALES VOLUME, REVENUES, AND PROFITS

A business absolutely devoted to service will have only one worry about profits.
They will be embarrassingly large.

Henry Ford

A company is a business entity established for the purpose of creating value for its stakeholders. Accordingly, managing company value is the fundamental aspect of a company's strategy, defining its very existence as a business enterprise. The key aspects of managing customer value are the focus of this chapter.

Creating Company Value

A company creates value for its stakeholders by developing and managing successful offerings. An offering can create company value in three different ways: by creating monetary value, by creating functional value, and by creating psychological value. These three dimensions of offering-created value are illustrated in Figure 1 and outlined in more detail below.

Figure 1. The Three Dimensions of Company Value

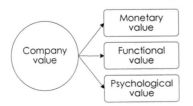

- **Monetary value** reflects the monetary benefits of the offering. Monetary value is directly linked to a company's desired financial performance and is typically measured in terms of net income, profit margins, sales revenue, earnings per share, and return on investment.

- **Functional value** reflects the degree to which an offering helps the company achieve functional goals, such as facilitating other strategically important and more profitable offerings. For example, a low-margin entry-level car can help a car manufacturer gain market share among younger customers so that they will be more likely to upgrade to this manufacturer's more profitable models. In the same vein, a free software program can provide a company with a technological platform for developing revenue-generating offerings.

- **Psychological value** stems from outcomes of psychological importance to the company employees and stakeholders. For example, psychological value might be derived from socially responsible actions, such as improving social welfare, preserving the environment, and supporting various social causes. Psychological value can also stem from working for a company known for its business, operational, technological, and/or customer leadership.

Because maximizing monetary value is the primary goal for most companies, the rest of this chapter focuses on understanding the key factors influencing profitability, as well as on identifying strategies for effectively managing profit growth.

Managing Profit Growth

Strategies for managing profit growth can be related to the key factors that determine a company's net income. A useful approach to identifying profit-growth opportunities is to map the net income tree and then determine areas in which changes will have the greatest impact on profits. Such an approach is illustrated in Figure 2 and discussed in more detail below.

Figure 2. Creating Company Value: Profit-Growth Analysis

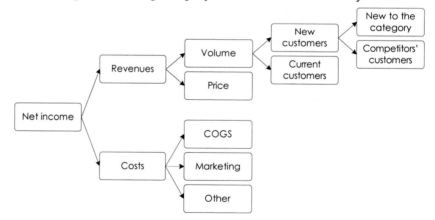

On the most general level, a company's net income is a function of revenues and costs. Consequently, income growth can be achieved by increasing revenues (also referred to as top-line growth) and reducing costs. Costs can be reduced by lowering one of the following three types of expenses: cost of goods sold (COGS), marketing costs, and other costs such as research and development costs, cost of capital, and general and administrative expenses. Revenue growth, on the other hand, can be achieved by an increase in sales volume and/or a change in per-unit price. Sales volume, in turn, can be increased either by attracting new customers or by increasing sales to the company's current customers. Sales volume to new customers can be increased either by growing the size of the entire market (attracting customers who are new to the particular product category) or by attracting competitors' customers (stealing customers from direct competitors).

The most effective strategy to achieve profit growth depends on a company's goals and the specific market conditions. In some cases, profit growth might involve lowering costs—for example, by streamlining operations or reducing marketing expenses. In other scenarios, profitability can best be achieved by increasing sales volume—for example, by generating incremental volume from current customers. Different strategies for achieving profit growth are outlined in more detail in the following sections.

Managing Profit Growth by Increasing Sales Revenues

There are two main strategies for increasing sales revenues: growing sales volume and optimizing price.

Increasing Sales Revenues by Growing Sales Volume

The development of a sales-volume strategy begins with identifying the best source of increased sales volume. In this context, there are three strategies for increasing sales volume: market growth, steal share, and market penetration. These strategies are illustrated in Figure 3 and briefly outlined below.

Figure 3. Strategies for Managing Sales Growth

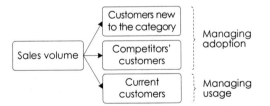

- **Market-growth strategy** involves increasing sales volume by attracting new-to-the-category customers who are currently using neither the company's nor competitors' offerings.

- **Steal-share strategy** involves growing sales volume by attracting customers who are already category users and are buying competitors' offerings.

- **Market-penetration strategy** involves increasing sales volume by increasing the quantity purchased by the company's own customers.

Note that the first two strategies, market-growth and steal-share, target customers who are new to the company, whereas the market-penetration strategy targets the company's existing customers. In this context, the market-growth and steal-share strategies are a part of a company's efforts to manage customer adoption, and the market-penetration strategy reflects a company's efforts to manage customer usage of the company's offerings.

Because increasing sales volume is the dominant approach to growing sales revenues, it is discussed in more detail later in this book (Chapter 15).

Increasing Sales Revenues by Optimizing Price

Setting prices is a vital component of managing sales revenues. The impact of pricing on sales revenues depends on the way customers react to changes in price. Thus, sales revenues can be increased by raising prices when the higher profit margin will exceed the corresponding decrease in sales volume. Alternatively, sales revenues can be increased by lowering price when the negative impact of the price drop is more than compensated for by the corresponding increase in sales volume.

In general, the impact of price on sales volume is a function of customers' price elasticity, which reflects the degree to which a change in price causes a change in quantity sold: The lower the price elasticity, the more likely it is that raising the price can increase sales revenues (see Chapter 9). Thus, in cases where the price elasticity is low and the decrease in sales volume caused by the higher price can be offset by the increase in revenues attributed to the higher price, raising prices can lead to greater sales revenues. In contrast, when the price elasticity is high and lost revenues from a price cut can be offset by an increase in sales volume, lowering price can lead to higher sales revenues.

Two issues in managing price merit attention. First, because a manufacturer's offerings are in most cases sold by a third party (wholesalers, retailers, distributors), its sales revenues are determined not only by the retail price that customers pay but also by the (wholesale) price it charges its channel partners. Second, the term "price" is used fairly broadly to reflect not only the "list" price of an offering but also various monetary incentives that include price reductions, coupons, rebates (in the case of customer transactions), and trade discounts such as volume discounts and allowances (in the case of collaborator transactions). Consequently, managing sales revenues can benefit from optimizing not only an offering's price but also its price incentives. A more detailed discussion of price and incentives management is offered in chapters 9 and 10.

Managing Profit Growth by Lowering Costs

An alternative strategy to growing revenues involves lowering costs. From a marketing perspective, costs can be classified into three categories: (1) cost of goods sold, (2) marketing costs, and (3) other costs such as research and development costs, cost of capital, and general and administrative costs.

- **Managing the cost of goods sold**. There are two basic ways to lower the cost of goods sold. The first is to lower the costs of *inputs*, such as raw materials, labor, and inbound logistics used in developing the company's offering. Lowering the costs of inputs can be achieved by outsourcing, switching suppliers, and adopting alternative technologies that use more cost-effective inputs. The second approach to managing the cost of goods sold is to lower the costs associated with the *processes* that transform the inputs into the end product, such as optimizing operations and adopting alternative technologies that use more cost-effective processes.

- **Managing marketing costs**. Marketing costs can be grouped into four categories: communication costs, costs of incentives, distribution costs, and miscellaneous marketing costs.

  - *Communication costs* comprise advertising expenditures (television, radio, print, outdoor, point-of-purchase, and event advertising); public relations expenditures (press coverage, product placement, and social media); and personal selling (sales force). Most communication expenditures are fixed costs and do not depend on the number of units sold.

  - The *cost of incentives* involves consumer-focused promotions such as price reductions, coupons, rebates, contests, sweepstakes, and premiums. Because most incentives are variable costs, increasing sales volume does not lower the per-unit cost of the incentives.

  - *Distribution costs* reflect the margins received by distributors, cost of the sales force, and trade incentives such as trade allowances, volume discounts, and co-op advertising allowances.

  - *Miscellaneous marketing costs* reflect the costs of factors such as marketing research and marketing overhead.

- **Managing other costs**. In addition to the cost of goods sold and marketing expenses, factors such as research and development costs, various administrative costs, legal costs, and cost of capital contribute to a company's overall expenses.

Managing Profit Growth via Mergers and Acquisitions

So far the discussion has focused on strategies to manage profit growth using internal resources—an approach commonly referred to as "organic growth." A popular alternative to organic growth is relying on mergers and acquisitions. In the case of an acquisition, one company (the acquirer) takes over another company. In contrast, in the case of a merger, two companies, typically similar in size, agree to go forward as a single new company in which they are more or less equally represented.

Companies pursue mergers and acquisitions when they believe that external opportunities present a better opportunity to achieve their goals than the internally available options. Mergers and acquisitions are typically aimed at (1) increasing sales volume by gaining access to new markets and gaining a competitive advantage in existing markets and (2) lowering costs by achieving economies of scale and scope.

Increasing Sales Volume via Mergers and Acquisitions

Mergers and acquisitions can facilitate sales volume growth in two ways: by providing access to new markets and by strengthening the company's competitive advantage in existing markets.

- **Increasing sales volume by gaining access to new markets.** Mergers and acquisitions can facilitate sales growth by providing access to untapped domestic markets and establishing a global presence.

  - *Gaining access to domestic markets.* Mergers and acquisitions are often motivated by a company's desire to gain access to new markets. For example, the largest banks in the United States—Citigroup, JPMorgan Chase, Bank of America, and Wells Fargo—have historically relied on acquisitions to fuel sustainable growth. Similar trends can be observed among large technology companies, including Cisco, Oracle, and Google. Combining companies with complementary products (e.g., banking and brokerage services) creates further opportunities for reaching new markets.

  - *Establishing a global presence.* Mergers and acquisitions can also facilitate sales growth by providing access to international markets. For example, hotel chains InterContinental Hotels Group, Hilton Hotels Corporation, and Starwood Hotels & Resorts Worldwide have established their worldwide presence by acquiring existing hotels in different parts of the globe.

- **Increasing sales volume by gaining competitive advantage.** Two common ways for a company to gain a competitive advantage involve eliminating key competitors and acquiring strategic resources that are in short supply.

  - *Eliminating key competitors.* By merging with or acquiring a key competitor, a company can effectively eliminate some of its strategically significant competition. For example, with the acquisition of Siebel Systems' leading CRM (customer relationship management) solutions in 2006, Oracle effectively eliminated one of its key competitors in the customer-centric applications market.

  - *Acquiring scarce resources.* Mergers and acquisitions can provide unique access to resources in short supply, such as scarce raw materials, proprietary technologies, and skilled personnel. For example, to stay on top of technological developments, medical, pharmaceutical, and high-tech companies often merge with or acquire firms with proprietary technologies. Thus, the pharmaceutical giant Johnson & Johnson acquired (in 2009) a stake in Elan Corporation to gain rights to use its research on treatment of Alzheimer's.

Lowering Costs via Mergers and Acquisitions

In addition to increasing sales volume, mergers and acquisitions can help lower a company's costs. The two most common ways in which mergers and acquisitions can lower costs are through economies of scale and economies of scope.

- **Lowering costs by achieving economies of scale.** Combining two companies often results in greater operational efficiencies due to the increased size of the combined assets and operations. Economies of scale typically can be achieved in several areas:

  - *Lower operation costs.* Combining the operations (manufacturing and supply-chain management) of two companies often leads to greater efficiency because of the larger scale and better coordination. Mergers and acquisitions also tend to lead to workforce reduction because duplicate functions are eliminated.

  - *Greater collaborator power.* Another reason companies favor mergers and acquisitions is to gain power over the other entities in the value-delivery chain. For example, the consolidation in the retail space that resulted in a market dominated by a few large retailers such as Walmart, Costco, and Home Depot significantly strengthened their power over manufacturers. This increased power subsequently translated into better trade margins, greater promotional allowances, and prioritized fulfillment.

  - *Lower financial costs.* Combining companies also can lead to a reduction in financial costs because larger firms often have an easier time raising capital and tend to have lower cost of capital than smaller companies.

- **Lowering costs by achieving economies of scope.** Economies of scope arise from synergies between the combined companies. The idea here is that combining two companies will result in greater operational efficiencies due to the complementarity of their assets and competencies. Economies of scope typically can be achieved in two main areas:

  - *Gaining operation synergies.* Combining companies can create operational efficiencies by optimizing complementary resources and processes. For example, mergers and acquisitions resulting in a vertical integration of entities in the value-delivery chain (e.g., a manufacturer acquiring a supplier) can lead to cost savings from optimizing joint operations, including production logistics, delivery schedules, and resource allocation.

  - *Optimizing financial performance.* Mergers and acquisitions can diversify a company's product line to hedge its financial performance in the case of an economic downturn. Combining diverse entities also can lower the cost of capital (in cases when diversification reduces financial risk), as well as offer certain tax advantages.

SUMMARY

Managing company value is an essential aspect of a company' strategy, affecting the very existence of the company as a business enterprise.

Achieving sustainable profit growth is the ultimate goal for most companies. Managing profit growth can be achieved by increasing sales revenues and/or reducing costs. Increasing sales revenues can be achieved by managing price and/or by increasing sales volume, which in turn can be achieved by stealing share from competitors, bringing new customers to the category, and increasing sales to existing customers. Managing costs involves decreasing costs of goods sold, optimizing marketing costs, as well as lowering various other costs (research and development costs, administrative costs, and cost of capital).

In addition to managing profit growth using internal resources, a company can grow profits through mergers and acquisitions. Companies tend to pursue mergers and acquisitions when they believe that external opportunities present a better opportunity to achieve their goals than the internally available options. Mergers and acquisitions can grow profitability in two ways: by increasing sales volume (by gaining access to new markets and gaining competitive advantage) and by lowering costs (through economies of scale and scope).

RELEVANT CONCEPTS

Economies of Scale: Cost savings arising from greater manufacturing and sales volume. Economies of scale occur when marginal production costs decrease with an increase in production output. In cases where marginal manufacturing and sales costs do not vary as a function of the output volume, there are no economies of scale. Typically, as the output volume increases, marginal costs initially decrease (economies of scale) until they reach the point at which they begin to increase (diseconomies of scale).

Economies of Scope: Cost savings arising from synergies among different offerings. Economies of scope are conceptually similar to economies of scale in that an increase in size typically leads to lower costs. Unlike economies of scale, however, where cost savings stem from increasing the scale of production of a single offering, economies of scope refer to cost savings resulting from synergies among different offerings in a company's portfolio.

Learning Curve: The curve describing how costs of production decline as cumulative output increases over time. The logic behind this concept is that labor hours per unit decline for repetitive tasks. The term learning curve is often used interchangeably with the term experience curve.

ADDITIONAL READINGS

Best, Roger J. (2008), *Market-Based Management: Strategies for Growing Customer Value and Profitability* (5th ed.). Upper Saddle River, NJ: Prentice Hall.

Henderson, Bruce, D. (1974), "The Experience Curve Reviewed: Why Does It Work?," in *Perspectives on Strategy: From the Boston Consulting Group* (1998), W. S. Carl and J. George Stalk, Eds. New York, NY: John Wiley & Sons.

Kotler, Philip, Dipak C. Jain, and Suvit Maesincee (2002), *Marketing Moves: A New Approach to Profits, Growth, and Renewal.* Boston, MA: Harvard Business School Press.

CHAPTER SIX

CREATING VALUE THROUGH COLLABORATION: MANAGING BUSINESS MARKETS

Coming together is a beginning. Keeping together is progress. Working together is success.

Henry Ford

Collaborators are entities that work with the company to create value for target customers. Because most collaborators are business entities, collaboration typically involves business-to-business relationships aimed at creating customer value. The key aspects of the process of creating value through collaboration is the focus of this chapter.

Overview

Value creation through collaboration reflects a fundamental shift away from the traditional business paradigm in which a company alone creates customer value to a new paradigm in which the value is jointly created by the company and its collaborators. Thus, value co-creation furthers a company's customer-centric business model by involving collaborators in the process of designing, communicating, and delivering value.

Collaboration involves entering into a relationship with an external entity and delegating to it a subset of the company's activities. With the rapid growth of outsourcing, collaboration has become the norm rather than the exception. The concept of a fully integrated company with its own supply, manufacturing, and distribution has been replaced with that of outsourcing, which delegates many business functions to external entities. This shift toward collaborative business enterprise stems from the belief that greater effectiveness and cost efficiency can be achieved from greater expertise and scale of operations. Accordingly, collaboration can bring together different entities, including suppliers, manufacturers, distributors (dealers, wholesalers, and retailers), research and development companies, service providers, external sales force, advertising agencies, and marketing research companies.

Collaboration typically follows one of two formats: vertical and horizontal collaboration. Vertical collaboration involves entities that occupy different places in the value-delivery chain—such as suppliers, manufacturers, wholesalers, and retailers. In contrast, horizontal collaboration occurs among entities that occupy similar positions in the value-delivery process—such as collaboration between different manufacturers or between different retailers. Given the mounting complexity of products and services and the increased market competitiveness, many businesses rely on a hybrid collaboration format that involves both vertical and horizontal collaboration.

Collaboration as a Business Process

As a business process, collaboration aims to improve a company's ability to create value for its target customers in a way that helps achieve its own strategic goals. The essence of collaboration, its advantages and drawbacks, levels of collaboration, and alternatives to collaboration are discussed in more detail below.

The Essence of Collaboration

Because it captures the relationships between business entities, collaboration is often viewed strictly as a business-to-business process unrelated to the company's consumer-focused activities. This is because business and consumer markets are very different on a variety of dimensions, including the type of customers served, the type of products and services offered, the selling process, and the nature of the relationship between the buyer and the seller. Yet, despite their differences, a company's business-focused and consumer-focused activities are closely related because they represent different aspects of an overarching value-creation process that determines the ultimate success of both business-to-business and business-to-consumer activities.

The key marketing principle—creating superior value for target customers in a way that benefits the company and its collaborators—is also the key principle that guides all forms of collaboration. Therefore, the relationship between a company and its collaborators should always be considered in the context of creating value for target customers. In this context, it can be argued that there are very few, if any, "pure" business-to-business relationships that can be considered independently from their ability to create customer value. Most business-focused relationships are in reality business-to-business-to-customer collaborations, meaning that the business-to-business component can meaningfully exist only as part of the overall value-creation process.

To illustrate, consider the typical vertical collaboration between a manufacturer and a retailer. The success of this collaboration is determined to a large degree by the ability of the manufacturer to create value not only for the retailer but for the end customer. If the manufacturer's offerings fail to create value for the customer, the retailer, in turn, will find it difficult to sell the company's offerings to these customers, which ultimately will hinder the collaboration between the manufacturer and the retailer. To succeed in the business-to-business aspect of collaboration, the manufacturer must envision the entire value-creation chain, including the end customer, and design its offering to create value for both its collaborators and end customers.

The same logic holds for entities involved in horizontal collaboration, such as research and development, product design, and manufacturing. The sustainability of this type of collaboration is also a function of the degree to which actions of the companies involved create value for target customers. Indeed, because target customers are the key source of revenues that are shared by collaborators, failure to create value for these customers will have a negative effect on the shared revenues, which, in turn, will threaten the sustainability of the collaboration.

Because collaboration is a value-creation process, it spans the processes of designing, communicating, and delivering value to target customers. Accordingly, collaboration can occur in three domains: (1) value-design collaboration—including product and service development, brand building, price setting, and incentive design; (2) value-communication collaboration—including advertising, public relations, and social media; and (3) value-delivery collaboration—including the actual delivery of a company's products and services.

It is important to note that even though they can serve different functions in the value-creation process, collaborating entities are often involved in all three aspects of designing, communicating, and delivering value. For example, in addition to delivering the company's offerings to target customers, distribution channels can play an important role in customizing the product, augmenting the service, setting the price, and managing incentives, as well as in communicating the offering's benefits by means of in-store advertisements, displays, and direct mail. In the same vein, in addition to communicating the value of an offering, advertising agencies can facilitate its branding, optimize its pricing, and design and distribute targeted incentives.

Pros and Cons of Collaboration

Like most business relationships, collaboration has its advantages and drawbacks. Specifically, collaboration offers several important *benefits* for participating entities: effectiveness, cost-efficiency, flexibility, and speed.

- **Effectiveness.** Collaboration enables companies to specialize in a particular aspect of the value-delivery process (e.g., research and development, manufacturing, and distribution). Because collaboration enables each party to take advantage of the other's expertise, it can provide both entities with a competitive advantage.

- **Cost-efficiency.** In addition to facilitating the effectiveness of the value-creation process, collaboration can also make it more cost efficient because by specializing in a given function, each collaborator can achieve greater economies of scale and experience. Specialization might also encourage a company to invest in cost-efficient solutions (e.g., an inventory-management system) that it would not invest in if it lacked scale of operations.

- **Flexibility**. Relative to developing the necessary in-house expertise, collaboration requires a lesser commitment of resources and, hence, offers much greater flexibility in terms of switching technologies, entering new markets, and exiting existing ones. For example, the development of a new distribution channel requires substantial resources and hence calls for a long-term commitment, whereas using an already existing distribution channel (e.g., renting rather than buying the shelf space) allows a company's commitment to a project to be much more flexible.

- **Time-to-market**. Collaboration enables a company to achieve the desired results much faster than building in-house expertise. For example, a manufacturer can gain access to target markets virtually overnight using an existing distribution chain, whereas launching its own distribution channel would take considerably longer.

Despite its numerous benefits, collaboration has several important *drawbacks* that include loss of control, loss of competencies, and empowering the competition.

- **Loss of control**. Delegating certain aspects of a company's activities to an external entity often leads to loss of control over the value-creation process. For example, outsourcing manufacturing operations frequently hinders the company's ability to monitor production processes and product quality. Outsourcing also diminishes the company's ability to monitor the financial aspects of the value-creation process.

- **Loss of competencies**. Outsourcing key activities tends to weaken a company's core competencies. For example, outsourcing research and development activities over time tends to diminish a company's ability to drive innovation.

- **Empowering the competition**. Outsourcing key activities also may enable collaborating entities to develop a set of strategic competencies, thus becoming a company's potential competitor.

When the benefits from collaboration outweigh the corresponding costs for each of the relevant parties, the collaboration tends to be sustainable. In contrast, when collaboration fails to create superior value for collaborators, they might pursue alternative options such as replacing collaborators or insourcing and terminating the collaboration.

Degree of Collaboration

A company's relationship with its collaborators can vary in the extent to which it is formalized. Based on the nature of the relationship between collaborating entities, collaboration can be either explicit or implicit.

- **Explicit collaboration** involves contractual relationships, such as long-term contractual agreements, joint ventures, and franchise agreements. The key advantage of explicit collaboration is that it fosters a long-term relationship among collaborating entities, which ultimately leads to greater effectiveness and cost efficiency. At the same time, explicit collaboration has certain drawbacks, such as lower flexibility, greater switching costs, and the strategic risk of creating a potential competitor by sharing proprietary information (e.g., pricing policies, profit margins, and cost structure).

- **Implicit collaboration** typically does not involve contractual relationships and, therefore, is much more flexible than explicit collaboration. This flexibility, however, comes at the cost of an inability to predict the behavior of various channel members. Another shortcoming of implicit coordination is the lower level of commitment, resulting in unwillingness to invest resources to customize the channel for a particular manufacturer. Implicit coordination is also likely to lead to lower cost efficiency (vis-à-vis explicit collaboration) resulting from a lower degree of coordination (for example, due to lack of systems integration).

Alternatives to Collaboration

A common alternative to collaboration involves insourcing the activities performed by collaborators by creating a new, company-controlled entity, or by acquiring (or merging with) an existing entity. Depending on the relative position of the entities in the value-creation process, there are two types of integration: vertical and horizontal.

- **Vertical integration** typically involves the acquisition of an entity occupying a different level in the value-delivery chain. Depending on the relative position of the entities, there are two common types of vertical integration: forward and backward. Extending ownership upstream (toward suppliers) is referred to as backward integration, whereas extending ownership of activities downstream (toward buyers) is referred to as forward integration. For example, a manufacturer acquiring a retailer to establish its own distribution system is a form of forward integration, and a retailer acquiring a wholesaler or a manufacturer is a form of backward integration.

  Vertical integration tends to be favored by companies seeking to control the key aspects of the value-delivery process. For example, ExxonMobil engages in worldwide oil and gas exploration, production, supply, and transportation. Starbucks directly manages all aspects of its business, including sourcing, roasting, distributing, and serving the coffee. American Express directly markets to customers, issues its cards, processes the payments through its own network, and directly acquires the merchant relationships.

- **Horizontal integration** involves acquiring a business entity at the same level of the value-delivery chain. For example, a retailer acquiring another retailer or a manufacturer merging with another manufacturer constitutes horizontal integration. Horizontal integration may occur among entities with similar core competencies—a common scenario for companies seeking economies of scale through consolidation, and for those seeking economies of scope through diversification.

Horizontal integration tends to be favored by companies for a variety of reasons, including gaining access to new markets, acquiring the rights to proprietary technology or research, reducing the competition in strategically important markets, and gaining power over the other entities in the value-delivery chain.

Managing Collaborator Relationships

Despite a company's efforts to optimize the value of its offerings for collaborators, often company and collaborator goals are not perfectly aligned. As a result, collaborator relationships can face tensions resulting from the different goal-optimization strategies pursued by collaborating entities. Such tensions are often facilitated by the power imbalance of the collaborating entities and frequently lead to explicit conflicts.

Collaborator Power

Collaborator power refers to the ability of a given company to exert influence over another entity. This influence often leads to an imbalance in the value exchange in favor of the more powerful entity and to market outcomes such as higher prices, margins, discounts, and allowances; preferential access to scarce resources; and premier shelf space and product-delivery schedules.

Power in collaborator relationships is a function of a number of factors, including the differentiation of collaborator offerings, collaborator size, strategic importance of the collaboration for each entity, and their switching costs.

- **Offering differentiation.** Companies with differentiated offerings in high demand are likely to have more power over their collaborators than companies with commoditized offerings. For example, companies with strong brands such as Coca-Cola, Adidas, and Samsung have more power dealing with their distribution partners than companies with lesser known brands.

- **Size.** Consolidated entities—both manufacturers and distributors—are likely to have more power over fragmented ones. For example, large consumer packaged goods manufacturers such as Procter & Gamble, Unilever, and Nestlé often receive preferential treatment (better shelf space, lower volume discounts, and lower promotional allowances) from retailers compared to smaller manufacturers. Similarly, relative to smaller retail stores, retail giants Walmart, Carrefour, and Home Depot often receive various monetary and nonmonetary benefits from manufacturers, including preferential volume discounts, greater promotional allowances, and customized product-delivery schedules.

- **Strategic importance**. An entity tends to have more power when it accounts for a significant portion of its collaborators' profits. For example, Walmart is in a position of power when negotiating with small manufacturers because their individual net contribution to Walmart's net income is low, whereas for many of them Walmart accounts for a substantial part of profits.

- **Switching costs**. An entity is likely to have more power when the switching costs of its collaborators are high and its own switching costs are low. Such switching costs may stem from a variety of factors, including a high level of systems integration between a company and its collaborator(s), long-term contractual obligations, and the learning curve associated with collaborating with a new entity.

Collaborator Conflicts

Tensions among collaborators are often caused by the differences in their profit-optimization strategies. Based on the nature of the collaborator relationship, there are two types of collaborator conflicts: vertical and horizontal.

Conflicts in Vertical Collaboration

Vertical conflicts typically depict tensions among entities occupying different levels in the value-delivery chain. The most common type of vertical conflict is that between a manufacturer and a retailer. Depending on the nature of the tension, there are two types of channel conflicts: vertical and horizontal. These two types of conflict are illustrated in Figure 1 (black arrows indicate the areas of conflict) and are described in more detail below.

Figure 1. Conflicts in Vertical Collaboration

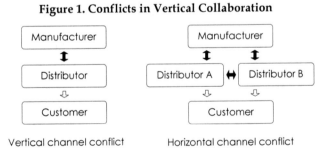

Vertical channel conflict   Horizontal channel conflict

- **Vertical channel conflict** depicts tensions between entities in a single distribution channel (e.g., a manufacturer and a retailer). For example, vertical conflict might involve tensions regarding the size and composition of the manufacturer's product line carried by the retailer. The conflict here stems from the gap between a manufacturer's desire that a retailer carry its entire product line and a retailer's desire to carry only the most profitable, non-competing offerings from individual manufacturers. Vertical conflict can also occur when collaborating entities exercise their power in the relationship to achieve their strategic goals (e.g., the supplier of a component in high demand raises the price, negatively affecting the manufacturer's sales volume).

- **Horizontal channel conflict** involves tensions among entities in multiple distribution channels (e.g., a manufacturer and two retailers). Horizontal conflicts occur when a manufacturer targets the same customers utilizing multiple distribution channels with different cost structures and profit margins. Consider a manufacturer that makes a product available through a high-margin, full-service retail store as well as through a low-margin category-killer. This manufacturer is likely to create channel conflict when the two retailers start selling the same product at different price points to the same customers.

Conflicts in Horizontal Collaboration

Horizontal conflicts typically depict tensions between entities occupying the same level in the value-delivery chain (Figure 2). For example, horizontal conflicts may occur between a manufacturer and a research-and-development company collaborating to develop a new product, between two entities collaborating to manufacture the product, and between a manufacturer and a service provider collaborating to offer post-purchase customer service.

Figure 2. Conflicts in Horizontal Collaboration

The tension between collaborating entities in this case can be caused by issues such as profit sharing, access to proprietary technologies, ownership of jointly developed intellectual property, and the sharing of core competencies and strategic assets. These tensions are often exacerbated when entities collaborating in one domain are competing in another.

SUMMARY

Collaborators are entities that work with the company to design, communicate, and deliver value to target customers. Common forms of collaboration involve suppliers, manufacturers, distributors (dealers, wholesalers and retailers), research and development companies, service providers, external sales force, advertising agencies, and marketing research companies.

Depending on the relative position of the collaborating entities in the value-delivery process, collaborators can be classified as either vertical—those located along the value-delivery chain (supplier–manufacturer–distributor–customer)—or horizontal—those usually occupying the same level of the value-delivery chain.

The key marketing principle—creating superior value for target customers in a way that benefits the company and its collaborators—is also the key principle that guides all forms of collaboration. Therefore, the relationship between a company and its collaborators should always be considered in the context of creating value for target customers.

An offering's value for company collaborators is a function of the degree to which this offering enables these collaborators to reach their goals. The benefits of collaboration include greater effectiveness, cost efficiency, flexibility, and time to market; the drawbacks include a loss of control, loss of competencies, and the possibility of strengthening the competition.

A common alternative to collaboration is integration, which involves insourcing the activities performed by collaborators by acquiring or merging with an existing entity. Depending on the relative position of the entities in the value-creation process, there are two types of integration: vertical and horizontal.

Despite a company's efforts to optimize the value of its offering(s) for collaborators, frequently the company's and collaborators' goals are not perfectly aligned. As a result, collaborator relationships often face tensions resulting from different goal-optimization strategies pursued by collaborating entities. Such tensions are often facilitated by the imbalance in power of the collaborating entities and often lead to explicit conflicts.

Collaborator power refers to the ability of a given company to exert influence over another entity. This influence often leads to an imbalance in the value exchange in favor of the more powerful entity and is often displayed in market behaviors such as higher prices, margins, discounts, and allowances; preferential access to scarce resources; and premier shelf space and product-delivery schedules.

Collaborator conflict describes tensions among collaborators, often caused by the differences in their goal-optimization strategies. Distribution channels face two common types of conflicts: vertical conflicts, which involve different levels of the same channel (a manufacturer and a retailer), and horizontal conflicts, which involve entities within the same channel level (two retailers).

ADDITIONAL READINGS

Anderson, James C., James A. Narus, and Das Narayandas (2008), *Business Market Management: Understanding, Creating, and Delivering Value* (3rd ed.). Upper Saddle River, NJ: Prentice Hall.

Anderson, Erin, Anne T. Coughlan, Louis W. Stern, and Adel I. El-Ansary (2006), *Marketing Channels* (7th ed.). Upper Saddle River, NJ: Prentice Hall.

Young, S. David and Stephen F. O'Byrne (2000), *EVA and Value-Based Management: A Practical Guide to Implementation*. New York, NY: McGraw-Hill.

CHAPTER SEVEN

MANAGING THE COMPETITION: CREATING A SUSTAINABLE COMPETITIVE ADVANTAGE

If you don't have a competitive advantage, don't compete.

Jack Welch, former CEO of General Electric

T he constantly evolving nature of the competitive landscape calls for developing dynamic strategies to manage a company's market position. Evaluating the competitive nature of the market and assessing a company's ability to create a sustainable competitive advantage are the focus of this chapter.

Competitive Analysis

The development of a competitive strategy begins with evaluating the competitive nature of the market in which the company competes. This involves two types of analysis: identifying the key competitors and evaluating the competitive intensity of the marketplace. These two aspects of competitive analysis are discussed in more detail below.

Identifying the Key Competitors

The first step in analyzing the nature of the competition is to identify the key competitors. Competitors are typically defined relative to the specific needs of a given customer segment rather than simply defined based on the industry in which the company operates. To illustrate, Canon's camera division competes not only with manufacturers of digital cameras, such as Sony and Nikon, but also with manufacturers of camera-equipped mobile phones, such as Apple, Nokia, and Ericsson. Starbucks competes not only with other coffee shops, such as The Coffee Bean & Tea Leaf, but also with manufacturers of caffeinated energy drinks, such as Red Bull and Monster Energy, and even with producers of caffeinated and vitamin-enhanced water, such as Water Joe and Glacéau. Coca-Cola competes not only with other cola producers, such as Pepsi, but also with the manufacturers of products such as juice, bottled water, and milk, which could potentially fulfill the same customer need.

Because most companies have a variety of offerings targeting multiple segments, competitive analysis is often limited to a given offering rather than to the entire company. This is because competition is customer-specific, such that companies competing for one target market might be collaborating to deliver value to another. To illustrate, Samsung and Sony compete in the flat-screen TV market but collaborate in the development and manufacturing of LCD panels. Thus, a company's competitors are business entities with offerings that target the same customers and strive to fulfill the same customer need(s).

Pinpointing key competitors involves identifying not only current competitors but potential competitors as well. Potential competitors are business entities that currently do not target the same customers to fulfill the same need(s), but nevertheless have the aspiration and the capability to satisfy the need(s) of the company's target customers. In this context, three groups of potential competitors can be identified.

The first type of potential competitors are companies with offerings that aim to satisfy the same need as the company's offering but, at present, target a different customer segment. Even though they do not currently compete with the focal company, their entry into a particular customer segment would be facilitated by their understanding of customer needs and their ability to deliver offerings that could fulfill those needs.

Potential competitors also include companies that currently target the same customer segment but aim to satisfy a different need. Although these potential competitors are not directly competing with the focal company, their entry into the company's market would be facilitated by their customer expertise, defined by their understanding, access to, and relationship with the target customers.

Finally, potential competitors include companies that currently satisfy a different set of needs of different customers. While these potential competitors do not compete directly with the focal company and have neither need-based nor customer-based expertise, they may have some of the key resources, such as strategic assets and core competencies, that could facilitate the development of successful competitive offerings.

Competitors that target the same customers and follow similar strategies to serve the needs of these customers are often referred to as a *strategic group*. Competitors in the same strategic group often have similar products and services, similar branding strategies, similar pricing and incentive strategies, similar communication campaigns, and similar distribution channels. As a result, competition among companies within the same strategic group tends to be more intense than competition among companies from different strategic groups.

Evaluating the Competitive Intensity of the Market

In addition to identifying the key competitors, competitive analysis involves evaluating the intensity with which companies are trying to steal share from one another to ensure growth. Market competitiveness is a function of five factors defined by the 5-C framework: customers, competitors, collaborators, company, and context (Figure 1). These factors are discussed in more detail below.

Figure 1. Evaluating the Competitive Intensity of the Market

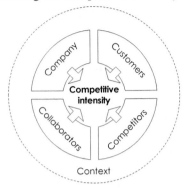

- **Customer factors**. The competitive intensity of the market is a function of the overall attractiveness of target customers, the growth of the target market, and customer loyalty in this market.

  - The *attractiveness of target customers* has a direct impact on the degree of competition the market attracts: the more attractive the segment, the greater the competition. Customer attractiveness is often linked to market size and profit margins. Because large markets have the potential to generate greater revenue streams, they tend to attract companies pursuing a high-volume strategy. Similarly, competition is likely to be more intense for customer segments with greater buying power because of the potential that these customers will generate a greater revenue stream.

  - *Market growth* has a direct impact on the nature of competition. Market competitiveness is typically greater when market growth is low, demand is stagnant, and companies have to grow sales by stealing share from one another rather than by attracting new customers.

  - *Customer loyalty* reflects the degree to which target customers are prone to switch offerings. Competition tends to be greater in markets where customer loyalty is low and where customers can easily be induced to switch.

- **Competitor factors**. The competitive intensity of a given market is a function of the diversity of the competitors and the rationality of competitors' behavior.

  - *Competitor diversity*. Markets in which competitors have similar goals, competencies, and assets tend to be more competitive than markets with diverse competitors because similar companies often belong to the same strategic group and tend to target the same customers.

  - *Competitor rationality*. The degree of competition is also a function of psychological factors such as the rationality of competitors' behavior. To illustrate, prior competitive history (e.g., price wars and comparative advertising campaigns) and the nature of the personal interactions among managers of competing organizations can have a significant impact on market competitiveness.

- **Collaborator factors**. Collaborators can influence the competitive intensity of a given market by directly entering the market or by exercising their power indirectly to influence market competitiveness.

  - *Market entry*. Collaborators can influence market competitiveness by taking over some or all of the functions currently performed by their partners in a way that makes them direct competitors. To illustrate, a retailer may insource the manufacturing, thus becoming a manufacturer's direct competitor. Similarly, a manufacturer may insource the distribution, thereby becoming a retailer's direct competitor.

  - *Market power*. Collaborators' actions can also influence competitors' profit margins, which, in turn, affect the intensity of the competition. For example, as retailers become more powerful, they are likely to squeeze manufacturers' margins, forcing them to compete more fiercely for market share to compensate for the eroding margins.

- **Company factors**. The competitive intensity of a given market is also a function of a company's own activities. For example, a company aggressively entering a particular market with a low-price strategy is likely to change the competitive dynamics by influencing overall market demand and customers' price sensitivity, and by potentially provoking a price war among the companies currently serving this market.

- **Context factors**. Market competitiveness can also be influenced by various economic, technological, sociocultural, regulatory, and physical factors. For example, government regulations such as import quotas, licenses, and tax exemptions can influence market competitiveness by favoring a particular company. In the same vein, changes in technology may lead to a shift in the strategic assets and core competencies defining the competitive advantage in a given market. For example, technological developments in digital photography and photocopying have weakened the dominant position of Kodak and Xerox in favor of companies with expertise in digital information processing, such as Sony and Canon.

Identifying key competitors and evaluating the competitive nature of the market serves as the basis for developing a competitive strategy that defines a company's position in the market.

Creating a Sustainable Competitive Advantage

A company's ability to create value for its customers, collaborators, and stakeholders is determined by its resources, specifically, its strategic assets and core competencies.

Strategic Assets

Strategic assets are resources that are essential for the success of the company's business and differentiate the company from its competitors. From a marketing standpoint, a company's strategic assets include some or all of the following factors: business infrastructure, collaborator networks, human capital, intellectual property, brands, customer base, synergistic offerings, access to scarce resources, and access to capital.

- **Business infrastructure** involves four types of assets: (1) manufacturing infrastructure, comprising the company's production facilities and equipment; (2) service infrastructure, such as call-center facilities and customer relationship management solutions; (3) supply-chain infrastructure, which aims to ensure an effective and efficient value-delivery process; and (4) management infrastructure, which involves the company's business management culture.

- **Collaborator networks** comprise two types of factors: (1) vertical networks, in which collaborators are located along the supply chain (suppliers and distributors), and (2) horizontal networks, in which collaborators are not an integral part of the company's supply chain (research and development, manufacturing, and promotion collaborators). The key to creating sustainable collaborator networks is designing offerings that deliver superior value to collaborators in a way that creates value for the company and its customers.

- **Human capital** involves the technological, operational, business, and customer expertise of the company's employees. The key to creating sustainable human capital is delivering superior value to the company's key employees and building relationships that enhance the loyalty of these employees.

- **Intellectual property** covers the legal entitlement attached to intangible assets. Two types of intellectual property can serve as sources of competitive advantage: (1) industrial property, which includes inventions, industrial designs, and identity marks such as trademarks, service marks, commercial names and designations, as well as indications of source and appellations of origin, and (2) copyrights, which include literary and artistic works such as novels, plays, films, musical works, drawings, paintings, photographs, sculptures, and architectural designs.

- **Brands** create competitive advantage in two ways: by identifying the company's offering and by differentiating it from the competition. The most common brand elements include the brand name, logo, symbol, character, jingle, and slogan, which can be used to create value for customers, the company, and its collaborators.

- **Existing customer base** creates competitive advantage by facilitating the acceptance of a company's current and new offerings and by impeding the acceptance of competitive products.

- **Synergistic offerings** are a strategic asset to the degree that they facilitate customer acceptance of related company offerings. For example, the Windows operating system can be viewed as a strategic asset for Microsoft because it facilitates customer adoption of related software offerings.

- **Access to scarce resources**, such as geographic locations and natural resources, provides the company with a distinct competitive advantage by restricting the strategic options of its competitors.

- **Access to capital** is a strategic asset when it provides the company with a unique competitive advantage. For example, access to capital can influence the resources at a firm's disposal to carry out its strategy, such as sustaining a price war, developing new products, or implementing a communication campaign.

Core Competencies

Core competencies reflect a company's ability to perform various business tasks in an efficient and effective manner in a way that strategically differentiates it from its competitors. A competency that is central to a company's business operations but is not unique is generally not considered a core competency because it does not meaningfully differentiate the company from its competitors. Thus, a core competency involves expertise in an area essential to the company's success, allowing the company to satisfy customer needs better than the competition. From a marketing standpoint, there are four key areas in which a company can develop a core competency: business management, operations management, technology development, and customer management.

- **Business management.** Competency in business management refers to proficiency in managing business processes such as identifying business goals, designing strategies and tactics to achieve these goals, and implementing a company's business plan. Business management competency also involves the company's ability to build the collaborator network required for efficient functioning of the business. This competency typically leads to strategic benefits such as business model leadership. To illustrate, Dell's core competency in business management resulted in a direct distribution business model that was one of the key reasons for its success. Other examples of companies with demonstrated competency in business management include McDonald's, Starbucks, Walmart, and Amazon.com.

- **Operations management.** Competency in operations management refers to expertise in manufacturing and supply-chain management. Companies with this competency are proficient in optimizing the effectiveness and cost-efficiency of their business processes. This typically leads to the strategic benefit of cost leadership in the marketplace. For example, Walmart's competency in operations management is reflected in its dominant position as the low-cost player in the market. Other examples of companies with demonstrated competency in operations management include Southwest Airlines, Costco, and Home Depot.

- **Technology development**. Competency in technology development refers to a company's ability to devise new technological solutions. This competency typically leads to the strategic benefit of technological leadership. Examples of companies that have demonstrated this competency include Motorola, BASF, Google, and Intel. Competency in developing new technologies does not necessarily imply competency in developing commercially successful products. To illustrate, Xerox and its Palo Alto Research Center (PARC) have invented numerous new technologies including photocopying, laser printing, graphical user interface, client/server architecture, and the Ethernet but have been slow in converting these technologies into commercial products.

- **Customer value management**. Competency in customer value management describes expertise in understanding, creating, and managing customer value. There are three common aspects of competency in customer value management: product management, service management, and brand management.

  - *Product management*. Competency in product management describes a company's ability to develop products that deliver superior customer value. This competency typically leads to the strategic benefit of *product leadership*. Examples of companies with demonstrated competency in this area include Microsoft, Merck, and Apple. Competency in product management is not contingent on the company's competency in technology management. In fact, technologically inferior products delivering need-based functionality are often more successful than technologically superior products that fail to meet customer needs.

  - *Service management*. Competency in service management describes a company's ability to develop services that deliver superior customer value. This competency typically leads to the strategic benefit of *service leadership*. Examples of companies with demonstrated competency in this area include Ritz-Carlton, American Express, and Nordstrom.

  - *Brand management*. Competency in brand management describes a company's ability to build strong brands that deliver superior customer value. This competency typically leads to the strategic benefit of *brand leadership*. Examples of companies with demonstrated competency in this area include Harley-Davidson, Lacoste, Nike, Procter & Gamble, and PepsiCo.

The relationship between strategic assets and core competencies is dynamic. Core competencies reflect the company's expertise in specific functional areas and result from a focused use of strategic assets. At the same time, a company's assets often stem from its competencies. For example, competency in database software development is likely to result in competency-specific assets such as business infrastructure, collaborator network, human capital, and intellectual property.

SUMMARY

Understanding the competitive environment in which a company operates is an essential factor for success in the marketplace. Competitive analysis begins with identifying key competitors—entities with offerings positioned to satisfy the same need of the same target customers. Competitors are typically defined relative to the specific needs of a given customer segment rather than simply defined based on the industry in which the company operates. The competitive intensity of a given market is a function of the relationships among the company, its customers, collaborators, and competitors, as well as the relevant context in which the company operates (the five "C"s).

To ensure its long-term success, a company must be able to create superior value for its target customers and collaborators—that is, it needs to gain a sustainable competitive advantage. Creating a sustainable competitive advantage is a function of a company's resources, namely its strategic assets and core competencies.

Strategic assets are the company's resources that are essential for the success of the company's business and differentiate the company from its competitors. From a marketing standpoint, a company's strategic assets include the following factors: business infrastructure, collaborator networks, human capital, intellectual property, brands, customer base, synergistic offerings, access to scarce resources, and access to capital.

Core competencies reflect a company's ability to perform essential business tasks in an efficient and effective manner. There are four key functional areas in which a company can establish a core competency: business management, operations management, technology development, and customer value management (product management, service management, and brand management).

RELEVANT FRAMEWORKS: SWOT

The SWOT framework is a relatively simple, extremely flexible, and very intuitive approach for evaluating a company's overall business condition. As implied by its name, the SWOT framework entails analyzing four key factors: the company's *strengths* and *weaknesses*, and the *opportunities* and *threats* presented to the company by the environment in which it operates. These four factors are typically organized in a 2 × 2 matrix based on whether they are internal or external to the company, and whether they are favorable or unfavorable from the company's standpoint. Analysis of the internal factors (strengths and weaknesses) focuses on the company, whereas analysis of the external factors (opportunities and threats) focuses on the market in which the company operates (Figure 2).

Figure 2. The SWOT Framework

To illustrate, factors such as loyal customers, strong brand name(s), strategically important patents and trademarks, know-how, experienced personnel, and access to scarce resources are typically classified as strengths, whereas factors such as disloyal customers, diluted brand name(s), and lack of technological expertise are classified as weaknesses. Similarly, factors such as emergence of a new, underserved customer segment and a favorable economic environment are typically classified as opportunities, whereas a new competitive entry into the category, increased product commoditization, and increased buyer and supplier power are classified as threats.

RELEVANT FRAMEWORKS: THE FIVE FORCES OF COMPETITION

The Five Forces framework was advanced by Michael Porter as a conceptual approach for industry-based analysis of the nature of competition and is often used for strategic industry-level decisions, such as evaluating the viability of entering (or exiting) a particular industry.[1] According to this framework, competitiveness within an industry is determined by evaluating the following five factors: bargaining power of suppliers, bargaining power of buyers, threat of new entrants, threat of substitutes, and rivalry among extant competitors (Figure 3). The joint impact of these five factors determines the competitive environment in which a firm operates and allows the firm to anticipate competitors' actions.

Figure 3. The Five Forces of Competition

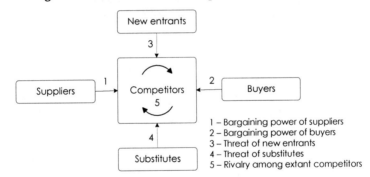

The five forces influencing the competition in an industry can be summarized as follows.

- *Bargaining power of suppliers.* A supplier is powerful when it is dominated by few companies; the product is differentiated, has switching costs, and has diverse applications (e.g., across industries); and there is a credible threat of forward integration.

- *Bargaining power of buyers.* A buyer is powerful when it has concentrated, large-volume purchases; the supplied product is undifferentiated and has no switching costs; the product represents a substantial part of buyers' costs (hence, encouraging more price shopping); the buyer's profit margins are low; the product is not crucial for the buyer; and there is a credible threat of backward integration.

- *Threat of new entrants.* The greater the threat, the greater the overall industry competitiveness. There are six common barriers to entry:
  - *Economies of scale* refer to the benefits from operating the business on a large scale (in terms of research, production, and distribution). As a general rule, large economies of scale tend to deter new entrants.

- *Product differentiation* reflects the degree to which competitive products are perceived by consumers to be different. In general, the presence of highly differentiated products is viewed as a deterrent for new entrants.
- *Capital requirements* refer to the magnitude of financial resources required to enter the industry. High capital requirements are likely to deter new entrants.
- *Cost disadvantages* (independent of size) capture factors such as experience curve effects, government subsidies, or favorable locations.
- *Access to distribution channels* refers to a new entrant's ability to ensure the availability of its products in distribution channels. In this context, limited access to distribution channels tends to serve as a deterrent for new entrants.
- *Government policy* involves factors such as government regulations, license requirements, and access to technologies (airlines, power generation, and liquor).

• *Threat of substitute products or services.* The introduction of new products tends to increase competition in an industry and limit its profitability. In general, the threat of substitutes tends to be greater in cases where the substitutes have clear advantages over existing products and where profit margins in the industry producing the substitute product are relatively high.

• *Rivalry among existing competitors.* Rivalry tends to be stronger when existing competitors are numerous and comparable in size and power (and hence are likely to have similar goals); industry growth is slow (leading to fights for redistribution of the existing market share); the product is undifferentiated (leading to price-based competition); fixed costs are high or the product is perishable; there is excess capacity; and exit barriers are high.

Additional Readings

Day, George S., David J. Reibstein, and Robert E. Gunther (2004), *Wharton on Dynamic Competitive Strategy*. New York, NY: John Wiley & Sons.

Prahalad, C. K. and Venkatram Ramaswamy (2004), *The Future of Competition: Co-Creating Unique Value with Customers*. Boston, MA: Harvard Business School Press.

Prahalad, C. K. and Gary Hamel (1990), "The Core Competence of the Corporation," *Harvard Business Review*, (May–June), 79–91.

Stern, Carl W. and George Jr. Stalk (1998), *Perspectives on Strategy: From the Boston Consulting Group*. New York, NY: Wiley.

Note

[1] Porter, Michael E. (1979), "How Competitive Forces Shape Strategy," *Harvard Business Review*, 57, (March–April), 137–145.

MARKETING TACTICS

INTRODUCTION

Strategy without tactics is the slowest route to victory.
Tactics without strategy is the noise before defeat.

Sun Tzu, Chinese military strategist

Tactics outline a set of specific activities employed to execute a given strategy. In the military, tactics refer to the deployment of troops during battle from their initial strategic position. In marketing, tactics refer to a set of specific activities — commonly referred to as the marketing mix — employed to execute a given strategy. The elements of an offering's marketing mix — product, service, brand, price, incentives, communication, and distribution — are the focus of Part Three.

- **Product** and *service* depict the functional characteristics of an offering. The key decisions involved in creating and managing the product and service aspects of an offering are discussed in Chapter 8.

- **Brand** serves to identify the company's offering, differentiate it from the competition, and create value that goes beyond its product and service attributes. The main aspects of creating and managing brand are the focus of Chapter 9.

- **Price** reflects the monetary aspect of the offering; it refers to the amount of money the company charges for an offering's benefits. The essential elements of pricing are outlined in Chapter 10.

- **Incentives** offer solutions, typically short term, aimed at enhancing the value of the offering by providing additional benefits and/or reducing costs. Managing incentives is discussed in Chapter 11.

- **Communication** aims to inform target customers about the availability of the offering and highlight its key aspects. The essential decisions involved in managing communication are discussed in Chapter 12.

- **Distribution** depicts the channels through which the offering is delivered to target customers. Managing distribution is the focus of Chapter 13.

CHAPTER EIGHT

MANAGING PRODUCTS AND SERVICES

Quality in a product or service is not what the supplier puts in.
It is what the customer gets out and is willing to pay for.

Peter Drucker

P roduct and service management aims to optimize the value that a company's products and services deliver to target customers and do so in a way that benefits the company and its collaborators. The key product and service decisions are the focus of this chapter.

Overview

The product and service aspects of an offering capture its key functional characteristics. Products typically change ownership during purchase; once created, they can be physically separated from the manufacturer and distributed to end users via multiple channels. Based on their consumption pattern, products are often classified as either durable or nondurable. Durable goods—cars, household appliances, and machinery—are consumed over multiple occasions and over an extended period. In contrast, nondurable goods—food, disposable items, and cosmetics—are typically consumed on a single occasion or over a short period.

Services are in many respects similar to products, with two main exceptions: change of ownership and inseparability. Unlike products, which typically change ownership during purchase (from the seller to the buyer), services do not necessarily imply a change in ownership; instead, the customer acquires the right to use the service within a given time frame. Furthermore, unlike products, which can be physically separated from the manufacturer, services are usually delivered and consumed at the same time.

Because services are created and delivered at the same time, they are difficult to standardize, and their quality varies depending on the interaction between the service provider and the customer. To illustrate, a customer may receive different levels of service from the same service provider at different times and in different locations, and the same service provider may have different interactions with different customers depending on customers' behavior. The inseparability of creating and delivering value also makes services perishable in the sense that they cannot be inventoried—an important consideration in industries such as airlines, hotels, and call centers, where companies with a fixed service capacity face fluctuating customer demand.

Based on the level of uncertainty, product and service attributes can be classified into one of three categories: search, experience, and credence.

- **Search** products and services are associated with the least amount of uncertainty and are typically identifiable through inspection before purchase.

- **Experience** products and services carry greater uncertainty and are revealed only through consumption.

- **Credence** products and services have the greatest amount of uncertainty and their quality is not truly revealed even after consumption.

For example, in the case of toothpaste, size is a search attribute, taste is an experience attribute, and cavity prevention is a credence attribute. In general, search attributes are more common for tangible offerings, whereas credence attributes are more typical for intangible offerings. Because services have more intangible properties relative to products, they are heavy on experience and credence attributes; in contrast, search attributes are more typical for products than services.

Product and Service Management as a Value-Creation Process

When designing products and services, a manager's goal is to create value for target customers in a way that benefits the company and its collaborators. To achieve this goal, a manager must consider five key factors—target customers, the company's goals and resources, its collaborators, competitors, and the context in which the company operates—and design products and services that deliver value for customers, the company, and its collaborators (Figure 1).

Figure 1. Product and Service Management as a Value-Creation Process

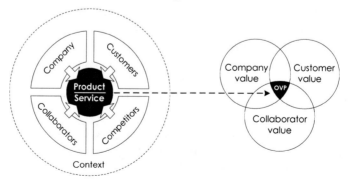

These five factors—customers, company, collaborators, competitors, and context (the 5-C framework)—are of strategic importance when designing the product and service aspects of offerings. Thus, because the primary function of an offering is to create value for its target customers, customers' needs play a key role in the development of the company's products and services. A company's products and services also depend on the company's collaborators. For example, a company might seek to optimize the channel's inventory costs by creating space-efficient packaging and/or extend the shelf life of perishable products. Because most consumer decisions involve a choice among competitive offerings, these offerings often serve as benchmarks for designing new products and services. A company's products and services to a large degree are also a reflection of its goals, core competencies, and strategic assets because they determine the capability of the company's products to fulfill customer needs. Finally, product and service design is also influenced by the economic, technological, sociocultural, regulatory, and physical *context*, including the technological specifications imposed by various government and nongovernment agencies, import/export regulations, and compatibility standards.

In addition to being a function of the five Cs, product and service design is also influenced by the other elements of the offering's marketing mix: its brand, price, incentives, communication, and distribution. Thus, an offering's products and services should be consistent with its brand, such that high-performance brands are represented by superior products and services and vice versa. Products and services are also contingent on price, such that higher priced offerings typically call for higher quality offerings. Products and services also depend on the offering's communications and should be designed in a way that facilitates informing customers about the key aspects of the offering. Finally, products and services are often designed to optimize their distribution—for example, by facilitating their transportation, storage, and on-shelf display.

Product and Service Decisions

Creating and managing products and services involves a series of specific decisions concerning factors such as performance, consistency, reliability, durability, compatibility, ease of use, technological design, degree of customization, form, style, and packaging. These factors are described in more detail below.

- **Performance**. Products vary in their performance on different attributes. For example, cars vary in engine power, acceleration, comfort, safety, and fuel efficiency. The key principle when deciding on the level of performance of a given offering is optimizing its value for target customers, the company, and its collaborators. In cases when a given offering is part of a product line, its performance also needs to be coordinated with the other offerings comprising this product line (see Chapter 17 for more details).

- **Consistency**. An important aspect of designing an offering is ensuring that in-kind products and services are identical and consistent with specifications. Because variability is a key characteristic of services, consistency is of vital importance in service delivery and is one of the main contributors to the success of companies like McDonald's, Starbucks, and Ritz-Carlton. A popular approach to managing product consistency is the Six Sigma method described in more detail at the end of this chapter.

- **Reliability**. Reliability refers to the probability that the product or service will operate according to its specifications and will not malfunction for the duration of its projected life cycle. Reliability is often used as a differentiating point to create a unique positioning for a company's offering. For example, FedEx promises "absolutely, positively overnight" next-day delivery service, the discount brokerage TD Ameritrade guarantees that certain trades will be executed within five seconds, and Verizon claims to be the most reliable wireless network in the United States with a call-completion rate of more than 99.9%.

- **Durability**. Another important consideration in product design involves the expected length of the offering's life cycle. Because durability is an important consideration in buyers' decision processes, products that are perceived to be more durable tend to be preferred by customers. At the same time, while durable products help companies attract new customers and build loyalty among existing customers, durability tends to have a negative impact on the frequency of repeat purchases since users are often reluctant to replace fully functioning products with new ones. As a result, manufacturers have to design superior models that will encourage customers to upgrade. This process of designing new products in a way that makes prior generations inferior is often referred to as planned obsolescence (see Chapter 17 for more details).

- **Compatibility**. Compatibility refers to the degree to which an offering is consistent with certain already existing standards and complementary products. Compatibility can be used strategically by companies to create barriers to entry by ensuring that offerings are uniquely compatible with customers' existing systems and processes. Product compatibility is also an effective strategy in networked environments, where users are forced to adhere to a certain standard. To illustrate, the popularity of Microsoft Office products is to a great degree a function of the need for compatibility when sharing information. Compatibility is also a key consideration in multipart pricing, where a company charges a relatively low price for the first part and higher prices for the complementary parts (e.g., razors and blades). In this case, unique (patented) compatibility is essential so that only parts manufactured by the same company can work together (e.g., only Gillette-manufactured blades will fit a Gillette razor).

- **Ease of use**. An important aspect of many products and services is their ease of use. There is a common misconception that greater functionality, such as a greater number of features, inevitably leads to greater satisfaction. In reality, however, this is not the case: Adding functionality in cases when customers lack the knowledge necessary to utilize it can backfire. To illustrate, in an attempt to incorporate the latest technology in its newly redesigned 7-series, in 2003 BMW introduced iDrive, an over-engineered computer system used to control most secondary functions of a car, including the audio system, climate, and navigation. Designed to manage more than 700 functions with a single knob, the iDrive had a steep learning curve and quickly became the most controversial feature of the 7-series.

- **Technological design**. Depending on the novelty of the offering, two technology-development methods can be identified: product innovation and product variation. The product-innovation approach involves technology-based innovations and innovative use of existing technology to design new offerings. Unlike the product-innovation strategy, which leads to substantive functional differences among offerings, the product-variation approach leads to offerings characterized by relatively minor variations in their functionality, such as adding different colors, flavors, tastes, sizes, designs, or packaging variations.

- **Degree of customization**. When designing its offerings, a company needs to decide on the degree to which these offerings will be customized for target customers. At one extreme, a company may decide to pursue a mass-production strategy, offering the same products and services to all customers. At the other extreme, the company might pursue a one-to-one customization in which the company's products and services are customized for each individual customer. A compromise between the mass-production approach and the one-to-one customization approach is segment-based customization. By developing offerings for groups of customers with similar needs, segment-based customization allows companies to develop fewer offerings while ensuring that these offerings fit customer needs. To illustrate, Dell offers more than a hundred options from which customers can choose to customize their computer; Porsche offers nearly a thousand customization options for its flagship 911 Carrera; and Nike offers more than 10,000 different design and color sport-shoe customization options through its website nikeid.com.

- **Form**. Product design typically involves decisions concerning the physical aspects of the offering, such as its size and shape. Design plays an important role in manufacturing, transporting, storing, inventorying, and consuming the product. Because customers vary in the amounts they consume, packaged goods are often available in a variety of sizes and shapes. For example, Johnson & Johnson's pain relief medicine Tylenol is available in more than fifty different SKU forms: regular, extra strength, and children's dosages; normal and extended relief; tablets, caplets, gelcaps, geltabs, and liquid—all in a variety of sizes.

- **Style**. The look and feel is particularly important for products that have a primarily hedonic and self-expressive function, such as luxury cars and fashion apparel, and could be somewhat less relevant for utilitarian products, such as manufacturing equipment. Because product styling can create value above and beyond the functional characteristics of the product, it is used by companies to differentiate their offerings from the competition. For example, Apple revolutionized the personal computer industry by designing computers that were not only powerful and fast but also aesthetically pleasing. Method Products, a home and personal cleaning products company, has managed to successfully differentiate its products through innovative, futuristic styling of the containers.

- **Packaging**. Packaging serves several key functions: *protecting* the product during transportation and storage; physically *containing* liquid, powder, and granular goods; *agglomerating* small items into larger packages; *preventing* tampering, counterfeit, and theft; providing *convenience* in transportation, handling, storing, display, sale, and consumption; offering *information* on how to transport, store, use, and dispose of the product; and *promoting* the product to potential buyers by providing them with reasons to choose it. Packaging can also be used to create value above and beyond the value created by the product itself. To illustrate, Tiffany's signature blue box highlights the exclusivity of the offering and at the same time strengthens its brand image and helps differentiate it from the competition.

In addition to deciding on the characteristics of the individual products and services, companies often must decide how to differentiate them from the other offerings in their product lines, as well as how to manage products and services over their life cycles. A more detailed discussion of managing the product and service life cycle and product-line management is offered in chapters 14 and 15.

SUMMARY

Product and service management aims to optimize the company's offering so that it delivers superior value to target customers, the company, and its collaborators. Products typically change ownership during purchase; once created, they can be physically separated from the manufacturer and distributed to end users via multiple channels. In contrast, services imply a right of use (rather than ownership) and are typically delivered and consumed at the same time.

Managing products and services is influenced by two types of factors: *strategic*, which include the offering's customers, the company, collaborators, competition, and context, and *tactical*, which depend on the other marketing mix variables: brand, price, incentives, communication, and distribution.

Product and service management involves deciding on factors such as performance, consistency, reliability, durability, compatibility, ease of use, technological design, degree of customization, form, style, and packaging. In addition to deciding on the characteristics of the individual products and services, companies often have to decide on how to differentiate them from the other offerings in their product lines.

RELEVANT CONCEPTS

Consumer Packaged Goods (CPG): A term used to describe consumer products packaged in portable containers: food, beverages, health and beauty aids, tobacco, and cleaning supplies.

Six Sigma: A methodology for managing process variations that cause defects, introduced by Motorola and later adopted by General Electric. (Sigma refers to the Greek letter σ, commonly used in statistics as a measure of the degree of variance in a given population.) The Six Sigma approach builds on the idea that for an offering to be consistent with specifications, the difference between the actual and the desired outcomes should not exceed six standard deviations. In this context, a widely accepted definition of a six sigma process is one that reduces defect levels below 3.4 defective items per million outcomes. Over time, the term "six sigma" has evolved beyond its literal definition as a specific metric and is often used in reference to a more general methodology of improving business processes that focuses on understanding customer needs and aligning the business processes to fulfill these needs with minimal variation.

Stock Keeping Unit (SKU): A unique identifier assigned to each distinct product or service.

ADDITIONAL READINGS

Berry, Leonard L. (2004), *Marketing Services Competing through Quality*. New York, NY: Free Press.

Lehmann, Donald R. and Russell S. Winer (2005), *Product Management* (4th ed.). Boston, MA: McGraw-Hill/Irwin.

Zeithaml, Valarie A., Mary Jo Bitner, and Dwayne D. Gremler (2006), *Services Marketing: Integrating Customer Focus Across the Firm* (4th ed.). Boston, MA: McGraw-Hill/Irwin.

CHAPTER NINE

MANAGING BRANDS

Any fool can put on a deal, but it takes genius, faith, and perseverance to create a brand.

David Ogilvy, founder of Ogilvy and Mather advertising agency

B rand management plays a pivotal role in marketing. Brands benefit customers by creating value that goes beyond the product and service characteristics of the offering. Successful brands are also among the most valuable strategic assets of a company. The key aspects of creating and managing brands are the focus of this chapter.

Overview

The increased commoditization in many categories has shifted the focus of differentiation from products and services to brands. Brands help differentiate the offering in two main ways: by creating a unique brand identity and by associating the brand with a meaning that resonates with its potential buyers.

- **Brand identity** includes the identifying characteristics of the brand such as brand name, logo, symbol, character, slogan, jingle, product design, and packaging. Brand identity elements should be unique, memorable, likeable, and consistent with the other brand elements and with the meaning of the brand. Brand elements should also be flexible to adapt to changes in the market environment (to accommodate shifts in consumer preferences) and the company's product-line strategy (to be extendable to other product categories). Furthermore, the company should be able to protect the uniqueness of its brand elements against infringement by competitors.

- **Brand meaning** reflects the brand-related perceptions and beliefs held by the buyers; it reflects buyers' understanding of this brand's value proposition, often referred to as a brand's promise. The meaning of the brand has a dual impact on customers' perceptions of value. First, it signals the quality of the products and services associated with the brand. Second, it creates additional emotional (satisfaction from using and owning the brand), social (group acceptance resulting from ownership of a particular brand), and self-expressive benefits (use of the brand as a means to express one's identity).

The primary function of brand identity is to identify the company's offering and differentiate it from the competition by creating value that goes beyond the product and service characteristics of the offering. To illustrate, the identity of BMW is captured by elements such as its distinct name and logo, whereas its meaning — "the ultimate driving machine" — reflects the mental associations that target customers make with the brand. A brand's identity can exist independently from its target customers; in contrast, a brand's meaning exists primarily in the minds of the buyers.

Branding as a Value-Creation Process

Brands aim to create value that goes beyond the functional benefits of the offering. To achieve this goal, a manager must consider five key factors — target customers, the company, its collaborators, competitors, and the context in which the company operates — and develop a brand that creates superior value for target customers in a way that enables the company and its collaborators to achieve their strategic goals (Figure 1).

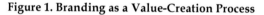

Figure 1. Branding as a Value-Creation Process

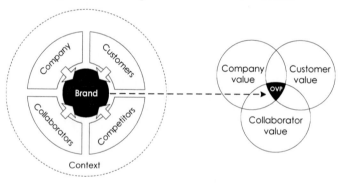

The five Cs — customers, company, collaborators, competitors, and context — define the strategy involved in building strong brands. Thus, because creating value for its target customers is a primary function of any brand, customer needs are the cornerstone for building successful brands. An offering's brand is also influenced by the company's core competencies and strategic assets, such that a company with an established reputation and expertise in a particular domain can use this reputation to build its brand. An offering's brand can be influenced by its collaborators, frequently leading to the development of co-branding strategies (e.g., Microsoft and Intel, Coca-Cola and Splenda, and Citibank and MasterCard). An offering's brand is also a function of the competition because it affects the brand's ability to create unique and shared associations (often referred to as points of difference and points of parity). Finally, an offering's branding is influenced by the various economic, technological, sociocultural, regulatory, and physical aspects of the environment in which it operates. For example, because they have become synonymous with a particular category and are commonly used as a generic term, Aspirin, Thermos, and Escalator have lost their legal trademark-protected brand status.

In addition to being influenced by the five Cs, branding decisions are also a function of the other aspects of the marketing mix, including product and service characteristics, price, incentives, communication, and distribution. Thus, the more commoditized a company's product or service is and the less observable its benefits are, the greater the importance of brands in differentiating the offering. An offering's brand must also be consistent with its price and incentives: low prices and frequent discounts can hurt the image of an upscale brand, just as high prices can hurt the image of a value brand. In the same vein, brand-focused communications tend to strengthen the brand, whereas price- and incentive-focused communications typically have the opposite effect, eroding the brand image.[1] Finally, an offering's brand is a function of its distribution channels, which often serve as a means for brand building (e.g., Disney World theme parks and Apple and Niketown retail stores function as channels delivering Disney, Apple, and Nike brands).

Brand Hierarchy

An important branding decision involves determining whether different offerings in a company's product line should be positioned as individual brands or share the same brand name. In this context, brand hierarchy (or brand architecture) reflects the relationship among different brands in a company's portfolio. There are two core approaches to managing multiple brands: individual branding and umbrella branding.

- **Individual branding** involves creating a separate brand for each product or product line. To illustrate, Tide, Cheer, Bold, and Era are individual brands of laundry detergents created by Procter & Gamble. Chevrolet, Buick, Cadillac, and GMC are individual brands of General Motors. Campbell Soup Company uses Campbell's for soups, Pepperidge Farm for baked goods, and V8 for juices. Sears uses Kenmore for appliances, Craftsman for tools, and DieHard for batteries. Diageo manages dozens of alcoholic beverage brands including Smirnoff, Ketel One, Tanqueray, Johnnie Walker, J&B, José Cuervo, Captain Morgan, Baileys, Hennessy, Guinness, Dom Pérignon, and Moët & Chandon.

- **Umbrella branding** involves using a single brand for all of a company's products. For example, General Electric, Heinz, Virgin, and Costco (Kirkland Signature) use a single brand for nearly all of their products. Umbrella branding often involves sub-branding, in which the umbrella brand is combined with a lower tier brand. For instance, Courtyard by Marriott, Residence Inn by Marriott, Fairfield Inn by Marriott, and SpringHill Suites by Marriott exemplify using sub-brands in the context of umbrella branding. Similarly, Porsche uses sub-branding for the different offerings in its product line: Carrera, Boxster, Cayenne, and Cayman. A more subtle form of sub-branding involves using brand names with the same origin: Nescafé, Nesquik, Nestea, and Nespresso are used by Nestlé to brand different beverages.

Companies with multiple product lines may also employ hybrid branding that involves a variety of individual, umbrella-branding, and sub-branding strategies. To illustrate, Chevrolet and Cadillac are individual brands of General Motors; at the same time, each one serves as an umbrella brand for its sub-brands (Camaro, Impala, Corvette, Malibu, Monte Carlo, and Blazer are Chevrolet sub-brands, and CTS, STS, XLR, and Escalade are Cadillac sub-brands).

A key advantage of an individual-brand strategy is that it enables a company to serve diverse customer segments in diverse product categories without diluting the image of its brands. Individual brands also tend to have greater brand equity because they are independent from the parent brand and can be the subject of acquisitions. On the downside, building new brands without the support of an existing brand takes a substantial amount of time and money.

A key advantage to using umbrella branding is that it leverages the equity of an existing brand, benefiting from the instant recognition of the core brand while avoiding the costs associated with building a new brand. Using umbrella branding in product-line extensions can strengthen the parent brand by raising its image, especially in the case of adding a high-end offering. Umbrella branding can also strengthen the existing brand by increasing its visibility to target customers. A drawback to using umbrella branding is that poor performance by any product carrying the brand name can easily hurt the reputation of the parent brand. For example, in 1986 General Motors introduced a Chevrolet-based compact car branded as Cadillac Cimarron and, by doing so, weakened the image of its upscale Cadillac brand.

Brand Dynamics

Once created, brands evolve over time. There are two common types of brand changes: *brand repositioning*, which involves changes to the identity and meaning of a company's brand, and *brand extensions*, which involve broadening the set of underlying offerings to which the brand is applied. These two types of brand dynamics are discussed in the following sections.

Brand Repositioning

Brand repositioning involves changing an essential aspect of the brand, most often to increase its relevance to target customers. Common reasons to reposition a brand include: (1) to respond to a change in target customers, (2) to reach a new target market, (3) to counteract a change in a competitor's branding strategy, and (4) to respond to legal challenges. These reasons are illustrated in more detail below.

- **React to the changing needs of target customers**. One of the most common reasons for repositioning a brand is to ensure that it remains relevant to the changing needs of its target customers. For example, to reflect the changing values and lifestyles of women, General Mills has consistently refined the image of Betty Crocker, a fictitious character designed to offer cooking advice to consumers. Over the years, she has had nearly a dozen different "looks," morphing from the stern, gray-haired, older woman in 1936 to today's olive-skinned, dark-haired Betty. Similarly, to increase its appeal to younger customers, Procter & Gamble repositioned its half-century-old beauty brand, Oil of Olay. The key changes introduced in 2000 included abbreviating the name to Olay (to avoid associations equating oil to "greasy"), streamlining its logo, replacing the woman's image (which resembled a nun) on the label with a younger one, and cleaning up the packaging design.

- **Reach a new target market**. Companies often reposition their brands when entering new markets to allow the brand image to reflect the specifics of that market and better resonate with the needs and values of target customers. For example, Philip Morris' Marlboro brand was originally introduced in 1924 as a women's cigarette, tagged "Mild as May"; in 1954 it was repositioned using the rugged cowboy image of the Marlboro Man, which was more likely to appeal to male smokers. Procter & Gamble's cleaning product Mr. Clean was introduced as Mr. Proper in Germany, Flash in the United Kingdom, Monsieur Propre in France, Mastro Lindo in Italy, Don Limpio in Spain (from *limpiar* — "to clean"), and Maestro Limpio in Mexico.

- **React to a change in a competitor's positioning**. Because companies strive to create superior customer value relative to that of other offerings in the marketplace, a change in the positioning of a competitor's offering often induces the company to reposition its brand to preserve and enhance its competitive advantage. To illustrate, the popularity of the Energizer Bunny in the United States forced Duracell to discontinue the use of its brand mascot — the Duracell Bunny — that is now used only outside of North America.

- **Respond to Legal Challenges**. In 1991 Kentucky Fried Chicken abbreviated its name to KFC to avoid paying license fees to the State of Kentucky, which trademarked the name in 1990. A decade and a half later, after reaching an agreement with the State of Kentucky in 2006, KFC begun to reintroduce its original name, rebranding itself once again as Kentucky Fried Chicken.

Brand Extensions

Brand extension refers to the strategy of using the same brand name in a different context, such as a different product category or a different price tier. For example, Starbucks, which has become synonymous with coffee, extended its brand to include ice cream sold in grocery stores. Montblanc — which over a century built a reputation for producing the finest quality pens — extended its brand to include items such as luxury watches, sunglasses, cufflinks, wallets, briefcases, and even fragrances. In the same vein, Oakley extended its brand from eyewear to unrelated domains such as apparel, footwear, bags, and watches.

The primary reason for extending an existing brand is to leverage its equity by applying it to a new offering. The popularity of brand extensions stems from the fact that building new brands is a costly and time-consuming task. As a result, when entering a new product category, companies often choose to leverage the equity of their existing brands rather than invest in creating new ones. Based on their relationship with the core offering, brand extensions can be vertical or horizontal.

- **Vertical brand extensions** stretch the brand to a product or service in a different price tier. Depending on the direction in which the original offering is being extended, two types of vertical brand extensions can be distinguished: upscale and downscale.

  Examples of *upscale brand extensions* include Gallo's entry into the premium wine segment with Gallo Family Vineyards Estate Series, Volkswagen's attempt to enter the luxury car market with the VW Phaeton in 2004, and Levi Strauss' attempt to enter the designer suit category in the 1980s. Because the image of the core brand generally hurts rather than helps the upscale extension, upscale brand extensions are not very common and companies often choose to launch a separate brand rather than extend an existing one. To illustrate, consider the decisions of Toyota and Volkswagen to enter the luxury car market. Both companies decided to extend their product line upscale but chose different branding strategies. Believing that its existing brand name could not convey the luxury image required to successfully compete with the Mercedes S-class and BMW 7-series, Toyota launched a new brand—Lexus—rather than try to extend its existing brand. In contrast, Volkswagen launched its upscale extension branded as Volkswagen Phaeton, prominently featuring the VW logo on the front and the back of the car. The aftermath is that Toyota succeeded in establishing Lexus as a premiere luxury brand, whereas Volkswagen failed to convince potential buyers that it could be a luxury brand.

  Examples of *downscale brand extensions* include the BMW 1-series, Porsche's Boxster, and Armani Exchange. Because they leverage the image of the core brand, downscale extensions tend to be more successful than upscale ones. The key shortcoming for downscale brand extensions is the potential dilution of the brand's image. To illustrate, the brand image of Lotus Cars (English manufacturer of sport cars) was negatively influenced by the introduction of Lotus Elise—a downscale extension featuring a Toyota-sourced engine that has been used in several Toyota models, including Celica and Corolla.

- **Horizontal brand extensions** involve applying the brand to a different product category in the same price tier. For example, Ralph Lauren successfully extended its Polo brand from clothing to home furnishings like bedding and towels, Timberland extended its brand from boots to outerwear and travel gear, and Porsche extended its brand from sport cars to sport utility vehicles. A potential downside of horizontal brand extensions is brand dilution, which is likely to occur when a brand is extended to diverse product categories that are inconsistent with its essence. For example, Heinz All-Natural Cleaning Vinegar—the company's first nonfood product launched in 2003—failed, in part, because consumers were confused by the Heinz-branded vinegar-based cleaning aid. In the same vein, Costco's strategy to use a single brand—Kirkland Signature—for all of its store-branded products, from food and wine to cleaning supplies, appliances, and clothes, curbs its ability to attach a specific meaning to its brand.

Brand Equity

The term brand equity refers to the financial value of the brand; it is the net present value of the financial benefits derived from the brand. Brand equity reflects the financial outcome from brand ownership and determines the premium that should be placed on a company's valuation because of brand ownership.

Brand Equity and Brand Power

A key driver of brand equity is the brand's power. Brand power reflects the brand's ability to differentiate the offering from the competition and create customer value through meaningful associations. Unlike brand equity, which reflects the value of the brand to the company, brand power reflects the value a brand creates in the minds of customers.

Brand equity is a function of brand power as well as a number of additional factors reflecting the company's utilization of the power of its brand, such as user base, sales volume, and pricing. A stronger brand does not automatically translate into greater brand equity. For example, although the Armani, Moët & Chandon, Audi, and Lexus brands are considered stronger than the Gap, McDonald's, Volkswagen, and Toyota brands, respectively (as measured by the greater price premium they command over identical unbranded products), the equity of the latter set of brands is estimated to be higher than that of the former: For example, the brand equity of Toyota is estimated to be higher than the brand equity of Lexus, even though Lexus commands a greater price premium compared to Toyota.[2]

Brand power can be defined as the differential impact of brand knowledge on consumer response to an offering's marketing efforts.[3] This means that a brand has greater power when customers react more favorably to an offering because they are aware of the brand name. To illustrate, one of the benefits of brand power is the price premium customers are willing to pay for the branded product compared to the identical unbranded product. In addition to the price premium, other dimensions of brand power include greater customer loyalty; enhanced perception of product performance; greater licensing, merchandising, and brand extension opportunities; less vulnerability to service inconsistencies and marketing crises; more elastic response to price decreases and more inelastic response to price increases; greater communication effectiveness; and increased channel power. Because powerful brands can influence all aspects of an offering, building strong brands is of crucial importance to sustainable growth.

Measuring Brand Equity

Knowing the monetary value of a company's brands is essential for company valuation, such as in the case of mergers and acquisitions, sale of assets, licensing, financing, and estimating benefits from or damages to the brand. Despite the importance of brand equity, there is no commonly agreed-upon methodology for its calculation; instead, there are several alternative methods, each placing emphasis on different aspects of brand equity. The three most common approaches to measuring brand equity are outlined below.

- **Cost-based approach** involves calculating brand equity based on the costs involved (e.g., marketing research, advertising, and legal costs) if the brand needs to be created from scratch at the time of valuation.

- **Market-based approach** involves calculating brand equity based on the difference in the cash flows generated from the branded product and a functionally equivalent but nonbranded product, adjusted for the costs of creating the brand. The market-based approach can be summarized as follows:

$$\text{Brand equity} = \text{Sales revenues}_{\text{Brand}} - \text{Sales revenues}_{\text{Generic}} - \text{Branding costs}$$

- **Financial approach** involves calculating brand equity based on the net present value of the cash flows derived from the brand's future earnings. This approach typically involves three key steps: (1) estimating the company's future cash flows, (2) estimating the contribution of the brand to these cash flows, and (3) adjusting these cash flows using a risk factor that reflects the volatility of the earnings attributed to the brand. The financial approach can be summarized as follows:

$$\text{Brand equity} = \text{NPV of future cash flows} \cdot \text{Brand contribution factor} \cdot \text{Risk factor}$$

The financial approach to estimating brand equity can be illustrated using Interbrand's methodology, which is the basis for *Business Week's* annual ranking of the top 100 brands. Interbrand's method involves three steps. The first step consists of estimating the percentage of the overall revenues that can be attributed to the brand. Based on reports from analysts at JPMorgan Chase, Citigroup, and Morgan Stanley, Interbrand projects five years of earnings and sales for the products and services associated with the brand. Interbrand then deducts the estimated earnings that can be attributed to tangible assets, on the assumption that the income generated beyond that point is the result of intangible assets. The next step involves stripping out the nonbrand intangibles such as patents, trademarks, technological know-how, and management strength to determine the portion of the company's income generated by intangible assets that can be attributed to the brand. The final step involves assessing the risk profile of these projected earnings based on a variety of factors such as market leadership, stability, market growth, global reach, trend, support (investment in the brand), and protection. The discount rate resulting from this risk analysis is applied to brand-related earnings to produce the net present value of the brand.

The validity of the above brand equity models is closely tied to the validity of their assumptions, such that small changes in the underlying assumptions can lead to significant changes in brand valuations. Therefore, using alternative valuation methods that employ different assumptions can greatly improve the accuracy and consistency of the resulting brand equity estimates.

SUMMARY

A brand is a marketing tool created for the purpose of differentiating a company's offering from the competition and creating value for customers, the company, and its collaborators. A brand has two key aspects: (1) brand identity, which includes identifying characteristics such as name, sign, symbol, character, and design, and (2) brand meaning, which reflects a set of offering-related associations in the mind of the buyer. Brand identity aims to *identify* the company's offering and *differentiate* it from the competition. In contrast, brand meaning aims to *create value* (for customers, the company, and its collaborators) that goes beyond the product and service characteristics of the offering.

Managing brands involves two types of decisions: (1) *strategic decisions*, which are a function of the offering's target market, defined by its customers, company, collaborators, competition, and context, and (2) *tactical decisions*, which are a function of the other marketing mix variables: product, service, price, incentives, communication, and distribution.

Two important branding decisions involve managing the brand hierarchy and managing the brand dynamics. Brand hierarchy reflects the relationships among different brands in a company's portfolio. The two popular approaches to managing multiple brands are individual branding and umbrella branding. Brand dynamics reflect the evolution of the brand over time. The two common types of brand dynamics are brand repositioning — which involves changes to an existing brand, most often to make the brand more relevant to its target customers — and brand extension — which involves broadening the set of underlying product categories to which the brand is applied without necessarily changing the core brand.

Brand equity is the net present value of the financial benefits derived from the brand. Brand equity is a function of brand power, as well as a number of additional factors reflecting the company's utilization of the strength of its brand. Brand power reflects the brand's ability to differentiate the offering from the competition and create customer value through meaningful associations. Unlike brand equity, which reflects the value of the brand to the company, brand power reflects the value the brand creates for customers. The three most popular approaches to measuring brand equity are cost-based (the cost of recreating the brand), market-based (the difference in the cost-adjusted cash flows of a branded and nonbranded product), and financial (the net present value of the cash flows of the offering's future earnings that are attributed to the brand). Using alternative valuation methods that employ different assumptions can greatly improve the accuracy and consistency of the resulting brand equity estimates.

RELEVANT CONCEPTS

Brand Audit: A comprehensive analysis of a brand, most often to determine the sources of brand equity.

Brand Essence: The fundamental nature of the brand, also referred to as "brand promise." Brand essence distills the meaning of the brand into one key aspect—the positioning of the brand. One way to think about brand essence is to think of the "ness" of the brand, such as "BMW-ness," "Apple-ness," and "Microsoft-ness."

Branded House: Term used in reference to the branding strategy in which a company's brand is used on all of the offerings in its brand portfolio. Companies using this strategy include General Electric, Ford, Heinz, and Virgin. See also *house of brands*.

Co-branding: Branding strategy that involves combining two or more brands, typically from different product categories. Examples of co-branding include United Airlines–JPMorgan Chase–Visa credit cards, Lexus "Coach edition" sport utility vehicles, and HP–iPod MP3 players. A form of co-branding involves ingredient branding in which an ingredient or component of a product has its own brand identity, such as Teflon surface protector, Gore-Tex fabrics, NutraSweet and Splenda sweeteners, and Intel microprocessors.

Copyright: A legal term describing rights given to creators for their literary and artistic works. The types of works covered by copyright include literary works such as novels, poems, plays, reference works, newspapers, and computer programs; databases; films, musical compositions, and choreography; artistic works such as paintings, drawings, photographs, and sculpture; architecture; and advertisements, maps, and technical drawings.

Fighting Brand: A downscale (lower priced) brand introduced to shield a major brand from low-priced competitors.

Generification: Colloquialized use of brand names (e.g., in reference to the products they are associated with). The use of a brand name as a generic term can lead to the loss of a company's right to the exclusive use of that brand name. To illustrate, Trampoline, Brazier, Escalator, Thermos, Yo-Yo, and Aspirin lost their trademark-protected status because of popular use; Xerox, Rollerblade, Velcro, and Google are considered to be at risk of following them.

Global Brand: A brand with a comprehensive international distribution system, such as Coca-Cola, Pepsi, and Sony.

House of Brands: Term used in reference to the umbrella branding strategy in which a company holds a portfolio of individual and typically unrelated brands. Companies using this strategy include Procter & Gamble, Unilever, and Diageo. See also *branded house*.

Industrial Property: A type of intellectual property that involves (1) *inventions* (patents), (2) *industrial designs*, and (3) *identity marks* such as trademarks, service marks, commercial names, and designations, including indications of source and appellations of origin. An invention is a product or process that provides a new way of doing something or offers new solutions to technical problems; a patent is an exclusive right granted for an invention. An industrial design is the aesthetic aspect of a product and may consist of three-dimensional features such as shape or surface, or two-dimensional features such as patterns, lines, or color. Industrial design is primarily of an aesthetic nature and does not protect any technical aspects of the product to which it is applied. Identity marks such as trademarks, service marks, commercial names, and designations are designed to identify an offering or a company and protect it from the competition. A trademark (or service mark in the case of services) is a distinctive sign that identifies certain goods or services as those produced or provided by a specific entity. A geographical indication is a sign used on goods that have a specific geographical origin and possess qualities or a reputation that stem from the place of origin. Geographical indications may be used for a wide variety of agricultural products, such as "Tuscany" for olive oil produced in the Tuscany region of Italy, or "Roquefort" for cheese produced in the Roquefort area of France.

Intellectual Property: The legal entitlement attached to the expressed form of an idea, or to some other intangible subject matter. Intellectual property is divided into two categories: (1) *industrial property*, which encompasses inventions, industrial designs, and identity marks such as trademarks, service marks, commercial names, and designations, including indications of source and appellations of origin, and (2) *copyright*, which includes literary and artistic works such as novels, poems and plays, films, musical works; artistic works such as drawings, paintings, photographs and sculptures; and architectural designs.

National Brand: A brand available nationwide.

Private Label: Branding strategy in which an offering is branded by the retailer (Kirkland Signature, Costco's private brand; Kenmore, Sears' brand for home appliances; White Cloud, Walmart's private label for laundry detergents). Private labels (also referred to as store brands) are often contrasted with national brands, which are branded by the manufacturer or a third party rather than by the retailer (Coca-Cola, IBM, and Nike). Typically, private labels tend to be less expensive than national brands, although there are many exceptions, such as private labels offered by upscale retailers (Nordstrom, Marks & Spencer).

Regional Brand: A brand available only in a particular geographic region.

Store Brand: See *private label*.

ADDITIONAL READINGS

Aaker, David A. (1996), *Building Strong Brands*. New York, NY: Free Press.

Keller, Kevin Lane (2007), *Strategic Brand Management: Building, Measuring, and Managing Brand Equity* (3rd ed.). Upper Saddle River, NJ: Prentice Hall.

Kapferer, Jean-Noël (2008), *The New Strategic Brand Management: Creating and Sustaining Brand Equity Long Term* (4th ed.). Sterling, VA: Kogan Page.

Kumar, Nirmalya and Jan-Benedict E. M. Steenkamp (2007), *Private Label Strategy: How to Meet the Store Brand Challenge*. Boston, MA: Harvard Business School Press.

Tybout, Alice M. and Tim Calkins (2005), *Kellogg on Branding*. Hoboken, NJ: John Wiley & Sons.

NOTES

[1] With the exception of companies such as Walmart, Home Depot, and Priceline.com, where low prices are directly related to the essence of the brand.

[2] *Business Week* (2008), "The 100 Top Brands," September 29.

[3] Keller, Kevin Lane (2007), *Strategic Brand Management: Building, Measuring, and Managing Brand Equity* (3rd ed.). Upper Saddle River, NJ: Prentice Hall.

Chapter Ten

Managing Price

Price is what you pay. Value is what you get.

Warren Buffett

Pricing plays an important role in determining the success of an offering because it directly influences the value that the offering creates for target customers, the company, and its collaborators. Moreover, from a company's perspective, price is the only marketing mix variable that produces revenue for the company; all other variables are costs. The main aspects of price management are the focus of this chapter.

Overview

Despite the fundamental role pricing plays in designing and managing a company's offerings, there is little consensus on what constitutes the optimal pricing strategy. Over time, three popular approaches to pricing have emerged: cost-based pricing, competitive pricing, and demand pricing.

- **Cost-based pricing** involves setting prices using the company's costs as a benchmark. In the most extreme case, referred to as *cost-plus pricing*, an offering's final price is determined by adding a fixed markup to the cost of the offering.

- **Competitive pricing** calls for using competitors' prices as benchmarks. A popular version of this approach, referred to as *competitive-parity pricing*, involves setting the offering's price in a way that puts it at parity with that of competitors.

- **Demand pricing** calls for setting prices based on customers' willingness to pay for the benefits afforded by the company's offering.

Each of these three approaches is correct in its own way; all three factors need to be taken into consideration when setting price. Yet, all three methods miss the point that the pricing decision is not made in isolation but is an integral component of the offering's strategy and tactics. Setting the price is a decision about value, not just price. The "optimal" price is a price that, in combination with the other marketing mix variables (product, service, brand, incentives, communication, and distribution), delivers superior value to target customers, the company, and collaborators.

Pricing as a Value-Creation Process

The "ideal" price must optimize the value of the offering for target customers, the company, and its collaborators. When setting prices, a manager must consider five key factors—target customers, the company's goals and resources, its collaborators, competitors, and the context in which the company operates—and identify the price that creates the optimal value proposition for customers, the company, and its collaborators (Figure 1).

Figure 1. Pricing as a Value-Creation Process

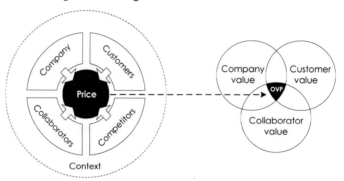

The five Cs—customers, company, collaborators, competitors, and context—are of strategic importance in setting and managing prices. Thus, price is a function of customers' willingness to pay for the offering's benefits, such that greater willingness to pay typically translates into higher prices. Pricing is also a function of the company's goals and cost structure, whereby aggressive sales goals, and/or lower cost structure often result in lower prices. Pricing is also influenced by the company's collaborators (e.g., channel partners), such that more powerful channels (e.g., Walmart, Costco, and Carrefour) require lower prices. Because most purchase decisions involve choosing between competing offerings, an offering's price is also influenced by competitors' prices. Pricing also is a function of various economic, technological, sociocultural, regulatory, and physical factors of the environment in which the company operates.

In addition to being a function of the five Cs, price is also influenced by the other marketing mix variables: product and service characteristics, brand, incentives, communication, and distribution. Thus, attractive and unique products and services command higher prices compared to less differentiated offerings. Price is also a function of the offering's brand, such that strong brands command substantial price premiums over weaker brands and unbranded offerings. Pricing also depends on the available incentives (e.g., promotional allowances, price discounts, and coupons), which determine the final amount buyers pay for an offering. Price can also be influenced by a company's communication and can be set in a way that facilitates communication (e.g., $5 footlong sandwiches at Subway). An offering's price is also a function of its distribution, such that channels with a lower cost structure tend to offer lower prices.

Customer-Based Pricing

Setting the optimal price is driven by a variety of considerations, including the size of the target segment, customers' price sensitivity, and the psychological aspects of customers' response to the offering's price. The role of these factors in setting the optimal price is discussed in more detail in the following sections.

Skim and Penetration Pricing

Because sales volume is a function of price, the company has to determine the price level at which it is most likely to achieve its goals. When launching a new offering, a company can employ one of two core pricing strategies: skim pricing and penetration pricing.

- **Skim pricing** involves setting a high price to "skim the cream" off the top of the market, represented by customers who value the offering and are willing to pay a relatively high price for it. By setting high prices, skim pricing maximizes profit margins, usually at the expense of market share. Skim pricing is more appropriate in cases where (1) demand is relatively inelastic and lowering the price is not likely to substantially increase sales volume, (2) there is little or no competition for the target segment, (3) cost is not a direct function of volume and significant cost savings are not achieved as cumulative volume increases, (4) being the market pioneer is unlikely to result in a sustainable competitive advantage, and (5) the company lacks the capital required for large-scale production.

- **Penetration pricing** involves setting relatively low prices in an attempt to gain higher sales volume, albeit at relatively low margins. Penetration pricing is more appropriate in cases where (1) demand is relatively elastic — that is, lowering the price is likely to substantially increase sales volume, (2) the target segment becomes increasingly competitive, (3) cost is a function of volume and, as a result, significant cost savings are expected as cumulative volume increases, and (4) being the market pioneer is likely to result in a sustainable competitive advantage

Price Sensitivity

Typically, sales volume is inversely related to price: Lowering the price results in an increase in the sales volume, and vice versa. The degree to which changing the price influences sales volume is a function of customers' price sensitivity. Lowering the price in order to increase volume is most effective in cases where demand is elastic, meaning that a small change in price leads to a large change in sales volume. In contrast, in cases where demand is inelastic, profits may often be increased by raising the price since the decrease in sales volume resulting from the change in price is likely to be relatively small.

The price–quantity relationship is specific to each offering and is quantified in terms of an offering's price elasticity. Price elasticity represents the percentage change in quantity sold ($\Delta Q\%$) relative to the percentage change in price ($\Delta P\%$) for a given product or service. Because the quantity demanded decreases when the price increases, this ratio is negative; however, for practical purposes, the absolute value of the ratio is used, and price elasticity is often reported as a positive number.

$$E_p = \frac{\Delta Q\%}{\Delta P\%} = \frac{\Delta Q \cdot P}{\Delta P \cdot Q}$$

To illustrate, a price elasticity of –2 means that a 5% price increase will result in a 10% decrease in the quantity sold. In cases where (the absolute value of) price elasticity is greater than one, demand is said to be elastic in the sense that a change in price causes a larger change in quantity demanded. In contrast, when (the absolute value of) price elasticity is less than one, demand is said to be inelastic, meaning that a change in price results in a smaller change in quantity demanded. When (the absolute value of) price elasticity is equal to one, demand is said to be unitary, meaning that a change in price results in an equal change in quantity demanded.

Because price elasticity reflects proportional changes, it does not depend on the units in which the price and quantity are expressed. Note also that because price elasticity is a function of the initial values, the same absolute changes in price can lead to different price elasticity values at different price points. For example, the volume decline resulting from lowering the price by five cents might be 5% when the initial price is $5.00 but only 1% when the initial price is $1.00.

Psychological Pricing

Consumers do not always evaluate prices objectively; instead, their reaction to an offering's price depends on a variety of psychological factors. The five most common psychological pricing effects—reference-price effects, price–quantity effects, price-tier effects, price-ending effects, and product-line effects—are outlined below.

- **Reference-price effects.** To assess the price of a given offering, people typically evaluate it relative to other prices, which serve as reference points. These reference prices can be either internal, such as a remembered price from a prior purchase occasion, or external, such as the readily available price of a competitive offering. By strategically choosing the reference price, a company can frame the price of its offering in a way that makes it more attractive to potential buyers, for example, by comparing it to a more expensive competitive offering.

- **Price–quantity effects.** People are more sensitive to changes in price than to changes in quantity. To illustrate, the sales volume of a ten-pack of hot dogs priced at $2.49 is likely to decline to a greater extent following a $.50 price increase (a ten-pack for $2.99) than following a two-item reduction in unit volume (an eight-pack for $2.49), even though on a per-item basis, the eight-pack is more expensive than the ten-pack.

- **Price-tier effects.** People encode prices in tiers, such that an item priced at $1.99 is typically encoded into the "$1+" price tier, whereas an item priced at $2.00 is typically classified into the "$2+" price tier. This tiered price encoding leads to the somewhat paradoxical perception that the difference between items priced at \$1.99 and \$2.00 is one dollar rather than one cent.

- **Price-ending effects.** Customers' perception of prices is also a function of price endings. For example, prices ending in "9" often create the perception of a discount, whereas prices ending in "0" tend to create the perception of quality.

- **Product-line effects.** Because many offerings are available as part of a company's product line, their relative prices can influence the demand for these offerings. To illustrate, restaurants often price wine they are trying to dispose of as the second cheapest in its assortment because many customers who are not willing to spend much on wine are often embarrassed to select the least expensive one.

Competitive Pricing

Price wars are very common in today's competitive markets. Price wars might involve price reductions offered directly from manufacturers to end users (price discounts, volume discounts, and coupons), as well as price cuts and incentives offered by manufacturers to channel partners (wholesale discounts and various promotional allowances). For example, a significant increase in a manufacturer's promotional allowances may prompt retailers to lower prices, thus provoking a price war.

Understanding Price Wars

Price wars often start when a company is willing to sacrifice margins to gain sales volume. Price wars usually begin with an action that results in a price cut on the customers' end. Price cuts, the forerunner of price wars, are popular among managers because they are easy to implement and typically produce fast results, especially when a company's goal is to increase sales volume. Not every price cut, however, leads to a price war. The likelihood of price wars is a function of the following factors:

- **Offering differentiation.** Price wars are more likely when offerings are undifferentiated and can be easily substituted.

- **Cost structure.** Companies are more likely to engage in price wars when significant economies of scale can be achieved by increasing volume.

- **Market growth.** Price wars are more likely to occur when markets are stagnant, and to grow sales a company has to steal share from its direct competitors.

- **Customer loyalty.** Companies are more likely to engage in price wars in markets in which customers are price sensitive and their switching costs are low.

Price wars are easy to initiate but costly to win. Winning a price war often comes at the expense of a significant loss of profits, making it more of a Pyrrhic victory than a true success. Price wars are detrimental to a company's profitability for several reasons:

- **Fixed-cost effect**. Price reductions have an exponential impact on profitability. To illustrate, reducing the price of an offering with a 10% profit margin by 1% will result in a 10% decrease in operating income unless there is a significant increase in sales volume.

- **Competitive reaction**. Because in most cases competitors can easily match price reductions, they are rarely sustainable. Firms with similar cost structures can quickly lower their prices in response to a competitor's action.

- **Increased price sensitivity**. Price wars often result in a shift in customers' future price expectations, such that the lowered prices become the reference points against which future prices are judged.

- **Brand devaluation**. Emphasis on price tends to erode brand power. This effect is exacerbated by the heavy price-focused communication campaigns that tend to accompany most price wars (because a company needs to promote the low price so that it can generate sufficient incremental volume to offset the lost profits resulting from the decrease in price).

Price wars rarely enable companies to achieve their strategic goals, and in most cases the only true beneficiaries of a price war are the company's customers. Quite often, the best strategy for a company to win a potential price war is to avoid it.

Circumventing Price Wars

Even companies not seeking a price war are often confronted with a scenario in which a competitor initiates a price cut. The gut reaction of most managers in such cases is to respond with a matching price cut. This, however, is often a premature and suboptimal reaction. Only after evaluating the antecedents and likely consequences of the price cut can a company identify the optimal response strategy. A relatively simple approach for developing a strategic response to a competitor's price cut is outlined below.

- **Verify the threat of a price war**. Price wars are often caused by miscommunication of pricing information or misinterpretation of a competitor's strategic goals. Thus, when competitive prices are not readily available (e.g., in contract bidding), a company may incorrectly believe that a particular competitor has significantly lowered its price. It is also possible that a competitor's price decrease is driven by internal factors, such as clearing the inventory (e.g., prior to introducing a new model), rather than by an intention to initiate a price war.

- **Evaluate the likely impact of the competitor's actions**. Identify customers most likely to be affected by competitors' price cuts and estimate their value to the company as well as their likely response to the price cut. In certain cases, a company might choose to abandon markets that have no strategic importance and in which customer loyalty is low.

- **Develop segment-specific strategies to address the competitive threat**. There are three basic strategies to respond to the threat of a price war: not taking an action, repositioning an existing offering, and adding new offerings (see Chapter 7 for more details).

  - *Not taking an action.* The decision to ignore a competitor's price cut reflects a company's belief that the price cut will not have a significant impact on the company's market position, that the price cut is not sustainable and will dissipate by itself, or that serving the customer segment targeted by the price cut is no longer viable for the company.

  - *Repositioning the existing offering by lowering the price or increasing the benefits.* This reduction in price can be accomplished either on a permanent basis by lowering the actual price or as a temporary solution by offering price incentives.

  - *Adding a new offering.* A common response to low-priced competitors involves launching a downscale extension, commonly referred to as a fighting brand. Using a fighting brand enables the company to compete for price-sensitive customers without discounting its premium offering (see Chapter 17 for more details).

SUMMARY

The key to determining the optimal price is to consider its implications on an offering's value for customers, collaborators, and the company in a broad context that involves all other aspects of the company's strategy and tactics. Setting the price is really a decision about value, not just price. Thus, the optimal price is one that, in combination with the other marketing mix variables (product, service, brand, incentives, communication, and distribution), delivers superior value to target customers, the company, and collaborators.

Managing price involves two types of decisions: *strategic decisions*, which are a function of the offering's target market defined by its customers, company, collaborators, competitors, and context, and *tactical decisions*, which are a function of the other marketing mix variables: product, service, brand, incentives, communication, and distribution.

Successful pricing strategies take into account that people do not always perceive pricing information objectively; instead, price perception is often a function of a variety of psychological effects such as reference-price effects, price–quantity effects, price-tier effects, price-ending effects, and product-line effects.

Competing on price often results in price wars, which typically start when companies are willing to sacrifice margins to gain market share. Price wars are likely to occur in the following cases: when offerings are undifferentiated, when capacity utilization is low, when significant economies of scale can be achieved by increasing volume, when markets are mature and a company has to steal share from its direct competitors to grow sales, and when customers' price sensitivity is high and switching costs are low. An effective approach for developing a strategic response to a competitor's price cut calls for verifying the validity of the threat of a price war, prioritizing customers that are most likely to be affected by the competitors' price cut based on their value to the company and price sensitivity, and developing segment-specific strategies to address the competitive threat.

RELEVANT CONCEPTS

Captive Pricing: See *complementary pricing*.

Complementary Pricing: Pricing strategy applicable to uniquely compatible, multipart offerings, whereby a company charges a relatively low introductory price for the first part and higher prices for the other parts. Classic examples include razors and blades, printers and cartridges, and cell phones and cell phone service. The unique compatibility is crucial to the success of complementary pricing: Only the printer manufacturer should be able to sell cartridges that fit its printers.

Cost-Plus Pricing: A pricing method in which the final price is determined by adding a fixed markup to the cost of the product. It is easy to calculate and is commonly used in industries where profit margins are relatively stable. Its key drawback is that it does not take into account customer demand and competitive pricing.

Cross-Price Elasticity: The percentage change in quantity sold of a given offering caused by a percentage change in the price of another offering.

Deceptive Pricing: The practice of presenting an offering's price to the buyer in a way that is deliberately misleading. Deceptive pricing is illegal in the United States.

Everyday Low Pricing (EDLP): Pricing strategy in which a retailer maintains low prices without frequent price promotions. See also *high–low pricing*.

Experience Curve Pricing: Pricing strategy based on an anticipated lower cost structure, resulting from scale economies and experience curve effects.

High-Low Pricing: Pricing strategy in which a retailer's prices fluctuate over time, typically a result of heavy reliance on sales promotions. See also *everyday low pricing*.

Horizontal Price Fixing: A practice in which competitors explicitly or implicitly collaborate to set prices. Price fixing is illegal in the United States.

Image Pricing: See *price signaling*.

Loss Leader: Pricing strategy that involves setting a low price for an offering (often at or below cost) in an attempt to increase the sales of other products and services. For example, a retailer might set a low price for a popular item in an attempt to build store traffic, thus increasing the sales of other, more profitable items.

Predatory Pricing: A strategy that involves selling below cost with the intent of driving competitors out of business. In most cases, predatory pricing is illegal in the United States.

Prestige Pricing: Pricing strategy whereby the price is set at a relatively high level for the purpose of creating an exclusive image of the offering.

Price Discrimination: A strategy that involves charging different buyers different prices for goods of equal grade and quality.

Price Fixing: A practice in which companies conspire to set prices for a given product or service. Price fixing is illegal in the United States.

Price Segmentation: See *price discrimination*.

Price Signaling: (1) Pricing strategy that aims to capitalize on price–quality inferences (higher priced products are also likely to be higher quality). Primarily used when the actual product benefits are not readily observable (also known as prestige pricing); (2) Indirect communication (direct price collusion is prohibited by law) between companies aimed at indicating their intentions with respect to their pricing strategy.

Product-Line Pricing: Pricing strategy in which the price of each individual offering is determined as a function of the offering's place in the relevant product line.

Second Market Discounting: Pricing strategy in which a company charges lower prices in more competitive markets, such as when exporting to developing countries.

Two-Part Pricing: See *complementary pricing*.

Vertical Price Fixing: The practice whereby channel partners (a manufacturer and a retailer) explicitly or implicitly collaborate to set prices. Price fixing is illegal in the United States.

Yield-Management Pricing: Pricing strategy whereby the price is set to maximize revenue for a fixed capacity within a given time frame (frequently used by airlines and hotels).

ADDITIONAL READINGS

Baker, Ronald J. (2006), *Pricing on Purpose: Creating and Capturing Value*. Hoboken, NJ: John Wiley & Sons.

Marn, Michael V., Eric V. Roegner, and Craig C. Zawada (2004), *The Price Advantage*. Hoboken, NJ: John Wiley & Sons.

Nagle, Thomas T. and John E. Hogan (2010), *The Strategy and Tactics of Pricing: A Guide to Growing More Profitably* (5th ed.). Upper Saddle River, NJ: Pearson/Prentice Hall.

CHAPTER ELEVEN

MANAGING INCENTIVES

But wait, there's more!

Ron Popeil, inventor and infomercial salesman

Incentives offer solutions, typically short-term, aimed at enhancing the value of the offering by providing additional benefits or reducing costs. Because they typically lead to an increase in sales volume, incentives are often referred to as sales promotions. The key aspects of managing incentives are the focus of this chapter.

Overview

Most incentives fall into one of three categories: incentives given to customers (coupons, loyalty programs, sweepstakes, contests, and premiums); incentives given to the company's collaborators, most often channel partners (price cuts, volume discounts, allowances, and co-op advertising); and incentives given to the company's employees (bonuses, rewards, and contests).

Incentives can be either monetary—such as volume discounts, price reductions, coupons, and rebates—or nonmonetary—such as premiums, contests, and rewards. Unlike monetary incentives, which typically aim to reduce an offering's costs, nonmonetary incentives typically aim to enhance the offering's benefits. The most popular incentives, organized by their focus (customers, collaborators, and company) and type (price and nonprice), are given in Table 1.

Table 1. Incentive Types

	Monetary incentives	Nonmonetary incentives
Customer incentives	Coupons, rebates, price reductions, volume discounts	Premiums, rewards, sweepstakes
Collaborator incentives	Advertising, slotting, stocking, display, and market-development allowances; spiffs; volume discounts; volume rebates; off-invoice incentives	Contests, bonus merchandise, buyback guarantees, sales support and training
Company incentives	Performance bonuses, monetary prizes, spiffs	Contests, recognition awards, free goods, vacation and travel incentives

Deciding on the optimal mix of these various incentives can be facilitated using a systematic approach, outlined in more detail in the following sections.

Managing Incentives as a Value-Creation Process

Incentives enhance the value of the offering by increasing its benefits and/or reducing its costs. When designing incentives, a manager must consider the five Cs—target customers, the company's goals and resources, its collaborators, competitors, and the context in which the company operates—and develop incentives that create value for customers, the company, and its collaborators (Figure 1).

Figure 1. Managing Incentives as a Value-Creation Process

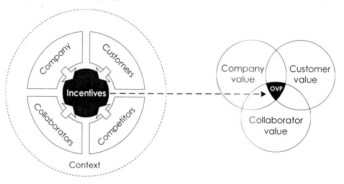

The five Cs—customers, company, collaborators, competitors, and context—are strategically important for managing incentives. Thus, incentives are a function of customers' needs and are more common for discretionary purchases and among price-conscious consumers. The use of incentives is also driven by a company's desire to achieve certain sales goals within a specific time frame. Incentives are also a function of the company's collaborators, such as distribution channels—many of which have gained considerable power and require significant concessions from manufacturers in the form of trade incentives. Competitors often influence incentives by making it necessary for companies to offer incentives to maintain competitive parity. The use of incentives is also a function of various context factors; for example, adverse economic conditions tend to lead to greater reliance on incentives to stimulate demand.

In addition to being influenced by the five Cs, incentives also depend on the other marketing mix factors: product, service, brand, price, communication, and distribution. Thus, incentives are a function of the product and service aspect of the offering, whereby the increased commoditization leads to increased use of incentives. In the same vein, incentives are a function of the offering's brand, such that luxury brands are less likely to utilize monetary incentives. An offering's incentives are often set as part of its overall pricing strategy—for example, everyday low pricing involves limited use of incentives, whereas high-low pricing (see Chapter 10) relies heavily on incentives. An offering's incentives are a function of its communication, such that consumer-focused communications (pull strategy) are often complemented by consumer incentives, and retailer-focused communications (push strategy) are often complemented with trade incentives. Incentives are also a function of an offering's distribution, whereby consolidated, powerful channels typically require greater trade incentives.

Customer Incentives

Customer incentives can be offered by either the manufacturer (manufacturer incentives) or the channel member (retailer incentives). Manufacturer incentives can then be delivered either directly by the manufacturer or indirectly by the retailer (pass-through incentives). Based on the type of reward, customer incentives can be divided into two types: monetary and nonmonetary.

- **Monetary incentives** aim to reduce an offering's costs by providing customers with a monetary inducement to purchase the offering. Most common forms of monetary incentives include coupons, rebates, price reductions, and volume discounts.
  - *Coupons* entitle the buyer to receive a price reduction for a given product or service at the time of purchase.
  - *Rebates* are cash refunds given to customers after they make a purchase.
  - *Price reductions* are price discounts that do not require any action from customers.
  - *Volume discounts* involve price reduction offers conditional upon the purchase of multiple items.
- **Nonmonetary incentives** typically aim to enhance the value of the offering. The most common forms of nonmonetary incentives are premiums, prizes, contests, sweepstakes, games, and loyalty programs.
  - *Premiums* involve bonus products or services offered for free or at deeply discounted prices as an incentive for purchasing a particular offering. Premiums can be delivered instantly with the purchase (packaged with the product) or may require the customer to send in a proof of purchase to receive the premium.
  - *Prizes* offer customers the opportunity to win an award as an incentive for purchasing a particular offering. Unlike premiums, where the reward is given with every purchase, in the case of prizes the actual reward is given to a relatively small number of participants. Prizes can be both monetary and nonmonetary.
  - *Contests, sweepstakes, and games* involve prizes that typically require customers to submit some form of entry and are usually not contingent on customers purchasing the offering. Winners are selected by a panel of judges (in the case of contests), by drawing (in the case of sweepstakes), or by an objective criterion, such as points collected (in the case of games).

- *Loyalty programs* involve rewards related to the frequency, volume, and type of products and services purchased. Loyalty programs can be both monetary (cash-back credit cards offering a reward based on purchase volume) and nonmonetary (frequent-flyer airline awards and frequent-stay hotel awards).

Companies typically use customer incentives to achieve three primary goals: to mange the timing of customers' purchases, to selectively reach specific segments, and to respond to competitive promotions.

- **Managing purchase timing.** Time-sensitive incentives can encourage customers to purchase a company's offering in a time frame consistent with the company's goals. Purchase timing is usually managed by offering widespread incentives available to all target customers (e.g., temporary price reductions).

- **Optimizing the value of the offering to different segments**. A company may offer incentives to selectively enhance the value of an offering for particular customer segments. For example, a company might give discounts to economically disadvantaged customers, repeat buyers, and high-volume buyers.

- **Responding to a competitor's promotion**. Companies often face competitive reaction, usually in the form of incentives given to potential buyers, which they must counter in order to make their offerings attractive to target customers.

Collaborator Incentives

Most collaborator incentives are offered to members of the distribution channel. These incentives, also referred to as trade incentives, can have multiple objectives, such as gaining distribution through a particular channel, encouraging channel members to stock the offering at certain inventory levels (to avoid stock-outs or to transfer the inventory from the manufacturer to retailers), and encouraging channel members to promote the company's offering. Similar to customer incentives, trade incentives can be either monetary or nonmonetary.

- **Monetary incentives** involve payments or price discounts given as encouragement to purchase the product or as an inducement to promote the product to customers. Typical monetary incentives include the following.
  - *Slotting allowance*: an incentive paid to a distributor to allocate shelf space for a new product.
  - *Stocking allowance*: an incentive paid to a distributor to carry extra inventory in anticipation of an increase in demand.
  - *Cooperative advertising allowance*: an incentive paid by the manufacturer to a distributor in return for featuring its offerings in a retailer's advertisements. The magnitude of the allowance can be determined as a percentage of the distributor's advertising costs or as a fixed dollar amount per unit.

- *Market-development allowance*: an incentive for achieving a certain sales volume in a specific customer segment.

- *Display allowance*: an incentive paid by the manufacturer to a distributor in return for prominently displaying its products and/or services.

- *Spiffs*: incentives such as cash premiums, prizes, or additional commissions given directly to the salesperson (rather than the distributor) as a reward for selling a particular item. Because they encourage the retailer's sales personnel to "push" the product to customers, spiffs are often referred to as "push money."

- *Volume discount*: price reductions determined based on purchase volume.

- *Volume rebate* (also referred to as *volume bonus*): an incentive paid by the manufacturer to a distributor as a reward for achieving certain purchase-volume benchmarks (e.g., selling 1,000 units per quarter).

- *Off-invoice incentive*: any temporary price discounts offered by manufacturers to distributors.

- *Cash discount*: price reductions for payments made instantly or within a short time frame.

- *Inventory financing* (also referred to as *floor planning*): loans provided to a distributor for acquiring manufacturers' goods.

- **Nonmonetary incentives** involve nonmonetary inducements designed to encourage channel support for a particular offering. Typical nonmonetary incentives include the following.

  - *Contests*: performance-based rewards (e.g., vacation trips, cars, and monetary compensation) given to the best achievers.

  - *Bonus merchandise*: free goods offered as a reward for purchasing a particular item.

  - *Buyback guarantees*: an agreement that the manufacturer will buy back from the distributor product quantities not sold within a certain time frame.

  - *Sales support and training*: various forms of aid offered to distributors that are designed to familiarize the distributor with the offering and facilitate sales.

Channel incentives have gained popularity for several reasons: to acquire shelf space for new products (e.g., through slotting allowances), to encourage distributors to carry higher levels of inventory to avoid stock-outs (e.g., through stocking allowances, inventory financing, and volume discounts), to encourage distributors to promote new products (e.g., through advertising and display allowances), and to offset the impact of competitive promotions (e.g., through competitive price-matching incentives).

Company Incentives

In addition to incentives focused on target customers and collaborators, companies often offer incentives to motivate and reward their own personnel. Company incentives commonly involve rewards for employees who meet certain performance benchmarks. The importance of incentivizing employees is effectively captured in the words of the founder of The Virgin Group, Richard Branson: "If you take care of your employees, your employees will take care of your customers, and your customers will take care of your shareholders."

Typical company incentives include performance-based awards such as contests, monetary bonuses, employee recognition awards, free goods and services, vacation and travel incentives, prizes, sweepstakes, and games. Some sales force incentives, such as spiffs, may be applied at the company level as well.

SUMMARY

Incentives offer solutions, typically short term, aimed at enhancing the value of the offering by providing additional benefits and reducing costs. Most incentives fall into one of three categories: incentives given to customers (coupons, loyalty programs, sweepstakes, contests, and premiums); incentives given to the company's collaborators, most often channel partners (price cuts, volume discounts, allowances, and co-op advertising); and incentives given to the company's employees (bonuses, rewards, and contests).

Managing incentives involves two types of decisions: *strategic* decisions — which are a function of the offering's target market defined by its customers, company, collaborators, competition, and context — and *tactical* decisions — which are a function of the other marketing mix variables: product, service, brand, price, communication, and distribution.

Most *customer incentives* serve one of two goals: temporarily increasing sales volume by giving target customers an additional reason to buy the offering, or serving as a segmentation tool by selectively enhancing the value of the company's offering for target customers. Customer incentives can be divided into two categories: monetary incentives that typically aim to reduce an offering's costs (coupons, rebates, price reductions, and volume discounts), and nonmonetary incentives, which often aim to enhance the offering's benefits (premiums, prizes, contests, and loyalty programs).

Most *collaborator incentives* are offered to members of the distribution channel and can have multiple objectives: (1) to gain distribution coverage, (2) to encourage channel members to stock the offering at certain inventory levels (to avoid stock-outs or to transfer the inventory from the manufacturer to distributors), and (3) to encourage channel members to promote the company's offering. Similar to customer incentives, trade incentives are either monetary (discounts and allowances) or nonmonetary (contests and bonus merchandise).

RELEVANT CONCEPTS

Freestanding Inserts (FSI): Leaflets or coupons inserted into newspapers.

Pull and Push Promotions: Based on the flow of promotions (i.e., incentives and communications) from the manufacturer to target customers, two core promotion strategies can be identified: pull and push. Pull strategy refers to the practice of creating demand for a company's offering by promoting the offering directly to end users, who in turn demand the offering from intermediaries, and ultimately "pull" it through the channel (Figure 2). To illustrate, the manufacturer may extensively advertise its products and services to end users and promote its offerings using means such as direct mail, coupons, and contests. In contrast, push strategy refers to the practice of creating demand for a company's offering by incentivizing channel members, who in turn push the product downstream to end users. For example, the manufacturer may offer high margins on its products and services so that retailers have a vested interest in selling them. The manufacturer may also educate a retailer's sales force about the benefits of its offerings and provide the retailer with promotional materials, thus facilitating the sales process.

Figure 2. Pull and Push Promotion Strategies

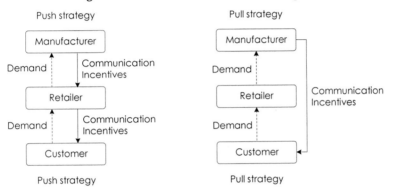

Run-of-Press Coupons: Coupons that appear in the actual pages of a newspaper (rather than being inserted as a separate page).

Slippage: The percentage of customers who fail to redeem a promotional offer made with the purchase.

Trade Allowance: A broad range of trade incentives, including slotting allowances, stocking allowances, and advertising allowances, offered as a reward for conducting promotional activities on behalf of the manufacturer. Trade allowances are typically implemented as a discount from the wholesale price rather than as a separate promotional payment. From an accounting standpoint, they are often considered as a discount to the channel rather than as a separate marketing expense.

ADDITIONAL READINGS

Blattberg, Robert C. and Scott A. Neslin (1990), *Sales Promotion: Concepts, Methods, and Strategies.* Englewood Cliffs, NJ: Prentice Hall.

Neslin, Scott A. (2002), *Sales Promotion.* Cambridge, MA: Marketing Science Institute.

Schultz, Don E., William A. Robinson, and Lisa Petrison (1998), *Sales Promotion Essentials* (3rd ed.). Lincolnwood, IL: NTC Business Books.

Chapter Twelve

Managing Communication

The single biggest problem in communication is the illusion that it has taken place.

George Bernard Shaw

Communication aims to inform the market—customers, collaborators, company stakeholders, competitors, and society in general—about the specifics of a company's offering. The main aspects of developing and managing a communication campaign are the focus of this chapter.

Overview

Communication is the most visible component of an offering's marketing mix. Thousands of companies spend millions of dollars each year to advise buyers about the availability of their offerings, explain the benefits of these offerings, spread the word about price cuts, and promote product and corporate brands. In the words of Leo Burnett, "Advertising says to people, 'Here's what we've got. Here's what it will do for you. Here's how to get it.'"

During the past decades there have been significant changes in the way companies design and manage communication. One of the most important changes is the evolution of the traditional forms of communication from mass media formats, including television and print, to one-on-one communication. Another important change involves the switch from company-driven communication to customer-driven social media interactions, whereby customers receive an increasing amount of information about the available offerings not from the companies but from other customers. These changes add an extra layer of complexity to the task of effectively managing communication, highlighting the importance of using a systematic approach to designing and implementing a communication campaign.

Communication as a Value-Creation Process

Communication informs target customers, collaborators, and/or the company employees and stakeholders about the benefits of the offering. The development of a communication strategy is influenced by five key factors—target customers, the company's goals and resources, its collaborators, competitors, and context—and aims to optimize the value of the offering for target customers, the company, and its collaborators (Figure 1).

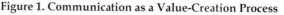

Figure 1. Communication as a Value-Creation Process

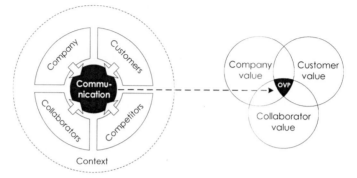

The five Cs—customers, company, collaborators, competitors, and context—are the key to designing the offering's communications. Thus, the choice of target customers plays an important role in managing communications: For customers unfamiliar with the offering, communication aims to create awareness of the offering, whereas for those already familiar with the offering, communication typically aims to strengthen their preferences and impel them to purchase the offering. Communication is also influenced by the company's goals and available resources, which determine the content (message), scale (budget), and the media selection (television, radio, print, or online). The communication campaign must be aligned with the company's collaborators, as in the case of co-developed and/or co-sponsored (co-op) advertising. Company communication is also often influenced by that of competitors, such that an increase in competitive spending frequently leads to a corresponding increase in the company's own communication budget. Communication is also a function of the context in which the company operates; it is influenced by technological advancements (e.g., the growth of online media), industry-specific regulations (e.g., tobacco, alcohol, and pharmaceuticals), and regulations concerning general advertising practices (e.g., claiming specific benefits and making product comparisons).

In addition to being driven by the five Cs, communication is also influenced by the other marketing mix factors: product, service, brand, price, incentives, and distribution. Thus, communication reflects the balance of the product and service aspects of the offering: In the case of services that are mostly intangible, communication often aims to highlight their tangible aspects (e.g., by creating tangible symbols such as the Rock of Gibraltar for Prudential), whereas for tangible products, communication often highlights their intangible characteristics (e.g., warranty, reliability, and durability). Communication also is a function the offering's brand, such that the message, media, and creative aspects fit the identity and the meaning of the brand. Communication is also influenced by the offering's price and incentives, such that low-priced offerings featuring monetary incentives call for a different communication strategy compared to high-priced offerings featuring nonmonetary incentives. An offering's communication is also influenced by its distribution strategy: for example, online retailers offer multiple opportunities for point-of-purchase communication using a variety of media formats.

The Communication Process

Managing communication involves six key decisions: setting the goal, developing the message, selecting the media, developing the creative solution, implementing the communication campaign, and evaluating the campaign results (Figure 2).

Figure 2. Developing a Communication Plan

```
┌─────────────────────────┐
│          Goal           │
└─────────────────────────┘
            ⇩
┌─────────────────────────┐
│        Message          │
└─────────────────────────┘
            ⇩
┌─────────────────────────┐
│         Media           │
└─────────────────────────┘
            ⇩
┌─────────────────────────┐
│    Creative solution    │
└─────────────────────────┘
            ⇩
┌─────────────────────────┐
│     Implementation      │
└─────────────────────────┘
            ⇩
┌─────────────────────────┐
│        Control          │
└─────────────────────────┘
```

- The **goal** identifies the criteria to be achieved by the communication campaign within a given time frame.

- The **message** identifies the information to be communicated to the target audience. The message can involve one or several of the other marketing mix variables: product, service, brand, price, incentives, and distribution. To illustrate, a company can choose to promote the benefits of its product and service, communicate the meaning of its brand, publicize its price, inform customers about its current incentives, and inform customers about the offering's availability.

- The **media** describes the means used by the company to convey its message. The media decision involves three key aspects: budget, media type, and scheduling.

- The **creative solution** involves the execution of the company's message. Among the key aspects of the creative solution is the type of appeal used in the campaign (information, humor, or fear) and execution style (text, format, and layout).

- The **implementation** aspect of marketing communication identifies the logistics and the timeline for executing the message, media, and creative decisions.

- The **control** aspect of marketing communication involves evaluating the success of the communication campaign with respect to its goals.

The key aspects of developing a communication campaign are discussed in more detail in the following sections.

Setting Communication Goals

Setting a goal typically involves two decisions: identifying the *focus* of the communication campaign and identifying the specific *performance benchmarks* to be reached.

- Identifying the **focus** of the communication campaign involves setting the ultimate criterion for success. There are three core goals, any of which can be the focus of a given communication campaign:
  - Create and raise *awareness* of the company's offering.
  - Create and strengthen buyer *preferences* for the company's offering.
  - Incite an *action* such as purchasing the offering or contacting the company for information.

  These goals are interdependent, such that some can be viewed as prerequisites for others. Thus, enhancing an offering's attractiveness implies that target customers are aware of the offering's existence. Similarly, a call for action implies that customers are already aware of the offering and find it attractive.

- The **benchmark** aspect of the goal provides measurable *criteria* for success (e.g., creating awareness among 40% of a given market), as well as an identifiable *time frame* for achieving these criteria (e.g., two weeks prior to product launch).

Developing the Message

The message can involve one or more marketing mix variables: product, service, brand, price, incentives, and distribution. For each of these marketing mix factors, the message articulates the specifics of the company's offering as follows:

- **Product- and service-related messages** inform target customers of the characteristics of the company's products and services.

- **Brand-related messages** focus on the identity and the meaning of the company's or offering's brand.

- **Price-related messages** communicate the offering's price.

- **Incentives-related messages** depict the incentives associated with the offering, such as temporary price reductions, volume discounts, rebates, coupons, and premiums.

- **Distribution-related messages** highlight the offering's availability in distribution channels.

The decision about which aspect of the offering to promote depends on a variety of factors such as the offering's competitive advantage, customers' perceptions of the offering, and competitive communications. The key principle when designing the message is that it should focus on the aspects of the offering that are likely to have the greatest impact. Thus, if customers are unaware of the benefits of the offering, the message should focus on its product and service aspects, whereas if customers are unaware of the offering's availability, the message should focus on distribution. A specific approach to identifying areas that can benefit from investing marketing resources, including communication, is outlined in Chapter 15.

Selecting the Media

The media decision involves deciding on the communication budget, selecting the type of media used, and setting a communication timetable. These three aspects are discussed in more detail in the following sections.

Media Budget

Deciding on the magnitude of communication expenditures is one of the key decisions in planning a promotional campaign, not only because it has a direct impact on the company's profitability but also because the overall budget often determines the type of media used. For example, mass-media television campaigns are predicated on the availability of substantial resources to secure this media. There are several approaches to determine the total communication budget:

- The **goal-driven** approach is based on an estimate of the resources required to achieve the company's strategic goal. This approach takes into account factors such as number of customers reached through a single exposure to the company's message per media dollar spent and the average number of exposures necessary to create awareness.

- The **percentage-of-sales** approach implies setting the budget as a fraction of the company's sales revenues.

- The **competitive-parity** approach implies setting the budget at par with that of a key competitor. The approach in which the budget is set proportionally to the desired share of total media expenditures in a given category is also referred to as share-of-voice budgeting.

- The **legacy** approach implies budgeting based on prior year expenditures.

- The **affordability** approach implies setting the budget based on resources available for promotional activities.

While all of the above budgeting strategies have merit (some more than others), the goal-driven approach dominates the others in its ability to estimate most effectively the resources required to achieve the company's communication goals. Competitive-parity and percentage-of-sales approaches can also provide useful insights into the budgeting decision. Because they are detached from market realities, the legacy and affordability approaches are the least likely to provide an accurate budget estimate.

Media Type

Media type involves the means used by the company to convey its message. The most popular types of media include advertising, public relations and social media, direct marketing, personal selling, event sponsorship, product-based communications, and product samples. These media types are discussed in more detail below.

- **Advertising** involves nonpersonal marketing communications in which the company develops the message and absorbs most or all of the media (air time and print space) costs. The most popular forms of advertising involve audio–visual (television, video, and film), radio, print (promotional brochures, advertisements in newspapers and magazines, and newspaper and magazine inserts), online, mobile, outdoor (posters and billboards), and point of sale (front-of-the-store, end-of-aisle, and shelf-talkers—signs displayed in close proximity to the promoted item). In the United States, advertising is the most popular media type, with most of the advertising dollars spent on television commercials.

- **Public relations and social media** involve communications by third parties that are not directly controlled by the company. Unlike advertising, with public relations the company does not pay for the media and therefore cannot control the content of the message. Instead, it aims to encourage a third party (opinion leaders and press) to promote the offering. Because the message comes from a third party that typically has no vested interest in the company's offering, public relations communications are often viewed as more credible than communications directly sponsored by the company.

- **Direct marketing** involves individually targeted communications (catalogs, direct mail, telemarketing, and online advertising), typically designed to elicit a direct response.

- **Personal selling** involves direct, typically face-to-face, interaction with a company representative (a salesperson).

- **Event sponsorship** involves sponsoring events and activities of interest to the offering's target customers. A form of event sponsorship is product placement, where the sponsor secures the rights to embed (place) its offering within a particular form of entertainment, such as a sports event, television show, or a movie.

- **Product-based communication** is embedded in the product itself, such as product labels, signs, and packaging.

- **Product samples** and **free trials** enable customers to experience product benefits directly. Samples and free trials are often used in new product introductions to encourage customers to try the offering. They are typically distributed via direct mail (in the case of consumer packaged goods); online (in the case of digital content products such as electronic newspapers, music samples, and movie trailers); or at the point of sale (in the case of items that can be readily consumed, such as food samples).

The allocation of resources across different media types is a function of the effectiveness and cost efficiency of each media format with respect to its ability to communicate the desired message. For certain types of products (gasoline, alcohol, and tobacco), the choice of advertising medium is also subject to significant legal regulations.

In addition to deciding on the allocation of resources across different types of media, the media decision involves determining the specific media channels within each of the media types. For example, within the domain of television advertising, the media channel decision involves selecting particular shows and time slots in which the company's message will be best positioned to reach and influence its target customers. Thus, beer companies often choose to advertise during popular sport events with predominantly male audiences, whereas beauty products are typically advertised during shows with predominantly female audiences.

Media Scheduling

Deciding on media scheduling involves identifying the pattern of communication, its reach, and frequency.

- The **pattern** of communication can be continuous, concentrated, or intermittent. Continuous communication (also referred to as flighting) involves allocating exposures evenly throughout the individual periods within a given time frame. Concentrated communication involves allocating the majority of exposures in a single period (e.g., spending the entire advertising budget on a single Super Bowl commercial). Intermittent communication (also referred to as pulsing) involves alternating periods with high and low (or no) levels of advertising (e.g., advertising every other week). The decision to use a particular timing format is a function of the characteristics of the company's offering and the pattern of product adoption/usage by target customers.

- The **frequency** reflects the number of times target customers are exposed to a particular message over a given period. The number of exposures necessary for the company's message to register in a customer's mind is a function of factors, such as communication goals, the novelty of the offering, the type of media (television, radio, print, mail, point of purchase, outdoor, or online), the creative solution used to generate awareness, and customers' level of involvement when viewing the advertisement. In some cases, a single exposure could be sufficient, although most often multiple exposures are required to achieve communication goals.

- The **reach** reflects the number of target customers that are exposed to a particular message at least once in a given period. The communication reach is typically a function of the size of the target market: the larger the market, the greater the potential reach.

Creative Solution

The creative solution involves translating the company's message into the language of the selected media format, such as television, print, radio, online, and point of purchase. Creative solutions vary on two main factors: their appeal and execution style.

- **Appeal** refers to the approach used to communicate the company's message. Most creative solutions involve at least one of two types of appeals: information-based and emotion-based. Information-based appeals typically rely on methods such as factual presentations (straightforward presentation of the relevant information), demonstrations (illustration of the offering's key benefits in a staged environment), slice-of-life stories (illustration of the offering's key benefits in everyday use), and testimonials (praise by an individual based on his or her experience with the offering and endorsements by ordinary users or celebrities). In contrast, emotion-based appeals typically play on emotions such as love, romance, humor, and fear. Some communication campaigns use a combination of the two approaches to achieve maximum impact.

- **Execution style** refers to the method used to convey a particular appeal using the language of the selected media format. Style decisions are media specific. Thus, print advertising involves decisions concerning the copy (wording of the headline and the body text), visual elements (pictures, photos, graphics, and logos), format (size and color scheme), and layout (the arrangement of different parts of the advertisement). Radio advertising involves decisions dealing with the text (wording of the dialogue and narration), audio (music, dialogue, and sound effects), and format (length). Television advertising involves decisions concerning the visual elements (imagery), text (wording of the dialogue, voice-over narration, and printed text), audio (music, dialogue, and sound effects), and format (length).

An important aspect of developing the communication campaign is keeping the balance between the marketing message and the entertainment component of the creative solution. Because of the ever-growing competition to capture buyers' attention, companies are often tempted to develop overly creative campaigns designed to break through the clutter of competitive messages. While creativity per se is a virtue, in business communication creativity should never be achieved at the expense of the content. "I do not regard advertising as entertainment or an art form, but as a medium of information," notes David Ogilvy, "A good advertisement is one which sells the product without drawing attention to itself."

Implementing the Communication Campaign

The implementation of a communication campaign involves setting up the necessary infrastructure to execute the campaign; setting up the processes necessary to execute the message, media, and creative solutions; and outlining the implementation schedule.

- Setting up the **organizational infrastructure** of the communication campaign involves identifying the relevant collaborators (advertising, public relations, and social media agencies) and forming a team to manage the campaign.

- Setting up the **processes** involves identifying the specific actions to be taken during preproduction (identifying the technical aspects of the message, media, and creative solution), production (the actual filming, videotaping, recording, or printing of the advertisement), postproduction (editing, duplicating, ensuring legal compliance, and obtaining client approval), and distribution (airing, printing, and shipping).

- The **scheduling** aspect of implementation involves deciding on the timing and the optimal sequence in which individual tasks should be performed to ensure effective and cost-efficient execution of the communication campaign.

Evaluating Communication Effectiveness

John Wanamaker's famous quote, uttered nearly a century ago, "I know that half of my advertising money is wasted. I just don't know which half," succinctly reflects the current state of evaluating communication effectiveness. There is little agreement on the part of marketers, advertising agencies, and research companies about the best way to measure advertising effectiveness. As a result, companies use diverse criteria to measure the effectiveness of an advertising campaign. The most commonly used criteria involve measuring six factors: exposure, comprehension, recall, persuasion, intent, and behavior.

- **Exposure** reflects the number of times a given advertisement has been seen by the target audience.

- **Comprehension** reflects the degree to which the target audience understands the message embedded in the advertisement.

- **Recall** reflects the degree to which the target audience remembers an advertisement. Recall can be either aided or unaided. In the case of aided recall, respondents are given a list of brand names following the presentation of a series of advertisements and are asked to recall whether they have seen any of these brands. In contrast, in the case of unaided recall, respondents are simply asked to recall all brands they have seen during the presentation.

- **Persuasion** reflects the degree to which the advertisement is able to strengthen or change preferences of the target audience. Because preferences for established brands (which often are among the largest advertisers) are difficult to change with a single advertisement, advertising agencies often measure the attitude toward the advertisement (rather than the attitude toward the brand) on the premise that if the target audience likes the advertisement, then this attitude will translate into liking the brand.

- **Intent** reflects customers' mental disposition to act favorably toward the offering, such as buy the product, visit the store, or contact the company. Intent is typically measured by asking respondents to indicate the likelihood of purchasing the product within a given time frame (see Chapter 15 for more details).

- **Behavior** reflects the impact of an advertisement on respondents' actual behavior, such as purchasing the product, inquiring about product features, and researching the product on the Internet. Behavior is typically measured by the number of sales, sales inquiries, and website visits.

A great deal of disagreement exists about which of the above measures is the most reliable indicator of advertising effectiveness. Intuitively, it may seem that sales volume is the best measure of communication effectiveness. This, however, is not the case. The problem with relying on customers' behavior as a measure of effectiveness is that most often the impact of communication is not immediate (especially in cases of brand-building communication). As a result, the impact of communication is typically confounded with a variety of nonrelated factors such as changes in price, incentives, competitive actions, and purchase cycle.

A more meaningful approach to measuring the effectiveness of a communication campaign should take into account three main factors: the goal of the campaign, the message being communicated, and the selected media format.

- **Communication goal**. Measuring the success of a communication campaign is a function of the nature of the communication goal. Thus, if the communication goal is to create awareness, then exposure, comprehension, and recall should be measured. If the communication goal is to strengthen preferences, then the persuasiveness of the advertisement should be measured. Finally, if the communication goal is to incite action, then behavior should be measured.

- **Communication message**. Evaluating the effectiveness of a communication campaign also depends on the type of message. Thus, communicating incentives tends to have an immediate impact on sales, whereas the impact of brand-building communication is delayed. As a result, using sales as a benchmark of effectiveness is likely to underestimate the impact of brand-building communication and overestimate the role of incentive-focused communication.

- **Media format**. Measuring the effectiveness of a communication campaign is also a function of the particular media format. Thus, in cases where the media are not directly linked to a particular performance measure, such as public relations and event sponsorship, performance tends to be gauged through indirect measures of awareness and preference. In contrast, in cases where the media are directly linked to performance measures (such as in direct marketing, personal selling, and click-through advertising), then actual behavior can be used to evaluate the effectiveness of the communication campaign.

SUMMARY

Managing communication involves *strategic* decisions—a function of the offering's target market defined by its customers, company, collaborators, competition, and context—and *tactical* decisions, which are a function of the other marketing mix variables: product, service, brand, price, incentives, and distribution.

Managing communication involves six key steps: setting the goal, developing the message, selecting the media, developing the creative solution, implementing the communication campaign, and evaluating the campaign results.

The *goal* identifies a set of criteria to be achieved by the communication campaign within a given time frame. The three most common communication goals are to create awareness, strengthen preferences, and incite action.

The *message* identifies the information communicated to target customers. The message can focus on one or several of the six value–design marketing mix variables: product, service, brand, price, incentives, and distribution.

The *media* describes the means used by the company to convey its message. The media decision involves three aspects: setting the media budget, deciding on the media type (advertising, public relations and social media, personal selling, product samples, event sponsorship, and product placement), and outlining the media scheduling (pattern, reach, and frequency).

The *creative solution* involves the execution of the company's message in a given media. Among the key aspects of the creative solution are appeal type (information-based or emotion-based) and execution style (text, format, and layout).

The *implementation* aspect of marketing communication identifies the timeline and the logistics of executing the message, media, and creative decisions.

The *control* aspect of marketing communication involves evaluating the success of the communication campaign with respect to achieving its goals. The most commonly used criteria involve measuring the following six factors: exposure, comprehension, recall, persuasion, intent, and behavior. The decision about which metric to use is a function of three key considerations: the goal of the campaign, the message being communicated, and the selected media format.

RELEVANT CONCEPTS

Above-the-Line Communications: Company communications are often divided into two categories: Above-The-Line (ATL) communications, which encompass mass media advertising such as television commercials, radio, and print advertisements; and Below-The-Line (BTL) communications, which include public relations, event sponsorship, personal selling, and direct mail. Historically, the term ATL was used in reference to communications for which an advertising agency charged a commission to place in mass media, whereas the term BTL was used in reference to communications that involved a standard charge rather than a commission. Currently, the terms ATL and BTL are loosely used to indicate an emphasis on mass media (ATL) versus one-on-one communications (BTL). The current use of BTL often includes customer and trade incentives as well.

Advertising Allowance: A form of trade promotion in which retailers are given a discount in exchange for advertising manufacturers' products.

Advertising Awareness: The number of potential customers who are aware of the offering. Awareness is a function of the total volume of advertising delivered to the target audience and the number of exposures necessary to create awareness. In cases where a single exposure is sufficient to create awareness, the awareness level equals the advertising reach.

$$\text{Awareness} = \frac{\text{Advertising reach} \cdot \text{Frequency of exposure}}{\text{Number of exposures necessary to create awareness}}$$

Advertising Reach: The size of the audience that has been exposed to a particular advertisement at least once in a given period (multiple viewings by the same audience do not increase reach). Reach may be stated either as an absolute number or as a fraction of a population. For example, if 40,000 of 100,000 different households are exposed to a given commercial at least once, the reach is 40%.

Advertising Frequency: The number of times the target audience is exposed to an advertisement in a given period. Also used in reference to the number of times an advertisement is repeated through a specific medium during a specific period.

Affiliate Marketing: A communication strategy that involves revenue sharing between advertisers and online content providers. An affiliate is rewarded based on specific performance measures such as sales, click-throughs, and online traffic.

Awareness Rate: The number of potential customers aware of the offering relative to the total number of potential customers. Depending on the manner in which it is measured, two types of awareness are commonly distinguished: aided awareness, in which respondents are provided with the name of the target offering (e.g., "Have you seen any advertisements for Coca-Cola in the past month?"), and unaided awareness, in which respondents are not provided with any offering-specific information (e.g., "Which soft drinks have you seen advertised during the past month?").

Below-the-Line (BTL) Communications: See *above-the-line communications*.

Carryover Effect in Advertising: Impact of an advertising campaign that extends beyond the time frame of the campaign. To illustrate, an advertising effort made in a given period may generate sales in subsequent periods.

Comparative Advertising: Advertising strategy whereby a given offering is directly compared with another offering.

Competitive Parity Budgeting: Budget allocation strategy based on (1) matching competitors' absolute level of spending or (2) the proportion per point of market share.

Cooperative Advertising: Advertising strategy in which a manufacturer and a retailer jointly advertise their offering to consumers. In this case, the manufacturer pays a portion of a retailer's advertising costs in return for featuring its products, services, and brands.

Cost Per Point (CPP): Measure used to represent the cost of a communication campaign. CPP is the media cost of reaching one percent (one rating point) of a particular demographic. See also *gross rating point*.

$$CPP = \frac{\text{Advertising cost}}{\text{GRP}}$$

Cost Per Thousand (CPM): Measure used to represent the cost of a communication campaign. CPM is the cost of reaching 1,000 individuals or households with an advertising message in a given medium (M is the Roman numeral for 1,000). For example, a television commercial that costs $200,000 to air and reaches 10M viewers has a CPM of $20. The popularity of CPM derives in part from its being a good comparative measure of advertising efficiency across different media (e.g., television, print, and Internet).

$$CPM = \frac{\text{Advertising cost}}{\text{Total impressions}} \cdot 1,000$$

Gross Rating Point (GRP): A measure of the total volume of advertising delivery to the target audience. It is equal to the percent of the population reached times the frequency of exposure. To illustrate, if a given advertisement reaches 60% of the households with an average frequency of three times, then the GRP of the media is equal to 180. GRP can also be calculated by dividing gross impressions by the size of the total audience. A single GRP represents 1% of the total audience in a given region.

$$GRP = \text{Reach} \cdot \text{Frequency}$$

Impression: A single exposure of an advertisement to one person.

Infomercial: A long-format television commercial, typically five minutes or longer.

Institutional Advertising: Advertising strategy designed to build goodwill or an image for an organization (rather than to promote specific offerings).

Integrated Marketing Communication (IMC): An approach to designing marketing communication programs that emphasizes the importance of consistency in all communication activities. In particular, this approach calls for consistency on at least three levels: strategic, tactical, and internal. *Strategic consistency* implies coordination between the different aspects of the communication campaign and the elements of the offering's overall marketing strategy. *Tactical consistency* implies coordination between communication and the other elements of the marketing mix to keep an offering's message consistent with the perceived product and service benefits, brand image, price, incentives, and distribution channel. *Internal consistency* implies that the message, media, creative solution, implementation, and control metrics evaluating the success of the campaign need to be consistent with the communication goal as well as in and of themselves. The concept of internal consistency can also be applied with respect to the different media types (e.g., advertising, public relations, and direct marketing) to ensure that they work in a coordinated fashion rather than independently of one another.

Net Promoter Score: A popular metric designed to measure customers' word of mouth about a company and/or its products. The basic idea is fairly simple: A company's current and potential customers are asked to indicate the likelihood that they will recommend the company and/or its products to another person (e.g., "How likely is it that you would recommend this company to a friend or colleague?"). Responses are typically scored on a 0–10 scale, with 0 meaning extremely unlikely and 10 meaning extremely likely. Based on their responses, customers are divided into one of three categories: promoters (those with ratings of 9 or 10), passives (those with ratings of 7 or 8), and detractors (those with ratings of 6 or lower). The net promoter score is then calculated as the difference between the percentage of a company's promoters and detractors. For example, if 40% of a company's customers are classified as promoters and 25% are classified as detractors, the company's net promoter score is 15%.

Point-of-Purchase Advertising: Promotional materials displayed at the point of purchase (e.g., in a retail store).

Public Service Announcement (PSA): Nonprofit advertising that uses free space or time donated by the media.

Reminder Advertising: Advertising strategy designed to maintain awareness and stimulate repurchase of an already established offering.

Share of Voice: A company's communication expenditures relative to those of the entire product category.

$$\text{Share of voice} = \frac{\text{An offering's communication expenditures}}{\text{Product category's communication expenditures}}$$

Target Rating Point (TRP): A measure of the total volume of advertising delivery to the target audience. TRP is similar to GRP, but its calculation involves using only the target audience (rather than the total audience watching the program) as the base. Thus, a single TRP represents 1% of the targeted viewers in any particular region.

Teaser Advertising: Communication strategy designed to create interest in an offering while providing little or no information about it.

Top-of-Mind Awareness: The first brand identified by respondents when asked to list brands in a given product category.

Wearout: A decrease in the effectiveness of a communication campaign from decreased consumer interest in the message, often resulting from repetition.

ADDITIONAL READINGS

Belch, George E. and Michael A. Belch (2007), *Advertising and Promotion: An Integrated Marketing Communications Perspective* (7th ed.). Boston, MA: McGraw-Hill Irwin.

Ogilvy, David (1983), *Ogilvy on Advertising* (1st American ed.). New York, NY: Crown.

Reichheld, Fred (2003), "The One Number You Need to Grow," *Harvard Business Review*, (December), 1–11.

Sutherland, Max and Alice K. Sylvester (2009), *Advertising and the Mind of the Consumer: What Works, What Doesn't, and Why* (3rd ed.). St. Leonards, NSW: Allen & Unwin.

Wells, William D., John Burnett, and Sandra E. Moriarty (2006), *Advertising: Principles & Practice* (7th ed.). Upper Saddle River, NJ: Pearson/Prentice Hall.

CHAPTER THIRTEEN

MANAGING DISTRIBUTION

If you make a product good enough, even though you live in the depths of the forest,
the public will make a path to your door . . . But if you want the public
in sufficient numbers, you better construct a highway.

William Randolph Hearst, American newspaper publisher

Distribution is a key aspect of an offering's marketing mix. Managing distribution involves the process of delivering a company's offering to target customers. The key aspects of managing distribution channels are the focus of this chapter.

Overview

Distribution typically involves collaboration between a company and a set of distribution partners—retailers, wholesalers, and distributors—for the purpose of delivering a company's products to target customers. Retail distribution channels are represented by a variety of business models such as traditional retailers (Target), franchises (McDonald's), personal selling (Amway), price clubs (Costco), and online retailers (Amazon.com).

One of the most important retail trends is the consolidation of fragmented retail outlets into powerful retail chains and superstores. In addition to creating large-scale mass merchandisers like Walmart, this consolidation has produced a number of specialized retailers concentrating on a single category like home repairs (Home Depot), electronics (Best Buy), and books (Barnes & Noble). In addition, online retailing has gained ground on the traditional brick-and-mortar stores, with online shopping becoming the norm rather than the exception in many product categories. This consolidation and specialization of retailers, and the increasing importance of online retail formats call for the development of effective distribution strategies that accommodate the complex and dynamic nature of the retail environment.

Distribution as a Value-Creation Process

Distribution aims to deliver the offering to target customers in a way that creates value for the company and its collaborators. When designing a distribution strategy a manager must consider the five Cs—customers, company, collaborators, competitors, and context—and design a distribution channel that optimizes the offering's value for target customers, the company, and its collaborators (Figure 1).

Figure 1. Distribution as a Value-Creation Process

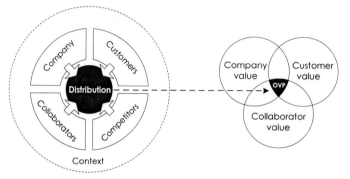

The five Cs—customers, company, collaborators, competitors, and context—are strategically important in designing the offering's distribution. Thus, the design of a distribution channel depends on the choice of target customers, such that offerings targeting mass markets are more likely to involve multiple distributors across different geographic markets, whereas niche offerings are likely to involve a more narrow distribution. The choice of a distribution channel is also a function of the company's goals and resources, such that a company seeking market dominance is likely to utilize diverse channels in order to achieve extensive coverage. An offering's distribution strategy also reflects the balance of power between the company and its collaborators, whereby a company may select multiple distributors or open its own retail stores in order to minimize the power of any particular channel. The choice of a distribution channel is also a function of competitors' offerings, such that companies seeking to avoid direct confrontation (e.g., to circumvent a price war) might seek alternative channels. Finally, distribution is a function of the economic, technological, sociocultural, regulatory, and physical context; for example, the preference for store size varies by culture and traditions, whereby many countries favor smaller, individually operated retail outlets to consolidated superstore chains.

In addition to being influenced by the five Cs, distribution also depends on the other marketing mix factors: product, service, brand, price incentives, and communication. Thus, an offering's distribution is a function of its product and service characteristics; for example, novel, complex, and/or undifferentiated products tend to benefit from channels offering higher levels of sales support. Distribution must also be aligned with the offering's brand, such that lifestyle brands (e.g., Ralph Lauren, Lacoste, and Cartier) benefit from using a direct distribution model that ensures a consistent brand image. Distribution is also a function of price, such that low-priced offerings are typically associated with channels offering lower levels of service, whereas high-priced offerings typically involve higher levels of service. The choice of distribution channel is also a function of the offering's use of incentives: Incentive-rich offerings typically call for channels that offer frequent sales (e.g., department stores), whereas offerings that do not rely on incentives are a better fit with retailers using everyday low pricing (e.g., Walmart, Target, and Home Depot). The selection and design of a distribution channel are often a function of the channel's ability to effectively communicate the offering's benefits and "push" the offering to target customers.

Distribution Channel Design

The process of designing and managing distribution channels involves several key decisions: channel structure, channel coordination, channel type, channel coverage, and channel exclusivity. The main aspects of these decisions are outlined in the following sections.

Channel Structure

Channel structure defines the members of the distribution channel and the flow of goods and services from the manufacturer to customers. Based on their structure, channels can be direct, indirect, and hybrid (Figure 2).

Figure 2. Distribution Channel Structure

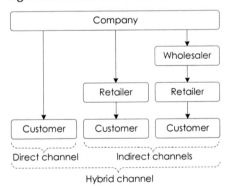

- **Direct channels** involve a distribution model in which the manufacturer and the end customer interact directly with each other without intermediaries.

  The direct distribution model affords multiple *advantages*: (1) a more effective distribution system resulting from better coordination of the different aspects of the value-delivery process; (2) greater cost-efficiency resulting from eliminating intermediaries; (3) greater control over the environment in which the offering is delivered to customers (level of service, product display, and availability of complementary offerings); and (4) closer contact with end users, allowing the manufacturer to obtain firsthand information about their needs and their reactions to its offerings.

Despite its numerous advantages, the direct-distribution model also has a number of *disadvantages*: (1) establishing a direct-distribution channel, especially a brick-and-mortar one, takes time; (2) in most cases, it is difficult to achieve the same breadth of distribution outlets with direct distribution as with multiple intermediaries; (3) launching and managing a distribution channel requires different assets and competencies that many manufacturers do not have readily available; and (4) in most cases, direct-distribution channels require a large upfront fixed-cost investment.

- **Indirect channels** involve a distribution model in which the manufacturer and the end customer interact with each other through intermediaries, such as wholesalers and retailers.

  The indirect distribution model has a number of *advantages*: (1) rapid distribution that can be implemented instantly; (2) broad coverage that enables the company to reach all or the majority of its target customers; (3) greater effectiveness of the value-delivery process since manufacturers can benefit from the assets and core competencies of intermediaries; (4) potential economies of scale because intermediaries perform similar activities for a variety of manufacturers; and (5) no large upfront investment necessary because a manufacturer using intermediaries is "renting" shelf space for its products.

  Despite its advantages, the use of intermediaries in the indirect distribution model is associated with a number of *disadvantages*: (1) a more complex channel structure that could have a negative impact on the efficiency of the distribution system; (2) potential for intermediaries to increase the overall distribution costs; (3) loss of control over the selling environment; (4) greatly diminished ability to communicate with and collect information directly from customers; and (5) potential for vertical channel conflicts resulting from different strategic goals and profit-optimization strategies for the manufacturer and its intermediaries.

- **Hybrid channels** involve a distribution model in which the manufacturer and the end customer interact with each other through multiple channels, both directly and through intermediaries (e.g., wholesalers and retailers).

  Hybrid channels have numerous advantages that stem from combining the benefits of direct and indirect distribution. At the same time, hybrid channels are also subject to many of the disadvantages of both direct and indirect channels. An additional problem with using hybrid channels is the potential for channel conflict in cases where both the company and its intermediaries target the same customers. Despite their disadvantages, hybrid channels are gaining popularity in categories where manufacturers can relatively easily establish direct online distribution.

Channel Coordination

Coordination benefits individual channel members by improving the effectiveness and cost efficiency of the channel as a whole. The conventional forms of coordination are: ownership-based, contractual, and implicit.

- **Common ownership** is a type of coordination in which different channel members are parts of the same company.

  Channel coordination based on common ownership of channel members offers numerous potential *advantages*: (1) better optimization of channel functions, resulting in greater effectiveness and cost-efficiency (through joint profit optimization and system integration), (2) greater degree of information sharing, and (3) better control and performance monitoring.

  Despite its multiple advantages, single-ownership distribution channels have a number of potential *disadvantages*: (1) high initial investment; (2) potential internal inefficiencies because of lack of competition; (3) lower cost-efficiency resulting from a smaller scale; and (4) the need to develop distribution channel expertise when moving from one business function to another (e.g., from manufacturing to distribution). In addition, in the case of hybrid distribution, in which some but not all channels are company owned, ownership often results in channel conflicts with independent distributors.

- **Contractual relationship** is a type of coordination that involves binding contractual agreements between channel members, including long-term contractual agreements, joint ventures, and franchise agreements.

  Channel coordination based on contractual relationships has several key *advantages*: (1) lower initial investment, (2) fast implementation, and (3) lower cost-efficiency resulting from partners' scale and/or specialization.

  Despite its advantages, contractual channel coordination has a number of *disadvantages*: (1) potential inefficiencies stemming from less coordination, (2) strategic risk of creating a potential competitor (through forward or backward integration) by sharing know-how and strategic information (pricing policies, profit margins, and cost structure), and (3) decreased ability to monitor performance.

- **Implicit channel coordination** is achieved without explicit contractual agreements. Implicit coordination is similar to contractual coordination, with the advantage of being much more flexible. This flexibility, however, comes at the cost of the inability to predict the behavior of various channel members. Another shortcoming of implicit coordination is a lower level of commitment, resulting in an unwillingness to invest resources to customize the channel for a particular manufacturer. Implicit coordination is also likely to lead to lower cost efficiency resulting from a lower degree of channel coordination.

Channel Type

Channels vary in terms of the breadth and depth of their assortments. Based on the *breadth* of their assortments, channels can be classified into one of two types: specialized or broad. Specialized retailers, such as Foot Locker, Office Depot, CarMax, and Toys"R"Us, tend to carry a relatively narrow assortment focusing on relatively few product categories. In contrast, mass retailers, such as Walmart, Costco, and Carrefour, tend to carry much broader assortments.

Based on the *depth* of the assortment, channels can be classified into limited and extensive. Limited-assortment retailers, such as 7-Eleven and Circle K, carry a relatively small number of items within each category, whereas extensive-assortment retailers, such as Carrefour and Walmart, carry a fairly large number of items in each category. Specialized retailers carrying extensive assortments of items, such as Home Depot, Best Buy, Office Depot, and SportMart, are often referred to as category killers.

Channel Coverage

Channel strategies vary in their coverage as defined by the number of outlets at which offerings are made available to target customers. Extensive coverage implies that an offering is readily accessible to a fairly large proportion of customers in a given market; in contrast, limited coverage implies that the offering is likely to be available only in select markets and/or through specialized retailers. The downside of extensive coverage is that it typically comes at a high cost and often leads to channel conflicts. The downside of limited availability, on the other hand, is that it runs the risk of the offering being unavailable to some target customers.

Channel Exclusivity

Channel exclusivity refers to the degree to which an offering is made available through different distribution channels. Channel exclusivity is commonly used to reduce the potential for horizontal channel conflicts, which occur when distributors with different cost structures and profit margins sell identical offerings to the same customers. To mitigate the negative impact of a direct price comparison of the same offering across retailers, manufacturers often release channel-specific product variants that vary in functionality and, therefore, cannot be directly compared.

Value-Delivery Functions of Distribution Channels

The primary function of distribution channels is to deliver the company's offering to its target customers. This involves delivering different aspects of the offering: product, service, brand, price, and incentives.

- **Delivering products** involves transfer of the physical possession and ownership rights (title) of the product from the manufacturer to intermediaries (wholesales, distributors, and retailers) and, ultimately, to end users. It can involve value-added functions.

- **Delivering services** involves customer-focused activities such as customization, repair, technical assistance, and warranty support as well as collaborator-focused activities such as storage, inventory management, sorting, and repackaging.

- **Delivering brands** provides customers with an opportunity to experience the brand. Disney, Sony, and Harley-Davidson retail stores function as channels delivering these brands to their customers.

- **Delivering prices** involves collecting and processing payments from customers. Unlike other marketing mix variables where the flow of items is from the company to its customers, in the case of pricing the flow is reversed: Payments are collected from customers and delivered to the company.

- **Delivering incentives** involves distributing incentives such as coupons, rebates, and premiums to customers, as well as processing some of these incentives (e.g., redeeming coupons).

Note that in addition to delivering value, distribution channels often participate in designing and communicating the value of the offerings they deliver. The value-design function of distribution channels can involve product assembly, financing and warranty services, enhancing the offering's brand, negotiating the sale price, and managing point-of-purchase incentives. In the same vein, the value-communication function of distribution channels can involve explaining product and service benefits of the offering, communicating the meaning of its brand, and informing customers about the offering's price and incentives. In addition to delivering the offering to target customers, the functions of distribution channels also involve managing reverse logistics, including processing returns and refunds. Channels also manage the reverse flow of information by soliciting and collecting customer feedback, suggestions, and complaints.

SUMMARY

Distribution decisions need to take into account two types of factors: strategic factors that involve customers, company, collaborators, competition, and context, and tactical factors that involve the other marketing mix variables: product, service, brand, price, incentives, and communication.

Designing and managing distribution channels involve several key decisions: channel structure (direct, indirect, and hybrid), channel coordination (ownership-based, contractual, and implicit), channel type (specialized vs. broad and limited vs. extensive), channel coverage (limited vs. extensive), and channel exclusivity.

Channels facilitate the value exchange between the company and its customers by delivering the different aspects of the company's offering to its target customers: they deliver the company's products and services, enhance the offering's brand, collect payments, and distribute and process incentives. Channels also facilitate reverse logistics by processing product returns and payment credits.

RELEVANT CONCEPTS

All-Commodity Volume (ACV): A measure of an offering's availability, typically calculated as the total annual volume of the company's offering in a given geographic area relative to the total sales volume of the retailers in that geographic area across all product categories (hence, the term "all-commodity volume"). Also refers to the gross sales in a specific geographic area (total sales of all stores).

$$ACV = \frac{\text{Total sales of stores carrying the company's offering}}{\text{Total sales of all stores}}$$

Category Killers: Specialty retailers that focus on one product category in which they offer a large assortment of options at very competitive prices. Category killers include retailers like Best Buy (electronics), Office Depot (office supplies), Home Depot (home improvement), and PetSmart (pet supplies).

Contractual Vertical Marketing System: Channel structure in which the relationships between channel members are set on a contractual basis (rather than common ownership).

Corporate Vertical Marketing System: Channel structure in which channel members have common ownership rather than a contractual relationship.

Detailers: Indirect sales force promoting pharmaceuticals to doctors and pharmacists so that they, in turn, recommend the brand to the consumer.

Direct Channel: Distribution strategy in which the manufacturer and the end customer interact directly with each other without intermediaries.

Forward Buying: Increasing the channel inventory, usually to take advantage of a manufacturer's promotion or in anticipation of price increases.

Gray Market: A market in which products are sold through unauthorized channels.

Horizontal Channel Conflict: Tension between entities in multiple distribution channels (e.g., a manufacturer and two retailers). *See Chapter 6 for more details.*

Hybrid Channel: Distribution strategy in which the manufacturer and the end customer interact with each other through multiple channels (directly and through intermediaries).

Indirect Channel: Distribution strategy in which the manufacturer and the end customer interact with each other through intermediaries.

Inventory Turnover: The number of times that inventory is replenished, typically calculated as the ratio of annual revenues generated by a given offering to average inventory.

Merchandisers: Indirect sales force that offers support to retailers for in-store activities, such as shelf location, pricing, and compliance with special programs.

Parallel Importing: The practice of importing products from a country in which the price is lower into a country in which the same product is priced higher. A hypothetical example of this practice is importing drugs from Canada to the United States. In most cases, parallel importing is illegal in the United States.

Reverse Logistics: The process of reclaiming recyclable and reusable materials and returns for repair, remanufacturing, or disposal.

Same-Store Sales: A metric used in the retail industry for measuring sales of stores that have been open for a year or more and have historical data by comparing the current year's sales to last year's sales. Same-store sales is a popular metric because it takes store closings and chain expansions out of the mix, indicating the portion of new sales that resulted from sales growth and the portion that resulted from the opening or closing of stores.

Share of Shelf Space: Shelf space allocated to a given offering relative to the total shelf space in a given geographic area.

Shrinkage: A term used by retailers to describe theft of goods by customers and employees.

Vertical Channel Conflict: Tension between entities in a single distribution channel (e.g., a manufacturer and a retailer). *See Chapter 6 for more details.*

Vertical Marketing Systems: Centrally coordinated distribution channel.

ADDITIONAL READINGS

Anderson, Erin, Anne T. Coughlan, Louis W. Stern, and Adel I. El-Ansary (2006), *Marketing Channels* (7th ed.). Upper Saddle River, NJ: Prentice Hall.

Rolnicki, Kenneth (1998), *Managing Channels of Distribution: The Marketing Executive's Complete Guide.* New York, NY: AMACOM.

Zoltners, Andris A., Prabhakant Sinha, and Sally Lorimer (2004), *Sales Force Design for Strategic Advantage.* Basingstoke, NH: Palgrave Macmillan.

PART FOUR

MANAGING GROWTH

INTRODUCTION

You will either step forward into growth or you will step back into safety.

Abraham Maslow, American psychologist

Managing growth is the most common route to profitability. Compared to cost-cutting—the alternative approach to profitability—ensuring top-line growth is the preferred strategy by most organizations. Unlike cost-cutting, which is only a temporary means to increase profits, top-line growth has the potential to provide the company with a viable solution for achieving sustainable profit growth. In addition to enhancing profits, focusing on growth adds vitality to organizations by providing challenges and fostering creativity.

Five key issues in managing growth merit attention: gaining and defending market position, growing sales revenues, managing customers, developing new products, and managing product lines.

- **Gaining and defending market position** deals with issues concerning creating and sustaining growth in a competitive environment. The common strategies for managing market position are discussed in Chapter 14.

- **Managing sales growth** involves increasing sales volume and is typically achieved by acquiring new customers and selling more to existing customers. These two strategies for increasing sales volume—product adoptions by new customers and product usage by existing customers—are discussed in Chapter 15.

- **Managing customers** involves optimizing a company's customer acquisition and retention efforts to cultivate a loyal customer base and ensure sustainable market growth. The key issues in managing customers—measuring customer equity, managing retention, and building customer loyalty—are discussed in Chapter 16.

- **New product development** is essential to ensure sustainable growth. The key issues in developing new offerings—understanding new product adoption, forecasting market demand, and designing new offerings—are the focus of Chapter 17.

- **Product-line management**. Most companies aim to grow by developing and managing a series of related offerings—or product lines—tailored to the diverse needs of their target customers. The key aspects of product line management are discussed in Chapter 18.

The selection of a growth strategy is ultimately determined by the company's strategic goals, core competencies, and strategic assets, as well as by its target customers, collaborators, competitors, and the overall economic, technological, sociocultural, regulatory, and physical context. An integrative approach to analyzing these factors, such as the one described in the following chapters, is essential for the development of a successful growth strategy.

CHAPTER FOURTEEN

GAINING AND DEFENDING MARKET POSITION

In football, everything is complicated by the presence of the other team.

Jean-Paul Sartre, French philosopher

T he constantly evolving nature of the competitive landscape calls for developing dynamic strategies to manage a company's market position. Managing market position presents companies with two perennial questions: how to gain market position and how to defend their current market position. These two questions and strategies to address them are the focus of this chapter.

Gaining Market Position

A company can gain share by using three core strategies: (1) stealing share from competitors already serving this market, (2) growing the market by attracting new customers to the category, and (3) creating new markets.

Steal-Share Strategy

The steal-share strategy refers to a company's activities aimed at attracting customers from its competitors rather than trying to attract customers who are new to the product category (Figure 1). Apple targeting Windows users (rather than aiming at customers who have never had a computer) is an example of a steal-share strategy. Because of its focus on attracting only competitors' customers, the steal-share focus is also referred to as *selective demand* strategy.

A company's steal-share strategy can vary in breadth: It can narrowly target customers of a specific competitor (e.g., Pepsi targeting Coke customers), or it can broadly focus on the competitor's market as a whole (e.g., RC Cola trying to steal share from all competitors, including Coke and Pepsi).

Figure 1. Steal-Share Strategy

To succeed in attracting competitors' customers, a company needs to present these customers with a compelling value proposition. In this context, there are two basic steal-share strategies: a differentiation-based strategy and a similarity-based strategy.

- *Differentiation strategy* aims to steal share from the competition by demonstrating the superiority of the company's offering. The differentiation may involve superior benefits, such as better performance and lower costs.

- *Similarity strategy*, also referred to as a "me-too" strategy, aims to establish multiple points of parity and steal share from a competitor, typically the market leader, by showing that a company's and a competitor's offerings are, in fact, identical. One particular form of the "me-too" strategy is cloning, which involves emulating the incumbent's offering, usually with slight variations to avoid patent and trademark infringement liability.

Market-Growth Strategy

Unlike the steal-share strategy, which competes for customers who are currently using competitors' offerings, the market-growth strategy aims to attract customers who are new to the category (Figure 2). For example, an advertising campaign promoting the consumption of milk (the "Got milk?" campaign) builds the entire category, whereby switching occurs between substitute products (milk vs. non-milk) rather than between different brands of milk. Because of its focus on increasing the overall category demand, the market-growth strategy is sometimes referred to as *primary demand* stimulation.

Figure 2. Market-Growth Strategy

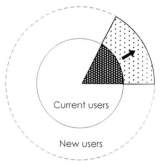

Because the market-growth strategy is aimed at growing the entire category, it typically benefits all companies competing in that category. Therefore, this strategy is usually adopted in the early stages of an offering's life cycle when the overall market growth is high and competition is not yet a primary issue. Moreover, because offerings tend to gain share proportionately to their current market position, in the case of relatively mature products the market-growth strategy is likely to benefit the market leader.

A notable exception to the scenario illustrated in Figure 3 involves a case in which a company's offering has a superior value proposition relative to the competition (because of a technological breakthrough, the addition of unique product benefits, or a price advantage), making it likely to gain a disproportionately large share (relatively to its current share) of new customers. In this case, a small-share offering can be as successful in growing the market as the leader (Figure 3).

Figure 3. Market-Growth Strategy for an Offering with a Superior Value Proposition

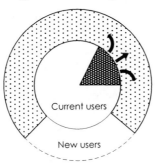

Market-Innovation Strategy

The market-innovation strategy is similar to the market-growth strategy in that a company gains market position by attracting customers who have not used any products and services in a given category (Figure 4). The key difference is that instead of converting new customers to the existing category in which the company faces its current rivals, it defines an entirely new category in which competition is limited or absent. Because of its focus on uncontested markets, the market-innovation strategy is sometimes referred to as the Blue Ocean Strategy (described in more detail at the end of this chapter).

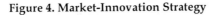
Figure 4. Market-Innovation Strategy

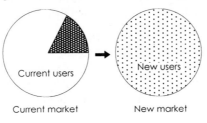

Because it targets customers that are new to the particular product category, the market-innovation strategy typically involves pioneering new markets.

Pioneering New Markets

The term *pioneer* or *first-mover* refers to the first company to establish its presence in a particular domain. Based on the domain in which the company is the first mover, there are four common types of pioneers.

- **Technology pioneer** is the company that first introduces a new technology to a category.

- **Product pioneer** is the company that is first to commercially introduce a conceptually new ("new-to-the-world") product aimed at satisfying a particular customer need.

- **Process pioneer** is the company that is first to introduce a particular business process, such as supply-chain management.

- **Market pioneer** is the company that first introduces a given offering to a particular target market.

For the purposes of marketing analysis, the term *pioneer* is used in reference to the first company to introduce its offering to a given market defined by a particular customer need. Thus, a pioneer in a market is the company that first reached a given segment with its offering. Even though, from a chronological standpoint, another company may have pioneered a product by introducing it to a different customer segment, the company that first introduced it to target customers is considered the pioneer for these customers. For example, Apple's iPod, which was introduced in the United States in 2001, is typically thought of as the pioneer of portable hard drive MP3 players, even though MPMan, which used the same technology, was introduced in Asia in 1998 by the Korean company Saehan.

The Benefits of Pioneering

Pioneering a market offers the incumbent several key advantages that are not available to later entrants. These advantages include shaping consumer preferences, creating switching costs, gaining access to scarce resources, creating barriers to competitive entry, and taking advantage of the learning curve.

- **Preference formation.** A pioneering company has the unique opportunity to shape customer preferences, creating a close association between its brand and the underlying customer need. For example, Coca-Cola, Jeep, Google, Amazon.com, eBay, Twitter, and Xerox not only helped shape customer preferences but also became synonymous with the entire category.

- **Switching costs.** As a pioneer, a company has the opportunity to build loyalty by creating switching costs for its customers. These switching costs could be functional (loss of the unique benefits of the pioneer's offering), monetary (the cost of replacing proprietary equipment or a penalty for breaking a contract), or psychological (the cost of learning the functionality of a competitor's offering).

- **Resource advantage.** The pioneer can benefit from preempting scarce resources such as raw materials, human resources, geographical locations, and collaborator networks. For example, the pioneer may be able to lock out the competition by securing exclusive access to strategically important mineral resources. Similarly, the pioneer may preempt competitors' access to a particular human resource in short supply, such as engineers, designers, and managers. The pioneer may also preempt strategically important geographic locations in both real space (Starbucks, McDonald's, and Walmart) and cyberspace (flowers.com, drugstore.com, and buy.com). The pioneer can also preempt the competition by forging collaborator alliances with strategically important partners such as distributors or advertisers. For example, sporting goods manufacturers offer exclusive long-term contracts to promising athletes early in their careers when they believe that these athletes will serve as a means for competitive differentiation.

- **Barriers to entry.** The pioneer can create technological barriers to prevent competitors from entering the market. For example, the pioneer may secure the exclusive rights to use a particular invention or design that is essential for developing offerings that will successfully address a specific customer need. Being the pioneer also enables a company to establish a proprietary technological standard (e.g., operating system, communication protocol, and video compression) that ensures the sustainability of the incumbent's technological advantage in the marketplace.

- **Learning curve.** The pioneer often benefits from learning curve advantages, allowing it to heighten production effectiveness and efficiency as its cumulative output increases over time. Simply put, being in business longer than its competitors often gives the pioneer a competitive edge in technological know-how, level of workforce experience, and production efficiency.

The Drawbacks of Being a Pioneer

Being a pioneer does not always benefit the company. Pioneers face a distinct set of disadvantages that may impede rather than facilitate their strategy. The three most common disadvantages include free riding, incumbent inertia, and market uncertainty.

- **Free riding.** A later entrant may be able to free ride on the pioneer's resources, including its investments in technology, product design, customer education, regulatory approval, infrastructure development, and human resource development. To illustrate, after spending millions of dollars to develop the technology and educate the American audience about the advantages of a personal digital recorder, the pioneer TiVo found itself in competition with cable and satellite operators selling similar services to its already educated target customers. Alternatively, a follower could reverse-engineer the pioneer's product and improve upon it, while investing only a fraction of the resources required to develop the original product. Federal Express built on DHL's idea to start overnight deliveries in the United States. IBM launched its PC, building on the earlier product introductions from Apple and Atari. Best Buy launched a rapid expansion of superstores based on the success of the Circuit City model.

- **Incumbent inertia.** Being a market leader often leads to complacency, thus leaving technological and market opportunities open to competitors. To illustrate,

IBM's reliance on mainframes, even when mainframes were being replaced by networked computers, enabled competitors such as Dell and Hewlett-Packard to gain a foothold in IBM's markets and steal some of its most valuable clients. Incumbent inertia may also be driven by a reluctance to cannibalize existing product lines by adopting a new technology or a new business model. For example, brick-and-mortar booksellers such as Barnes & Noble and Borders failed to recognize the importance of e-commerce, allowing Amazon.com to establish a dominant presence in online book retailing. Incumbent inertia may also result from a "sunk-cost mentality," whereby managers feel compelled to utilize their large investments in extant technology or markets, even when technological advancements and market forces make these investments unfeasible. For example, one of the reasons Ford lost its leading market position to General Motors in the 1930s was its reluctance to make the necessary investments to modify existing manufacturing facilities to diversify its product line.

- **Market uncertainty.** Another potential disadvantage in being a pioneer is the uncertainty associated with the offering. Indeed, whereas the pioneer has to deal with the uncertainty surrounding the technology and market demand, a follower can learn from the pioneer's successes and failures and design a superior offering. Because of the uncertainty associated with the introduction of a new offering, companies with strong brands and distribution capabilities often choose to be late market entrants, which enables them to learn from the pioneer's experience and develop an effective and cost-efficient market entry strategy. These companies use their brand and channel power to manage the risk associated with new product development and new market entry, allowing them to be successful late entrants into a given market. To illustrate, the first sugar-free soft drink was introduced in the United States by Cott in 1947, and the first sugar-free cola was introduced by Royal Crown in 1962, only to be overtaken by Coke and Pepsi, which used their branding and distribution power to dominate the consumer soft drink market.

The numerous drawbacks of being a market pioneer suggest that when entering new markets, a company should strive not only to gain share but also to create a business model that cannot be easily copied by its current and future competitors. Because market success inevitably attracts competition, creating a sustainable competitive advantage is the key to a successful pioneering strategy.

Defending Market Position

Because business success inevitably attracts competition, a company needs to develop strategies to defend its market position. There are three basic ways in which a company can react to a competitor's activities: not taking action, repositioning its existing offering(s), and adding new offerings. These strategies are illustrated in Figure 5 and discussed in more detail below.

Figure 5. Defensive Marketing Strategies[1]

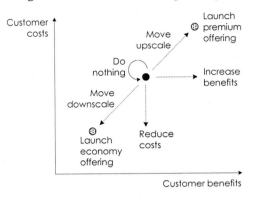

Not Taking Action

The decision to ignore a competitor's action(s) reflects a company's belief that these actions either will have no material impact on the company's market position or that the competitive threat is not sustainable and will dissipate by itself. For example, a company may decide that its upscale offering will not be affected by the entry of a low-price, low-quality competitor and therefore not consider this action a direct threat. In the same vein, a company may not react to a competitor's price reduction if it believes that this low-price position is not sustainable in the longer term.

Repositioning the Existing Offering

A company may choose to reposition its offering in one of two ways. It may change the offering's value proposition to increase its appeal to current customers or, alternatively, it may reposition the offering to target a different customer segment.

- **Repositioning to increase the offering's value for current customers**. Because value is a function of benefits and costs, enhancing the value of an offering may be achieved in two ways: by increasing benefits and by decreasing costs.
  - *Increasing an offering's benefits.* To increase the customer benefits of its offering, a company may choose to (1) enhance the functional benefits of its offering (by improving the offering's performance), (2) increase the monetary benefits (by adding monetary rewards), and (3) increase the psychological benefits (by enhancing the offering's image). For each of these strategies to succeed, the increase in benefits must actually be perceived as such by customers; improving the offering's performance on attributes that are unobservable by customers is not likely to enhance its customer value.
  - *Decreasing an offering's costs.* As in the case of increasing benefits, decreasing an offering's costs can be achieved by decreasing its functional, monetary, and psychological costs. Because the price of an offering is typically the most important component of customers' costs, price reduction and adding monetary incentives are the most common form of cost decreases.

- **Repositioning to attract new customers.** In addition to increasing an offering's value for existing customers, a company may decide to reposition its offering to better address the needs of target customers. Repositioning implies a change in the value proposition of a given offering in one of two ways: vertical or horizontal.

  - *Vertical repositioning* refers to a scenario in which a company modifies the value proposition of an offering by moving it into a different price tier. Vertical repositioning can be either upscale or downscale. In the case of upscale repositioning, the company increases the price of an offering while augmenting its benefits. In contrast, downscale repositioning involves a decrease in an offering's price and a corresponding decrease in benefits.

  - *Horizontal repositioning* refers to a scenario in which a company modifies the value proposition of an offering by altering its benefits without necessarily moving it to a different price tier. To illustrate, in an attempt to break away from the traditional association of prunes as a means to regularity for the elderly and make them appealing to younger customers, California prune manufacturers began marketing prunes as "dried plums," highlighting their high level of antioxidants.

Extending the Product Line

In addition to repositioning its existing offerings, a company can respond to competitive actions by adding new offerings to its product line. Product-line extension is similar to repositioning, with the key distinction that instead of modifying the value proposition of an existing offering, the company launches a new offering with a different value proposition. There are two common product line extension strategies: vertical and horizontal.

- **Vertical extensions** are new offerings differentiated by both benefits and price (e.g., an economy car vs. a luxury car). A company can use both upscale and downscale extensions to defend its market position. One popular strategy to fight low-price rivals involves launching a *fighting brand*—a downscale offering introduced to shield the core offering from low-priced competitors. A slightly more complex approach to dealing with low-priced competitors is the *sandwich strategy*, which involves both the introduction of a downscale offering and upscale repositioning of the core brand. A third commonly used approach to deal with low-priced rivals is the *good-better-best strategy*, which involves introducing both an upscale and a downscale offering, resulting in a three-tier product line.

- **Horizontal extensions** are new offerings that are differentiated primarily by functionality and not necessarily by price (e.g., a sedan vs. a minivan). As product categories mature, their user base becomes more diverse, calling for specialized offerings customized to the needs of different customer segments. Consequently, the pioneer might preempt the competition by extending its product line with offerings tailored to each strategically important customer segment.

A more detailed discussion on managing product lines is offered in Chapter 17.

SUMMARY

The constantly evolving nature of the competitive landscape calls for developing dynamic strategies to manage a company's market position. There are three basic strategies to gain market position: stealing share from competitors serving this market (steal-share strategy), growing the market by attracting new customers to the category (market-growth strategy), and creating new markets (market-innovation strategy).

Gaining market position often involves pioneering new markets. The key benefits of market pioneering include the opportunity to shape customer preferences, create switching costs, preempt scarce resources, create technological barriers to entry, and reap learning curve benefits. The key drawbacks of being a pioneer include free riding by competitors, incumbent inertia, and uncertainty associated with the offering's technology and with customer demand.

Because business success inevitably attracts competition, a company needs to develop strategies to defend its market position. There are three basic ways in which a company can react to a competitor's actions: by not taking an action, by repositioning its existing offerings (increasing benefits, decreasing costs, and moving upscale or downscale), and by adding a new offering to its product line.

RELEVANT CONCEPTS: THE BLUE OCEAN STRATEGY

The Blue Ocean strategy argues that instead of competing in overcrowded existing markets (red oceans), a company should focus its efforts on uncovering new, uncontested markets (blue oceans). Consistent with the concept of product life cycle, the Blue Ocean Strategy argues that mature markets are red oceans that should be avoided and priority given to the search for the blue oceans—new markets that a company can shape and in which it can be the dominant player.

According to this strategy, technology innovation is most often not the key driver in discovering uncontested markets; instead, it is the company's ability to find an innovative way of creating value for target customers that determines its success in discovering blue oceans. The Blue Ocean Strategy further asserts that the competition should not be used as a benchmark in strategic planning. Instead of focusing on the competition, the company should focus on creating value for its target customers in a way that benefits the company itself. With its focus on optimizing value for target customers and the company, the Blue Ocean Strategy is aligned with the 3-V framework advanced in this book.

RELEVANT FRAMEWORKS: PRODUCT-MARKET GROWTH FRAMEWORK

The product-market growth framework (also referred to as the Ansoff matrix) offers a practical approach to evaluating market opportunities by linking customer segments to product development opportunities.[2] This framework is often presented as a 2 × 2 matrix in which one of the factors is the type of offering (existing vs. new) and the other factor is the type of customers (current vs. new). The resulting four product-market strategies are commonly referred to as market penetration, market development, product development, and diversification (Figure 6).

Figure 6. Product-Market Growth Matrix

Current customers   New customers

	Current customers	New customers
Current products	Market penetration	Market development
New products	Product development	Diversification

- *Market-penetration* strategies aim to increase sales of an existing offering to a company's current customers. A common market-penetration strategy involves increasing usage rate. To illustrate, airlines stimulate demand from current customers by adopting frequent-flyer programs, cereal manufacturers enclose repurchase coupons in their offerings, and orange juice producers promote drinking orange juice throughout the day rather than only for breakfast.

- *Market-development* strategies aim to grow sales by promoting their existing offering to new customers. Popular market-development strategies include price promotions (e.g., price reductions, coupons, and rebates), new distribution channels, and communication strategies focused on new customer segment(s).

- *Product-development* strategies endeavor to grow sales by developing new (to the company) offerings for existing customers. The two most common product-development strategies include developing entirely new offerings or extending the current product line by modifying existing offerings.

- *Diversification strategies* aim to grow sales by introducing new offerings to new customers. Because both the offering and the customers are new to the company, this strategy tends to be riskier than the other product-market strategies. The primary rationale for diversification is to take advantage of growth opportunities in areas in which the company has no presence.

The four strategies identified above are not mutually exclusive: A company can pursue multiple sales growth strategies. However, the company needs to prioritize these strategies and focus on those that will enable it to achieve its strategic goals.

Additional Readings

Day, George S., David J. Reibstein, and Robert E. Gunther (2004), *Wharton on Dynamic Competitive Strategy*. New York, NY: John Wiley & Sons.

Kim, W. Chan and Renée Mauborgne (2005), *Blue Ocean Strategy: How to Create Uncontested Market Space and Make the Competition Irrelevant*. Boston, MA: Harvard Business School Press.

Kotler, Philip, Dipak C. Jain, and Suvit Maesincee (2002), *Marketing Moves: A New Approach to Profits, Growth, and Renewal*. Boston, MA: Harvard Business School Press.

Notes

[1] Adapted from Hoch, Stephen J. (1996), "How Should National Brands Think about Private Labels?" *Sloan Management Review*, 37 (2), 89–102.

[2] Ansoff, H. Igor (1979), *Strategic Management*. New York, NY: John Wiley & Sons.

CHAPTER FIFTEEN

MANAGING SALES GROWTH

He who moves not forward, goes backward.
Johann Wolfgang von Goethe, German writer and philosopher

S ales growth is an essential component of a company's efforts to achieve sustainable profitability. Sales growth can be achieved by two core strategies: acquiring
new customers and increasing sales to existing customers. Understanding the main
factors influencing sales volume and identifying strategies for effectively managing
sales growth are the focus of this chapter.

Overview

There are two basic strategies for managing sales growth: increasing the rate of
adoption of a company's offering by new customers and increasing the offering's
sales to existing customers (Figure 1). Balancing a company's resources across these
two strategies and optimizing the implementation of each of these strategies is essential
for a company's ability to gain and defend its market position and ensure long-term
profitability.

Figure 1. Managing Sales Growth

The two strategies for increasing the sales volume of a company's offerings—
managing product adoptions by new customers and managing product usage by
current customers—are discussed in more detail in the following sections.

Managing Adoption

To identify the optimal strategy for increasing sales volume, a company first needs to understand the process by which its target customers adopt new products, then identify the impediments to new product adoption in different stages of the process, and, finally, develop an action plan to remove these impediments. These aspects of managing product adoption are discussed in more detail below.

Understanding the Adoption Process

From a customer's perspective, product adoption can be viewed as a multistage process comprising a sequence of four key steps: awareness, attractiveness, affordability, and availability. This view implies that for customers to adopt an offering, they should (1) be aware of its availability, (2) find its benefits attractive, (3) perceive the offering to be affordable, and (4) have access to purchase the offering. Because the number of potential customers who ultimately purchase the offering tends to decrease with each step, the steps in the adoption process are also referred to as an *adoption funnel* (Figure 2).[1]

Figure 2: The Adoption Funnel

The adoption funnel illustrates how users progress through the experience of purchasing a new offering. The key steps of the adoption funnel are as follows:

- **Awareness** reflects customers' knowledge that the offering is available. Awareness can be generated by the company's direct communications to its target customers, by communications initiated by its collaborators (distribution partners, supplier partners, co-developers, and co-promoters), as well as by third-party communications, such as social media and press coverage.

- **Attractiveness** reflects the benefits buyers expect to receive from the offering. An offering's attractiveness reflects its ability to satisfy a particular need of target customers better than competitors' offerings. Attractiveness implies that buyers are not only aware of the offering but also understand and value its benefits.

- **Affordability** reflects customers' perceptions of the costs associated with the offering and their ability to cover these costs. Considered together, affordability (costs) and attractiveness (benefits) determine the overall value (utility) of the offering to target customers. Affordability can involve monetary as well as nonmonetary costs (e.g., time and effort involved in acquiring and using the offering). Affordability related to monetary costs is often the key impediment to adoption of an offering in developing countries and in financially strained demographic areas.

- **Availability** reflects the degree to which customers have access to the offering. An offering's availability is a function of the density of the distribution channels catering to a given customer segment and the in-stock availability of the offering in these channels on a day-to-day basis.

Identifying and Closing Adoption Gaps

Managing product adoption calls for identifying and eliminating impediments at different stages of the adoption process. These impediments, often referred to as *adoption gaps*, can be illustrated by mapping the dispersion of customers across different stages of the adoption process. The goal of this analysis is to provide a better understanding of the dynamics of the adoption process and identify problematic areas that require specific actions.

To visualize the potential hurdles in the adoption process, the dispersion of customers across different stages of the adoption process can be represented by a series of bars, as shown in Figure 3. Here, the blank part of each bar corresponds to the share of potential customers who have not transitioned to the next stage of the adoption process. The ratio of the blank part to the shaded part reflects the effectiveness of the company's actions at each step in acquiring new customers.

Figure 3: Identifying Adoption Gaps

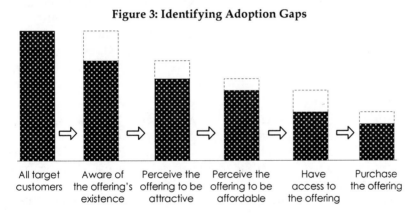

| All target customers | Aware of the offering's existence | Perceive the offering to be attractive | Perceive the offering to be affordable | Have access to the offering | Purchase the offering |

Evaluating the loss of potential customers at each step of the process offers a simple way to identify steps with a disproportionate drop in product adoption. These disproportionate drops in the product adoption process are the adoption gaps. The gap analysis can be used both to pinpoint the problem spots in product adoption and to identify specific solutions to close adoption gaps. Some of the common solutions for closing these performance gaps at the different stages of the adoption process are outlined below.

- **Awareness gaps** call for increasing awareness of the offering among target customers. This type of gap calls for increasing the effectiveness of company communications (by increasing overall communication spending, streamlining the message, developing a better creative solution, and using more effective media in a more cost-efficient manner). In addition to directly communicating the availability of the offering to target customers, the company can also involve its collaborators in creating awareness of the offering among target customers (e.g., by joint advertising). Finally, the company may foster third-party communications that promote the offering (e.g., by encouraging product adoption by opinion leaders and facilitating publicity about the offering).

- **Attractiveness gaps** call for improving the benefits of the offering. This typically is achieved by reformulating/redesigning the offering, which can involve permanent changes in the product, service, branding, and pricing aspects of the offering, as well as temporarily enhancing the value of the offering through incentives. Note that attractiveness gaps do not always imply that the offering lacks the benefits desired by target customers; they can also stem from the fact that buyers do not understand the offering's benefits. Such gaps in customers' understanding of the offering's benefits can be closed by improving communication by using various types of media, as well as by providing target customers with an option to experience the offering via product samples and demonstrations.

- **Affordability gaps** call for lowering the costs of the offering. Lowering monetary costs might involve lowering the offering's price, adding monetary incentives, as well as redesigning the offering to improve its affordability. Lowering nonmonetary costs might involve decreasing the amount of time and effort involved in acquiring and using the offering. Note that affordability gaps do not always imply that the actual costs of the offering are high; they might also result from customers' perception of the offering's actual costs. Such gaps in customers' understanding of the offering's costs can be closed by communicating the costs of the offering in a way that leads to a more accurate perception of these costs.

- **Availability gaps** indicate that target customers do not have access to the offering. For example, an offering may be in short supply because a company underestimated its appeal to target customers or because of inadequate distribution coverage. Depending on the cause of the availability gap, improving an offering's availability can involve ramping up production to meet demand, improving the geographical coverage of distribution channels to give target customers better accessibility to the offering, and improving channel operations to reduce stock-outs.

- **Purchase gaps** indicate that even though customers may find the company's offering attractive, affordable, and accessible, they have not purchased the offering within the time frame defined by the company's goals. This can result from the fact that customers have not formed an intent to purchase the offering in the near future or that they have formed such an intent but have fail to act upon it—for example, because of time or budgetary constraints. Closing purchase intent gaps typically involves introducing time-sensitive incentives such as short-lived price discounts, coupons, and financing options.

Managing Usage

The discussion so far has focused on growing sales volume by increasing product adoption by new customers. An alternative approach to growing an offering's sales volume involves increasing its consumption by current customers. This approach is discussed in more detail in the following sections.

Understanding Consumption

Most purchases are recurring in nature, be it products for daily usage like food, apparel, and cosmetics or durable goods like cars, household appliances, and electronics. Therefore, managing recurring consumption can have a significant impact on sales volume.

The total quantity of offerings purchased over time by individual customers depends on several key factors, including the overall satisfaction with the offering, the frequency with which consumers use the offering, the quantity used on each usage occasion, the frequency of replacement, and the availability of the offering (Figure 4). These five factors are summarized in more detail below.

Figure 4: Key Factors Influencing Consumption Quantity

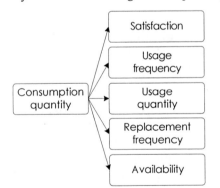

- **Satisfaction** reflects customers' experience of the offering. Unlike the attractiveness stage in product adoption, which is based on expectations of an offering's value, satisfaction reflects the postconsumption evaluation that takes into account customers' actual use of the offering.
- **Usage frequency** reflects the number of occasions on which the offering is used. For example, for cars, usage frequency refers to how often customers drive; for toothpaste, it refers to the number of times people brush their teeth.

- **Usage quantity** is particularly relevant when customers determine the quantity consumed on each occasion. For example, usage quantity for toothpaste depends on the amount of toothpaste people use to brush their teeth.

- **Replacement frequency** is particularly relevant in cases of unit-based products such as cars, printer cartridges, water filters, and razor blades, where customers determine when to replace the item.

- **Availability** indicates whether customers have a replacement at hand or can conveniently repurchase it.

Identifying and Closing Consumption Gaps

A practical approach to managing usage calls for identifying and eliminating impediments at the different stages of the repurchase process. This can be achieved by analyzing the consumption process (Figure 5).

Figure 5: Identifying Consumption Gaps

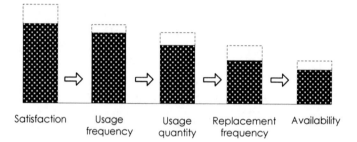

| Satisfaction | Usage frequency | Usage quantity | Replacement frequency | Availability |

Evaluating the effectiveness of each stage of the repurchase process offers a simple way to identify disproportionate drops in product usage. The most common solutions for closing these usage gaps at the different stages of the repurchase process are outlined below.

- **Satisfaction gaps** call for improving customers' experience with the offering. Depending on the cause of the satisfaction gap, this might involve enhancing the benefits and reducing the costs of the offering to make it more competitive, better aligning the offering's value proposition with changes in customer preferences, and adding variants to the offering's product line to reduce boredom and address variety seeking.

- **Usage-frequency gaps** call for increasing the frequency with which customers use the offering. For example, sales of a laundry detergent can be increased if customers wash their clothes more often; sales of toothpaste can be increased if customers brush their teeth more frequently; and sales of razors can be increased if customers shave more frequently. Sales volume can also be increased by identifying new ways to use the offering. To illustrate, Campbell Soup Company promotes the use of its soup (usually consumed in winter time) during summer and Arm & Hammer promotes baking soda not only for baking but also as a household cleaner and deodorizer.

- **Usage-quantity gaps** call for increasing the amount of product that customers use on each occasion. One approach to increasing usage quantity is to educate customers about the optimal usage quantity. A classic example of this approach is the "rinse and repeat" shampoo instruction. Another approach involves increasing the size of the packaging in categories where bigger package size typically leads to using a larger quantity. For example, Pepsi's introduction of the two-liter bottle in 1970 resulted in increased consumption of its products. Usage volume also can be increased by designing the product in a way that ensures dispensing the optimal quantity per usage occasion. For example, Heinz introduced a plastic squeeze bottle, increased the size of the opening in the bottle neck, and designed the "upside-down bottle" so ketchup can be poured without having to wait for the contents to slide down to the opening of the bottle. Similarly, laundry detergents often include measuring cups to determine the optimal usage quantity.

- **Replacement-frequency gaps** call for increasing the frequency with which customers replace the product. This type of gap is particularly relevant when consumption is defined by the number of occasions on which the same item is used, as in the case of durable goods. For example, to encourage customers to replace their toothbrush, Gillette added blue bristles on its Oral-B Indicator toothbrush, which fade halfway to alert users that they need to replace their brush.

- **Availability gaps** call for ensuring continuous consumption without disruptions due to stock-outs. For example, printer manufacturers include toner-level indicators to alert users that the cartridge will soon need replacement. Repurchase can also be facilitated by incentives that encourage customers to buy the offering in advance of having to replace it. A side benefit of advance purchasing and stockpiling is that it can promote consumption in categories where usage is "elastic" with respect to the quantity available. For example, the consumption of food and beverages is often influenced by the quantity at hand, such that greater quantity leads to greater consumption (often referred to as the "pantry effect").

Because they deal with recurring purchases, consumption gaps often hold greater potential to increase sales volume than acquisition gaps. This is especially true for companies with a dominant position in the market because of the relatively large installed base of users. Optimizing the consumption experience in this case can have a significant impact on the company's ability to grow sales volume.

SUMMARY

Sales growth is a key factor for achieving sustainable profitability. The two core strategies for increasing the sales volume of a company's offerings are (1) increasing product adoptions by new customers and (2) increasing product usage by current customers.

Product adoption can be viewed as a multistage process comprising four key factors: awareness (knowledge of the existence of the offering), attractiveness (perceived benefits that customers expect to receive from the offering), affordability (perceived costs associated with the offering), and availability (degree to which the offering is accessible by target customers). A useful approach to managing product adoption involves identifying and eliminating impediments (adoption gaps) at the different stages of the adoption process.

In addition to increasing adoption by new customers, in many cases an offering's sales volume can also be increased by influencing its usage (and, hence, repurchase frequency) by current customers. Product repurchase is a function of the following five factors: satisfaction (the degree to which customers find the offering attractive after having experienced it), usage frequency (rate at which customers use the offering), usage quantity (amount of the offering that customers consume on each usage occasion), replacement frequency (the rate at which consumers replace the offering), and availability (the extent to which the offering is readily available for repurchase and use). A practical approach to managing product usage involves identifying and eliminating impediments (usage gaps) at the different stages of the repurchase process.

RELEVANT CONCEPTS

Conversion Rate: The number of potential customers who have tried the product/service relative to the total number of customers aware of the product/service.

$$\text{Conversion rate} = \frac{\text{Current and former customers}}{\text{Potential customers aware of the offering}}$$

Penetration Rate: The number of customers who have tried the offering at least once relative to the total number of potential customers.

$$\text{Penetration rate} = \frac{\text{Current and former customers}}{\text{Potential customers}}$$

ADDITIONAL READINGS

Aaker, David A. (2009), *Strategic Market Management* (9th ed.). New York, NY: John Wiley & Sons.

Best, Roger J. (2008), Market-Based Management: Strategies for Growing Customer Value and Profitability (5th ed.). Upper Saddle River, NJ: Prentice Hall.

Kumar, Nirmalya (2004), *Marketing as Strategy: Understanding the CEO's Agenda for Driving Growth and Innovation.* Boston, MA: Harvard Business School Press.

NOTE

[1] The sequence of these steps in the adoption process may vary across products and customers. The model presented in Figure 2 reflects the most common sequence.

CHAPTER SIXTEEN

MANAGING CUSTOMERS

We see our customers as invited guests to a party, and we are the hosts. It's our job every day to make every important aspect of the customer experience a little bit better.

Jeff Bezos, founder of Amazon.com

Customer management involves a company's activities aimed at retaining and growing its user base. The development of a successful customer management strategy requires understanding the value that each customer brings to the company and designing strategies to create value for these customers. These two aspects of customer management are the focus of this chapter.

Value-Based Customer Management

Customer management aims to identify the optimal balance between the value created by the company for its target customers, on the one hand, and the value created by these customers for the company and its collaborators, on the other. Because customers vary in the value they create for the company, companies often prioritize their efforts to develop superior offerings for customers with higher profit potential. Accordingly, a manager's goal is to assess the profit potential of a company's customers and modify the company's offering to reflect the value of these customers for the company.

Customer Value and Customer Equity

When evaluating the viability of targeting a particular customer segment, a manager needs to answer two key questions: (1) Can the company create superior value for these customers? and (2) Can these customers create value for the company and its collaborators? The answer to the first question is determined by the degree to which the company's core competencies and strategic assets are aligned with the needs of target customers. The answer to the second question is determined by customers' lifetime value — that is, the monetary and strategic value customers are likely to create for the company during their tenure with this company. The monetary aspect of lifetime customer value is commonly referred to as customer equity.

Customer equity goes beyond the current profitability of a customer to include the entire stream of profits (adjusted for the time value of money) that a company is likely to receive from this customer. Although customer equity is relevant for both product-focused and service-based companies, it is particularly important for service-based companies, where customer equity is often a large component of the overall valuation of the company.

Recent technological developments have enabled companies to track real-time revenues and costs associated with their customers, allowing them to more precisely estimate the value of each customer. This, in turn, enables a company to segment its customer base according to customer profitability and to deliver a level of service based on each customer's equity. The result is a value-based stratification that is used to define the benefits offered to each individual customer. The customer equity value-allocation principle is straightforward: customers with greater value to the company (e.g., profit potential and strategic importance) receive superior benefits compared to less valuable customers For example, frequent flyers receive different levels of service based on their flying patterns, including dedicated customer service, faster check-in, waived fees, exclusive flight bonuses, and expanded seat availability. In the same vein, high rollers receive exclusive casino benefits, including free private jet transfers, limousine use, and complementary hotel suites.

This "value-per-equity" approach follows from the principle of value optimization, whereby the company needs to create value for target customers in a way that enables it to achieve its and its collaborators' goals. In this context, it is logical for companies to focus their efforts on customers with the highest value and the greatest profit potential. To follow this value-optimization strategy, however, the company needs to know the lifetime value of its customers. The basics of understanding and measuring customer equity are discussed in more detail below.

Understanding and Measuring Customer Equity

A customer can create value for the company in at least three different ways: (1) by directly generating revenues (and profits) for the company through purchase of the company's products and services, (2) by promoting the company's products and services to other buyers, and (3) by providing the company with information that can help increase the effectiveness and efficiency of its operations. These three sources of customer equity are illustrated in Figure 1 and outlined in more detail below.

Figure 1. The Three Dimensions of Customer Equity

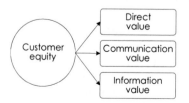

- **Direct value** reflects the monetary value received by a company from its transactions with a particular customer. A customer's direct value is typically calculated as the difference between the revenues generated and costs incurred during a customer's lifetime, discounted for the time value of money. The assessment of a customer's direct value typically includes the following six factors: (1) number of transactions during the customer's tenure with the company, (2) average transaction profitability, (3) customer acquisition costs (i.e., expenses incurred in acquiring the customer), (4) customer maintenance costs (i.e., expenses incurred for post-purchase support), (5) customer retention costs (e.g., the cost of loyalty programs), and (6) the discount rate (i.e., the interest rate used to determine the present value of future cash flows).

- **Communication value** reflects a customer's potential to influence other buyers' behavior with respect to the company's offerings. Communication value is often measured in terms of referrals generated by customers who share their experience with the company in order to influence other buyers. Note, however, that depending on the nature of the experience, customer referrals — and hence the communication value — can be either positive (in the case of satisfied customers) or negative (in the case of dissatisfied customers). Accordingly, the goal of customer management is to maximize the number and potency of the positive referrals and at the same time minimize the quantity and the impact of the negative ones. Because communication among customers cannot be readily observed by the company, identifying methods for tracking and assessing a customer's social impact is a key challenge in the development of quantifiable models for measuring customer equity.

- **Information value** reflects the value of the information provided by a customer. This includes two types of information: customer-specific and company-specific. Customer-specific information involves data about a customer's needs and profile that can help the company design, communicate, and deliver value to this customer, as well as to customers with similar needs. For example, enrolling in a loyalty program requires customers to share their purchase history, which helps the company understand buyer behavior and design its activities in a way that optimizes the value-creation process. Company-specific information, on the other hand, reflects customer feedback regarding the viability and effectiveness of the company's activities. For example, a (complaining) customer who informs the company about shortcomings of its offering de facto creates value for the company by alerting it to the problem and enabling it to address the situation before it affects other customers.

Of the above three sources of customer equity, the one that traditionally has been the focus of attention is direct value. This is because direct value, unlike the other two sources of customer equity, is readily observable and measurable. More recently, however, communication value has gained prominence, largely because of the growth and increased importance of social media. As companies realize the impact of peer-to-peer communication, they are beginning to view the social influence of their customers as a key component of customer equity valuation models.

Managing Customer Loyalty

A key question facing companies is identifying strategies for increasing customer retention and building customer loyalty. Three such strategies — retention-driven targeting, balancing acquisition and retention, and product-line retention — are discussed in the following sections.

Retention-Driven Targeting

Creating a loyal customer base begins with selecting the "right" target customers for whom the company can create a sustainable value proposition. Identifying loyal customers, however, requires thinking about retention *before* developing a customer acquisition strategy. Yet, companies often think about retention only *after* they realize that they are losing customers. Because a company's ultimate goal is not to gain transient customers but to cultivate a loyal customer base, thinking about customer retention should precede the development of an acquisition strategy. This focus on retention prior to acquisition is the essence of retention-driven targeting.

Retention-driven targeting begins with identifying customers for whom the company can create superior value and whose lifetime value fits the company's goals. It then involves designing an offering that creates superior customer value by minimizing the use of short-term incentives and ensuring the sustainability of the company's value proposition. The final step is the development of an acquisition strategy targeting high-value customers whose lifetime value is aligned with the company's strategic goals. Development of an acquisition strategy is the final step; it should take place only after the company identifies the high-value customers and develops a superior value proposition for them, the sustainability of which ensures customer loyalty.

Building a loyal customer base calls for replacing the traditional acquisition-focused *targeting → acquisition → retention* approach with the retention-driven *retention → targeting → acquisition* strategy. This retention-driven targeting approach implies that before developing a strategy to acquire new customers, a company should have a clear understanding of how to retain these customers.

Balancing Customer Acquisition and Customer Retention

Most companies spend a large portion of their promotional budget on acquiring new customers rather than on trying to retain their existing customers. This acquisition bias is paradoxical because even though most of a company's promotional efforts are spent on noncustomers, the majority of its revenues and profits come from current customers. Thus, by allocating most resources to new customers while neglecting existing ones, companies often end up substituting customer rotation for customer retention, replacing profitable customers with less profitable ones.

The focus on acquisition at the expense of retention stems from viewing current customers as a captive market that is inherently loyal — an approach that is ultimately detrimental to customer loyalty and often promotes customer attrition. Yet, despite the fact that defection rates of 10 to 30 percent per year are not unusual, many companies do not allocate sufficient resources to retain their existing customers and instead focus on acquiring new customers to replace the ones that have defected.[1] This customer-rotation strategy is based on the erroneous assumption that newly acquired customers have the same value to the company as its current customers.

There are multiple reasons for investing in retaining current customers and building customer loyalty. Lowering customer attrition can help lower the company's expenses due to reduced acquisition costs and the lower costs involved in serving existing customers. Indeed, because existing customers are familiar with the company's offerings, policies, and procedures, the cost of serving these customers is typically lower than the cost of serving customers who are new to the company. Customers familiar with the company are also more likely to adopt other products and services offered by this company, thus generating additional revenues and profits. Another important reason to develop customer loyalty is that loyal customers are often the company's best advocates, promoting the company's products and services and bringing in new customers. The above reasons underscore the value of loyal customers, validating a company's investment in cultivating loyalty and increasing customer retention.

Product-Line Retention Strategies

One of the key causes of customer defection is the inability of the company's offerings to fulfill customer needs. This is often a result of changes in the offering (e.g., using subpar materials to lower production costs) that end up diminishing its value to the customer. On many occasions, however, the mismatch between customer needs and the offering's benefits is not caused by changes in the company's offering but by the changing needs of its current customers.

Customer needs vary not only across segments; they also vary over time. This means that a company's customer base is constantly evolving. An important implication of this evolution is that with time a company might end up serving customers whose needs are very different from those of customers initially targeted by that company. Consequently, to fulfill the evolving needs of its customers, a company's offering must also evolve to align its value proposition with customers' needs (Figure 2).

Figure 2. Product-Line Management for Customer Retention

The retention-focused view of product-line management is a departure from the conventional view of new product introduction as a tool for acquiring new customers. Indeed, when introducing a new product the question managers typically ask is: *How many customers would I gain if I launch this offering?* Instead, what they should be asking is: *How many customers would I lose if I don't introduce a new offering?* The challenge here is that measuring an offering's success in terms of customers *not lost* is far more difficult than measuring the number of customers *gained* by the new offering. Yet, the difficulty of measurement notwithstanding, the ultimate result of both strategies is the same: the company has one more or one fewer customer. Given that attracting new customers is usually more costly and ultimately less profitable than retaining current customers, retention-based rather than rotation-based customer management strategies are likely to yield greater value for the company, its collaborators, and ultimately its customers.

SUMMARY

Customer management aims to find the optimal balance between the value created by the company for its target customers, on the one hand, and the value created by these customers for the company and its collaborators, on the other. A key concept in customer management is that of customer equity, which reflects the monetary value a company is likely to receive from a customer during this customer's tenure with the company.

Customer equity draws on three different sources: (1) direct value, which reflects the monetary value received by a company from its transactions with a particular customer, (2) communication value, which reflects a customer's potential to influence other buyers' behavior with respect to the company's offerings, (3) and information value, which reflects the value of the information provided by a customer.

Creating a loyal customer base begins with selecting the "right" target customers for whom the company can create a sustainable value proposition. Identifying loyal customers requires thinking about retention before developing a customer acquisition strategy. This focus on retention prior to acquisition is the essence of retention-driven targeting. There are multiple reasons for investing in retaining current customers and building customer loyalty: lower acquisition costs, lower customer maintenance costs, higher revenues due to upselling, and positive word of mouth.

Because customers' needs change with time, to effectively fulfill these needs and serve these customers a company's offerings need to evolve as well. The retention-focused view of product-line management is a departure from the conventional view of new product introduction as a tool for acquiring new customers.

RELEVANT CONCEPTS

Customer Relationship Management (CRM): A set of strategies used to manage a company's relationship with its current and potential customers. The term is also used in reference to specialized software developed to facilitate a company's customer management processes.

Customer Attrition Rate (Churn Rate): The number of customers who discontinue using a company's product or service during a specified period relative to the average total number of customers during that same period.

$$\text{Customer attrition rate} = \frac{\text{Number of customers who disadopt an offering during a specific period}}{\text{Total number of customers during that period}}$$

Pareto Principle: The 80/20 relationship discovered in the late 1800s by the economist Vilfredo Pareto.[2] Pareto established that 80% of the land in Italy was owned by 20% of the population. He later observed that 20% of the peapods in his garden yielded 80% of the peas that were harvested. The Pareto Principle, or the 80/20 Rule, has proven its validity in a number of other areas. In marketing, the most common illustration of the 80/20 rule is that 80% of revenues (or profits) are often generated by 20% of customers (or products).

Retention Rate: The number of customers who have repurchased the offering during the current buying cycle (month, quarter, or year) relative to the number of customers who purchased the offering during the last cycle. Also used in reference to the number of customers who have repurchased the offering relative to the total number of customers who have tried the product at least once.

$$\text{Retention rate} = \frac{\text{Active customers during the current period}}{\text{Active customers during the last period}}$$

RELEVANT FRAMEWORKS: THE CUSTOMER EQUITY PYRAMID

The customer pyramid method uses value-based segmentation to help companies identify the value derived from each of its customers and identify strategies for maximizing profit growth.[3] The name of the method follows from the fact that in many industries customer value stratification yields a pyramid-like pattern with relatively few high-value customers at the top of the pyramid.

The customer pyramid method involves rank-ordering customers based on their value to the company, as indicated by their score on a key value metric (profitability, sales, or revenues). A popular way of categorizing is by small customers (80% of all active customers) and large customers (the remaining 20% of the active customers)—a division consistent with the Pareto principle, according to which 80% of revenues come from 20% of customers. Further categorization of large customers (e.g., into medium customers, big customers, and top customers—accounting for 15%, 4%, and 1% of all active customers, respectively), as well as alternative classifications of a company's customer base, are also possible.

The rationale for dividing customers into groups is to enable the company to optimize the value it delivers to its customers based on their value to the company. Thus, a company should take special care of top customers to protect the company's market position while at the same time cultivating small customers to turn them into large customers. The customer pyramid method offers a systematic approach to aligning a customer's value to the company with the value the company delivers to each customer. At the same time, a potential limitation of the customer pyramid method is that it does not reflect a customer's true profit potential: for example, a small customer today can grow to be a large customer tomorrow. In addition, because it is implicitly based on the 80/20 rule, it has limited validity when applied to companies and industries for which the 80/20 rule does not hold.

REFERENCES

Blattberg, Robert, Gary Getz, and Jacquelyn Thomas (2001), *Customer Equity: Building and Managing Relationships as Valuable Assets*. Boston, MA: Harvard Business School Press.

Curry, Jay and Adam Curry (2000), *The Customer Marketing Method: How to Implement and Profit from Customer Relationship Management*. New York, NY: Free Press.

Griffin, Jill (2002), *Customer Loyalty: How to Earn It, How to Keep It*. New York, NY: Jossey-Bass.

Ofek, Elie (2002), *Customer Profitability and Lifetime Value* (Case 9-503-019). Boston, MA: Harvard Business School Press.

Rust, Roland, Valerie Zeithaml, and Key Lemon (2000), Driving Customer Equity: How Customer Lifetime Value Is Reshaping Corporate Strategy. New York, NY: Free Press.

NOTES

[1] Reichheld, Frederick and Thomas Teal (1996)., The Loyalty Effect. Boston, MA: Harvard Business School Press.

[2] Koch, Richard (1998), *The 80/20 Principle: The Secret to Success by Achieving More with Less*. New York, NY: Doubleday.

[3] Lowenstein, Michael (1997), *The Customer Loyalty Pyramid*. Westport, CT: Quorum.

CHAPTER SEVENTEEN

MANAGING NEW PRODUCTS

I don't design clothes. I design dreams.

Ralph Lauren, founder of Polo Ralph Lauren

New products and services are the key to sustainable growth; they enable companies to gain and sustain their market position by taking advantage of the changes in the market to create superior customer value. The main aspects of designing and managing new product offerings are the focus of this chapter.

Overview

The term "new products" is used in reference to two types of offerings: those that are new to the company but not new to target customers ("new-to-the-company" products) and those that are new both to the company and its target customers ("new-to-the-world" products). New-to-the-company offerings usually involve using new processes to create the product, devising new ways to communicate its benefits, and finding new distribution channels to deliver the product to target customers. Even though these innovations are novel to the company, they have already been adopted by competitors and are already familiar to target customers. In contrast, new-to-the-world innovations are novel not only to the company but to target customers as well.

Depending on their novelty to target customers, new-to-the-world products can be either extensions of an existing category or can create their own category. Common category extensions typically involve variants of existing offerings (different colors, flavors, tastes, sizes, designs, or packaging variations of an existing core product). In contrast, new category offerings involve products and services with a fundamentally different value proposition that extends beyond the existing categories. Examples of new category offerings include Amazon.com (online retailing), eBay (consumer-to-consumer online auctions), Priceline.com (reverse-price auctions), and Groupon (reverse promotions).

Forecasting Market Demand

The decision to launch a new offering stems from a company's belief that there is market demand for the benefits provided by this offering. To define the strategy and design tactics involved in the development of the new offering, the company needs to know the specifics of the target market and, in particular, the size of the market for its offering. This process of estimating the size of the potential market is referred to as demand forecasting.

There are two common types of demand forecasts: market forecasts and sales forecasts. *Market forecasts* estimate the total sales volume that ultimately can be achieved by all companies in a given market. Forecasts of market potential are typically used to make market entry and exit decisions, resource allocation decisions, and to set goals and evaluate performance. Unlike market forecasts, which indicate the sales volume that potentially could be achieved in a particular market, *sales forecasts* impose a specific time frame for achieving the sales volume. Thus, sales forecasts are an estimate of the total sales volume attainable within a given time frame. Similar to estimates of market potential, sales forecasts typically are used to make entry and exit decisions, allocate resources, plan production capacity, and evaluate the impact of various marketing mix variables on sales.

Based on the type of data they utilize, there are two types of demand-forecasting methods: collecting and analyzing primary data (data collected especially for the purpose of demand forecasting) and analyzing secondary data (existing data). These two types of methods are discussed in more detail in the following sections.

Forecasting Demand Using Primary Data

Primary-data forecasting involves collecting and analyzing new data to gain insight into the adoption process and estimate the potential market size and speed of adoption. There are two types of primary-data demand forecasts: expert-judgment forecasts and customer-research forecasts.

- **Expert-judgment forecasting** relies on experts' opinions to estimate market demand. Depending on the nature of the expert's background, there are three main categories of forecasts: executive forecasts, sales force forecasts, and industry forecasts.

  - *Executive forecast* is a top-down approach in which the forecast is based on the aggregated opinion of a company's top executives and senior managers.
  - *Sales force forecast* is a bottom-up approach in which the forecast is based on the aggregated opinion of a company's sales force and sales managers.
  - *Industry forecast* is based on the aggregated opinion of industry experts, such as industry analysts, executives, managers, and sales forces from competitive companies.

  Because most expert-judgment forecasts are based on aggregating the opinions of multiple experts, an important issue concerns the process of aggregating individual judgments to arrive at the final estimate. A popular method for eliciting expert judgments is the Delphi method, described in more detail at the end of this chapter.

- **Customer-research forecasting** examines customers' reaction to the offering at different stages of the product development process. The two most popular methods of customer-based forecasting are concept testing and market testing.

  - *Concept testing* is the process of evaluating consumer response to a particular offering prior to its introduction to the market. Concept testing can be based on a description of the offering or, alternatively, can involve a fully functional prototype. One approach to concept testing involves using a representative sample of the target segment (a focus group) for the purpose of revealing insights, ideas, and observations related to the key aspects of the offering. Another methodology involves estimating the probability of the offering's purchase by target customers based on a description of its main benefits and costs. Because it is based on customers' estimates of their future behavior, concept testing provides only rough estimates of sales volume.

  - *Market testing* relies on test markets to estimate market potential and future sales volume. It is often used as the litmus test for a go or no-go decision to launch a new product, as well as for testing specific aspects of the offering's marketing mix. Test markets aim to replicate all relevant aspects of the environment in which the company's offering will be launched (offering-related advertising and incentives, competitive offerings, and point-of-purchase environment) so that the test market outcome can be extrapolated to more general (national) sales forecasts. To ensure greater validity of the results, multiple test markets, typically located in different geographic areas, are used. Because of its relatively high costs, market testing is normally used only for products that successfully pass the concept testing stage.

Forecasting Demand Using Secondary Data

Secondary-data forecasting relies on already existing data. Based on the type of data, three different secondary-data forecasting methods can be used:

- **Offering-specific forecasting** is based on past data from the sales of the same offering for which the demand is being forecast. A popular approach relies on past sales data to identify trends, then extrapolates these trends to a sales forecast. A variety of time-series statistical approaches may be employed for this type of analysis, such as linear trend analysis, moving-average analysis, and exponential smoothing. Another popular approach involves identifying the relationships between the offering's sales and a variety of internal (the offering's price, incentives, and communication) and external factors (competitors' price, incentives, and communication) to predict the likely sales volume.

- **Forecasting by analogy** involves forecasting an offering's performance by comparing its adoption cycle to a functionally similar product for which sales data are available. This approach is useful for new-to-the-world products for which adoption data are not available, or for nontraditional marketing activities involving existing products (drastic price change, novel incentives, non-traditional communication campaign) for which market reaction is unknown. For example, one could forecast the adoption of 3-D TVs by comparing it to the adoption of analogous products such as color, flat-screen, and high-definition TVs. The key assumption of analogy-based forecasts is that the pattern of adoption of the new product (speed and depth of market penetration) follows a similar pattern to that of the analogous product.

- **Category-based forecasting** involves utilizing available product-category data to estimate a particular product's performance. One category-based forecasting approach to quantifying sales potential involves estimating the degree to which sales in a given category have captured the total market potential in a particular geographical area based on the population of that area and average consumption per user nationally (also referred to as the Category Development Index, or CDI). An alternative approach to category-based demand forecasting involves estimating the degree to which sales of a specific offering (rather than the entire category) have captured the total market potential in a particular market (also referred to as the Brand Development Index, or BDI). Comparing these two indexes reveals an offering's performance relative to the category. Thus, a combination of high BDI and low CDI indicates that the brand is doing better than competitive offerings, whereas a combination of low BDI and high CDI indicates that the brand is doing worse than competitive offerings.

Understanding New Product Adoption

Managing new products calls for understanding how customers adopt these products—a process often referred to as diffusion of innovations. The diffusion of new products is often represented by an S-shaped curve, which depicts the total number of adoptions at any given point in time (Figure 1A). The pattern of the diffusion process can be defined by two factors: (1) the size of the potential market, indicating the total number of users that will ultimately adopt the innovation, and (2) the speed of diffusion, which can be defined by the time frame for reaching the inflection point—the point at which the rate of growth slows down and starts declining (and where the shape of the diffusion curve turns from convex to concave).

The diffusion process can also be represented by the number of new (rather than total) adoptions of the innovation at any given point in time. In this context, new product adoption can be represented by a bell-shaped curve, whereby, after a relatively slow start, an increasing number of people adopt the innovation until it reaches a peak, then starts declining as the number of potential adopters decreases. The pattern of new adoptions directly corresponds to that of total adoptions, with the key difference that it represents the dispersion of new adoptions over time instead of the total number of current users (Figure 1B). A popular interpretation of the bell-shaped curve of noncumulative product adoptions involves classifying customers into distinct categories based on their adoption pattern. The two most influential frameworks offering such classifications — Rogers' and Moore's models — are discussed at the end of this chapter.

Figure 1. New Product Adoption

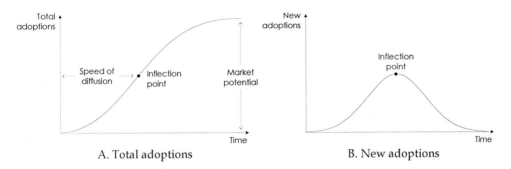

A. Total adoptions   B. New adoptions

The adoption of an innovation does not always follow a normal distribution represented by the bell-shape curve: Some innovations are adopted very rapidly, whereas others take a substantial amount of time to achieve their peak adoption period. A new offering may be adopted almost instantly by a large segment of the population, then it may be diffused at a much slower rate until it is adopted by all target customers; alternatively, adoption might start at a much slower rate and reach the point at which the majority of target customers have adopted it relatively late in the adoption process. The speed with which customers adopt a new offering is a function of the value provided by the offering. Specifically, several factors can influence the diffusion of new offerings:

- **Inherent value of the offering**. The greater the inherent value of the new offering, the more likely it is to be adopted.

- **Relative advantage**. The greater the relative advantage of an offering over the product it replaces, the more likely it is to be adopted.

- **Transparency**. An offering is more likely to be adopted when its relative advantage is readily observable and can be experienced by customers (e.g., due to the shared nature of the consumption experience).

- **Compatibility**. An offering compatible with customers' existing systems and processes is more likely to be adopted than an incompatible one.

- **Perceived risk**. An offering is more likely to be adopted when the level of customer uncertainty is low. This might involve customer uncertainty about their own preferences, uncertainty about the product's future performance, and uncertainty about the magnitude of the risks associated with the new product.

In addition to being a function of the offering's inherent benefits, the likelihood that customers will adopt a new offering is a function of a company's promotional and distribution activities. Thus, the greater the promotional activity (advertising, public relations, monetary and nonmonetary incentives) associated with a new offering and the greater the availability of the offering across distribution channels, the more likely it is to be adopted.

Communications associated with a new offering can be initiated by the company, its collaborators, and by a third party. Company and collaborator communications include advertising, press releases, event sponsoring, product placement, trade shows, free samples, free trials, sales force communications, and various other promotional incentives. In contrast, third-party communications involve sources like word of mouth and social media (e.g., comments, reviews, and noncompensated endorsements). From a chronological perspective, a company's own communications typically precede third-party communications, although on many occasions third-party communications precede the company's promotions. For example, Google, eBay, and Facebook relied primarily on word of mouth to build their initial customer base.

Third-party communications can both help and hurt new product adoptions. Offerings that appeal to customers are likely to generate positive word of mouth that can facilitate their adoption. Consider the movie *My Big Fat Greek Wedding*, released by IFC Films in 2002 and launched with a relatively small advertising budget. Ranked twentieth at the box office its first week, it steadily gained share from positive word of mouth and twenty weeks later became the second highest grossing movie. In contrast, unattractive offerings can generate unfavorable third-party communications that may slow down the rate of adoption and decrease the market potential of the offering. To illustrate, helped by a massive advertising campaign, the movie *Hulk*, released by Universal Pictures in 2003, became number one at the box office, with one of the highest grossing opening weekends of all time, only to be followed by a record 70% drop in ticket sales the second week—a drop that stemmed from mixed reviews and unfavorable word of mouth.

Managing the Product Life Cycle

The product life cycle describes the general trend of products and services as they progress through different stages in the marketplace. It can be defined in terms of a product category (e.g., flat screen TVs), a product class (e.g., 3-D TVs), or a particular product form (e.g., 55" 3-D TVs). The concept of a product life cycle is based on the idea that products have a limited life in which they pass through distinct stages. Because the stages in the product life cycle are characterized by different market conditions, different stages require different marketing strategies. In this context, four key product life cycle stages are identified: introduction, growth, maturity, and decline.

During the introduction stage, product awareness is low and there are very few competitors. As the product takes off during the growth stage, the number of competitors entering the market increases. At maturity, the number of competitors tends to peak, the market becomes saturated, and industry profitability starts to decline because of intensifying competition. Finally, the decline stage is characterized by falling demand for the product, relatively low profitability, and a decreasing number of competitors stemming from consolidation and exit from the market. The four stages of the product life cycle and the corresponding market conditions at each stage are illustrated in Figure 2.

Figure 2. Managing the Product Life Cycle[1]

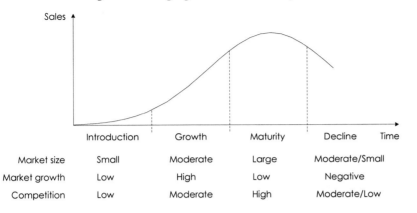

	Introduction	Growth	Maturity	Decline
Market size	Small	Moderate	Large	Moderate/Small
Market growth	Low	High	Low	Negative
Competition	Low	Moderate	High	Moderate/Low

Product strategies vary across an offering's life cycle. At the introduction stage, companies typically offer a single product variant targeted at the most likely adopters. As the product enters the growth stage, the number of customers adopting the product increases, and so does the heterogeneity of these customers. To address the diverse needs of current and potential customers, companies add product extensions designed to better meet the needs of various customer subsegments. The number of product variants typically peaks at maturity and starts decreasing as the product enters its decline stage; profit margins shrink, and companies focus on best-selling products, phasing out products with insufficient volume to meet their profitability benchmarks.

In the same vein, the stage of an offering's life cycle can influence its communication. Thus, in the early stages of product introduction, the communication campaign aims primarily at creating awareness among early adopters, as well as among channel partners. As the product enters the growth stage, a company's communication goals shift to creating awareness of the product within the mass market while at the same time differentiating its offerings from those of competitors. As the product enters its maturity stage and the majority of customers are aware of the category benefits, the communication focus shifts from creating awareness of the category benefits to differentiating the company's offering by highlighting its benefits vis-à-vis the competition. This emphasis on product differentiation continues as the product enters its decline stage; however, at this point overall communication expenditures tend to decline.

An important aspect of new product decisions involves managing the evolution of the company's products over time. As products become obsolete, they are often replaced by a new generation of products that take advantage of changes in target markets, such as changes in customer preferences, alterations in the competitive landscape, advances in technology, and changes in the regulatory environment. Innovation enables companies to extend the life cycle of their individual products (Figure 3). To illustrate, consider Gillette's product development strategy leading to the introduction of Fusion, its eighth-generation wet-shaving razor. Gillette's original razor, introduced in 1903 was replaced by the second-generation razor Trac II (1971), followed by Sensor (1990), Sensor Excel (1995), MACH3 (1998), MACH3 Turbo (2002), M3Power (2004), and Fusion (2006).

Figure 3. Extending Product Life Cycle through Innovation[2]

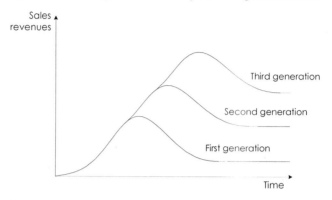

When developing a new generation of products, companies often develop strategies to make the earlier generation obsolete, a process often referred to as planned obsolescence. Planned obsolescence involves designing new products in a way that makes prior generations inferior (and, therefore, obsolete) on key dimensions such as functionality, compatibility, and style. To illustrate, to facilitate user migration to later versions of their software, companies systematically terminate support (e.g., software upgrades) for earlier versions. In addition, the added functionality of the new generation of software often limits its backward compatibility; as a result, once the new software has been adopted by a critical mass of users, the earlier versions become obsolete because of their incompatibility.

One important implication of planned obsolescence for new product design involves managing a new product's costs by optimizing its performance during its expected lifetime, a process often referred to as value engineering. For example, a company expecting its product to be obsolete within a given time frame may optimize costs by designing the durability of a product's components according to the expected product lifetime.

SUMMARY

The term "new product" is used in reference to offerings that are new to the company but not new to target customers (new-to-the-company products), as well as to products and services that are new to both the company and its target customers (new-to-the-world products).

Understanding market demand is essential for managing new products. There are two basic types of demand forecasting methods: methods that involve collecting primary data (data collected especially for the purposes of demand forecasting) and methods that involve analyzing secondary data (existing data). Primary-data forecasting comprises two types of methods: expert-judgment forecasts and customer-research forecasts. Forecast methods involving already existing (secondary) data include offering-specific forecasting, forecasting by analogy, and category-based forecasting. Because most forecasting methods are based on a variety of assumptions, a more accurate forecast can be achieved by using multiple methods.

The process of new product adoption can be represented by an S-shaped curve that depicts the total number of adoptions at any given point in time, as well as by a bell-shaped curve depicting the number of new (rather than total) adoptions of the innovation at any given point in time. The product life cycle describes the general trend of products and services as they progress through different stages in the marketplace: introduction, growth, maturity, and decline. Because the stages in the product life cycle are characterized by different market conditions, different stages require different marketing strategies.

RELEVANT CONCEPTS

Brand Development Index (BDI): A measure of the degree to which sales of a given offering (or a product line associated with a particular brand) have captured the total market potential in a particular geographical area. BDI quantifies the sales potential of a given brand in a particular market.

$$BDI = \frac{\text{Percent of an offering's total U.S. sales in market X}}{\text{Percent of the total U.S. population in market X}}$$

Category Development Index (CDI): A measure of the degree to which sales in a given category have captured the total market potential in a particular geographical area. CDI quantifies the sales potential of a given category in a particular market.

$$CDI = \frac{\text{Percent of a category's total U.S. sales in market X}}{\text{Percent of the total U.S. population in market X}}$$

Delphi Method: A popular method for eliciting group expert judgments, named after the site of the most revered oracle in ancient Greece, the Temple of Apollo at Delphi. The Delphi method involves multiple rounds of collecting anonymous expert opinions. The primary goal of the Delphi method is to ensure an accurate forecast from a group of experts by controlling for many of the potential decision biases, such as social conformity (agreeing with the majority), status (seniority within the organization), confirmation bias (ignoring new information that is inconsistent with the original forecast), and other related effects (experts' ability to eloquently articulate their forecast). To achieve this degree of control, individual forecasts are collected by a moderator who ensures anonymity of the experts' opinions. Each forecast typically consists of two parts: the forecast and its rationale. In the Delphi method, after each round of forecast elicitation, the moderator provides the experts with the anonymous forecasts and their rationale, and gives them the option to revise their opinion. This process is repeated until a consensus is reached. In cases where consensus is unlikely after several rounds, the individual forecasts are typically aggregated into an overall estimate (e.g., by averaging the individual numeric forecasts).

RELEVANT FRAMEWORKS: ROGERS' MODEL OF ADOPTION OF INNOVATIONS

The key premise underlying the Rogers model is that some consumers are inevitably more open to innovations than others.[3] Based on the relative time of adoption of innovations, the Rogers model distinguishes five categories of customers (Figure 4): innovators (the first 2.5% of the adopters), early adopters (the 13.5% of the adopters following the innovators), early majority (the next 34% of adopters), late majority (the next 34%), and laggards (the remaining 16%).

Figure 4. Rogers' Categorization of Customers Based on the Time of Adoption of Innovation

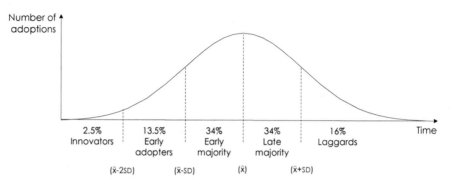

The respective percentage values associated with each category are based on the assumption that the process of adoption of innovations can be represented by a normal distribution, which is defined by two key parameters: its mean ($\bar{x}$) and its standard deviation (SD), a measure of the variation from the mean. In this context, the early and late majorities are defined as being one standard deviation from the mean (34%), whereas early adopters are defined as being two standard deviations from the mean. This classification is not symmetric: There are three categories on the left of the mean and only two on the right. The reason is that the segment on the far left end is further divided into two categories: innovators and early adopters, which cumulatively add up to the size of the laggards segment on the right. The rationale for this division is that these two categories display distinct patterns of adoption behavior and, therefore, from a theoretical standpoint, need to be considered separately.

Despite its popularity, the Rogers model has a number of limitations. One of its key limitations is that it is essentially a classification model; although it identifies the five different categories of adopters of innovation, it does not explain the factors that determine this classification. For example, this model does not offer a decision rule to determine whether a particular individual will become an early adopter or a laggard. Another limitation is that individuals' classification into one of the five categories is linked to relatively stable personality traits, even though in reality individuals who are innovators in one domain often may be laggards in another. Additional limitations can be traced back to some of its assumptions, such as the normally shaped distribution of adoption of innovation across the population and the preset percentage allocation of individuals into each of the five categories. As a result, the application of the Rogers model is limited to a general description of the adoption of innovations process and to classifying adopters into one of the five categories for descriptive purposes.

RELEVANT FRAMEWORKS: MOORE'S MODEL OF ADOPTION OF NEW TECHNOLOGIES

A popular application of Rogers' diffusion theory to technology products is Moore's[4] "chasm" model.[5] Moore argued that the adoption of technology-based innovations is discontinuous because different groups of adopters have different adoption patterns and, therefore, require different marketing strategies. Moore's model identifies five distinct categories of customers based on their attitudes toward technology, which correspond to Rogers' five categories: technology enthusiasts (innovators), visionaries (early adopters), pragmatists (early majority), conservatives (late majority), and skeptics (laggards). These five categories of adopters can be described as follows:

- **Technology enthusiasts** (innovators) are fundamentally committed to new technology and derive utility from being the first to experience new technologies.

- **Visionaries** (early adopters) are among the first to apply new technologies to solve problems and exploit opportunities in the marketplace.

- **Pragmatists** (early majority) view technology innovation as a productivity tool. Unlike enthusiasts, they do not appreciate technology for its own sake. Unlike visionaries, they do not use technology innovations to change existing business models but rather to optimize the efficiency and effectiveness of existing business models.

- **Conservatives** (late majority) are generally pessimistic about their ability to significantly benefit from new technological innovations and are reluctant to adopt them.

- **Skeptics** (laggards) are critics of any innovative technology and are not likely to adopt such technologies even when they offer distinct benefits.

Unlike Rogers' model, which implies smooth and continuous progression across segments over the life of an offering, Moore's model assumes that the adoption of technology-based innovations follows a discontinuous pattern. This discontinuity in the adoption process is attributed to the fact that different groups of adopters have different adoption patterns and, therefore, require different marketing strategies. Thus, once a technology has reached its market potential within a given segment, it may not naturally roll over to the next segment.

To illustrate, even though an innovation has been adopted by technology enthusiasts, it may never be widely accepted by the next segment, the visionaries. In this context, a company's biggest hurdle in promoting technology innovations is to bridge the gaps among different segments. According to Moore, the key gap among segments—typically referred to as a "chasm"—is the one between the early market (enthusiasts and visionaries) and the mainstream market (pragmatists, conservatives, and skeptics). In this context, the chasm describes the impediments to mainstream commercialization of technology innovations that prevent pioneers from gaining mainstream acceptance of their offerings (Figure 5). Thus, to be successful, an offering needs to "cross the chasm" between the early and the mainstream market.

Figure 5. Moore's Application of Rogers' Model to Technology Markets

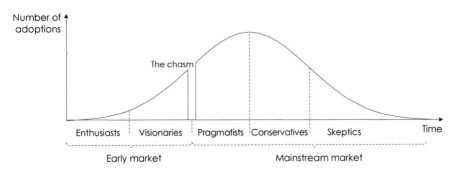

To avoid the perils of discontinuity of adoption of innovations, Moore's model suggests promoting innovations first to technology enthusiasts so that they help educate visionaries. Visionaries, in turn, are likely to serve as a reference for pragmatists, one of the two largest market segments. Leveraging its success with pragmatists, the company should be able to gain the know-how and achieve the economies of scale necessary to make the product reliable and inexpensive, allowing it to meet the needs of conservatives. With respect to skeptics, referred to as the "gadflies of high tech," the prescription is to let them be and not promote the innovation to them.

Despite the intuitive appeal of the idea that customers vary in terms of the speed and likelihood of adopting new technologies, Moore's model of technology adoption is subject to several important assumptions that limit the validity of its predictions. Dividing adopters into five distinct categories, as well as predefining the size of each category (e.g., enthusiasts/innovators are the first 2.5% of adopters), often involves an unrealistic assumption that does not apply to all high-tech innovations. This assumption is not an issue for Rogers' model, which assumes continuous adoption across different segments. In contrast, because the presence of gaps among segments is the cornerstone assumption for Moore's model, the identification and size of each segment are crucial. To illustrate, the assumption that a pronounced discontinuity (chasm) in the adoption process is likely to occur after 16% of customers (the "early market") have adopted the product is not likely to hold universally across different innovation types and industries. In the same vein, relative segment sizes are likely to be a function of the degree to which the technology appeals to the broader market. Indeed, certain types of innovations are likely to have much broader appeal than others and, as a result, the dynamics of their adoption patterns are likely to vary.

Additional Readings

Christensen, Clayton (1997), *The Innovator's Dilemma: When New Technologies Cause Great Firms to Fail*. Boston, MA: Harvard Business School Press.

Davidow, William H. (1986), *Marketing High Technology: An Insider's View*. New York, NY: Free Press.

Rogers, Everett M. (2003), *Diffusion of Innovations* (5th ed.). New York, NY: Free Press.

Grieves, Michael (2006), *Product Lifecycle Management: Driving the Next Generation of Lean Thinking*. New York, NY: McGraw-Hill.

Notes

[1] Adapted from Levitt, Theodore (1965), "Exploit the Product Life Cycle," *Harvard Business Review*, 43, (November–December), 81–94.

[2] Adapted from Christensen, Clayton (1997), *The Innovator's Dilemma: When New Technologies Cause Great Firms to Fail*. Boston, MA: Harvard Business School Press.

[3] Rogers, Everett M. (1962), *Diffusion of Innovations*. New York, NY: Free Press.

[4] Not to be confused with Intel's cofounder, Gordon E. Moore, widely known for "Moore's Law."

[5] Moore, Geoffrey A. (1991), *Crossing the Chasm: Marketing and Selling High-Tech Products to Mainstream Customers*. New York, NY: HarperBusiness.

CHAPTER EIGHTEEN

MANAGING PRODUCT LINES

The essence of the beautiful is unity in variety.
William Somerset Maugham, English writer

Product line refers to a set of related offerings that function in a similar manner, are sold to the same target customers, and/or are distributed through the same channels. Product-line management aims to optimize the value delivered by the individual offerings comprising a company's product line. The key aspects of managing a company's product line—managing vertical and horizontal extensions, managing product-line cannibalization, and using product lines to gain and defend market position—are the focus of this chapter.

Overview

The increased fragmentation of many markets calls for developing customized offerings that create value for each individual segment. The times when a company can fulfill the needs of all its customers are long gone; to successfully compete in today's environment, a company must develop and manage a portfolio of offerings that targets the "long tail" of the market. Even companies like Coca-Cola and PepsiCo that once were able to cover the market with a single product now find it imperative to extend and constantly reinvent their product line to address the needs of different customer segments.

The process of developing offerings that are part of a company's product line is similar to developing freestanding offerings—each offering should target a distinct customer segment and deliver superior value to these customers in a way that benefits the company and its collaborators. The main difference is that in the case of targeting multiple segments, in addition to developing a strategy to manage each individual offering, a company needs to develop a product-line strategy that delineates the relationship between the individual offerings in the company's product line.

Product-line management involves extending a company's product line by introducing new offerings as well as managing the existing offerings in the product line. Extending a company's product line creates customer value by offering a better match between a customer's preferences and the benefits provided by the company's offerings: The more extensive a company's product line, the greater the chance that each individual customer will find the "ideal" option. Extensive product lines are also preferred by customers who seek to explore new options and might feel that their choice is constrained by a limited roster of options.

Despite its apparent advantages, extending a company's product line can also have a negative impact on customers. Increasing the number of available options can lead to customer confusion stemming from the inability to choose among the options. Indeed, the premise for offering a greater variety of options is that it allows consumers to identify the "ideal" option. However, in cases when consumers do not have well-defined preferences, offering more choice can backfire, leading to greater confusion. As a result, buyers might defer their choice or choose an offering from a (competitor's) product line that offers greater simplicity of choice.

In addition to providing customer value, product-line extensions can create value for manufacturers by helping them manage their relationship with channel partners. Specifically, product-line extensions can help minimize conflicts that are likely to occur among distribution channels (e.g., mass-market retailers and specialty stores) that offer the same product at different price points to the same customers. Manufacturers can address such conflicts (also referred to as horizontal channel conflicts) by developing product lines comprising different versions of the same product that vary on minor attributes (color, packaging, and optional features), which makes their offerings in different distribution channels difficult to compare.

Developing an extended product line can also increase the adoption of offerings by distribution channels seeking a single supplier to provide the entire range of products sought by this channel's customers. Moreover, product-line extensions create value for manufacturers by helping deter market entry by competitors. The rationale is that competitors are less likely to enter markets with established offerings. Having an extensive product line also enables a company to literally "crowd out" the competition by taking up premiere shelf space in distribution channels featuring its entire product line.

On the downside, however, extending a company's product line leads to an increase in product development, production, distribution, and management costs. There is also the potential danger that instead of stimulating new customer demand, the new offerings will ultimately cannibalize sales of the company's existing offerings. Finally, a manufacturer's desire that a retailer carry its entire product line may clash with a retailer's profit optimization strategy, which often includes carrying only the most profitable, bestselling offerings from competing manufacturers.

Depending on the relationship between the individual offerings in a company's product line, there are two types of extensions: vertical and horizontal. These two types of extensions are discussed in more detail in the following sections.

Managing Vertical Extensions

Vertical extensions involve adding new offerings that are in different price tiers. Because a higher price is typically associated with better performance, vertically differentiated offerings differ in benefits such that more attractive offerings come at a higher price (Figure 1).

Figure 1. Vertical Extensions

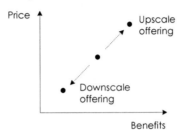

Depending on the price tier of the newly added offering, there are two basic types of vertical extensions: upscale extensions in which the newly added offering is in a higher price tier and downscale extensions in which the new offering is in a lower price tier.

Upscale Extensions

Upscale extensions involve extending the company's product line by adding an offering that delivers a higher level of benefits at a higher price. One of the main reasons for introducing an upscale extension is that it enables a company to capture a more lucrative, higher margin market. For example, to gain a foothold in the growing market for professional tools, leading home improvement company Black & Decker introduced DeWalt—a line of professional, high-end power tools.

In addition to providing access to higher end markets, upscale extensions can provide synergies with existing offerings. For example, adding an upscale offering can lift the image of the lower end offerings in the company's product line. Thus, by introducing a line of premium, award-winning Gallo-branded wines, E. & J. Gallo Winery aimed in part to strengthen the image of its lower end offerings.

Upscale extensions are often used to follow customers through different stages of their life cycle by creating offerings that fit their evolving needs and changing buying power. For example, building on the success of its low-priced cars, Volkswagen introduced the more upscale Jetta, Passat, and Phaeton, aimed at customers who seek larger, better performing vehicles.

Companies often introduce upscale extensions to gain a competitive advantage in developing advanced technologies. For example, car manufacturers often develop high-performance versions of their vehicles to strengthen their core competencies and further the advancement of technologies that can be used in their mass-produced lower end models.

Despite their multiple advantages, upscale extensions present numerous challenges. Developing upscale offerings usually requires specific resources—core competencies and strategic assets—that a company specialized in lower tier offerings might not readily possess. The lack of such resources might prevent a company from developing an offering that can successfully compete in the upscale market. For example, launching an upscale apparel brand requires a variety of specific resources, such as knowledge of fashion trends, product development know-how, high-end manufacturing capabilities, a reputable brand, and access to specialized suppliers and upscale distribution channels.

Because most companies do not readily have the resources necessary to introduce higher quality offerings, "organic" upscale extensions (internally developed by the company) usually take time to implement and are not very common. Instead, companies often gain access to upscale markets by acquiring existing high-end offerings. This acquisition strategy is illustrated by Fiat's entry into the racing car market with the acquisition of Ferrari, Gap's purchase of Banana Republic, and Marriott's acquisition of Ritz-Carlton.

Downscale Extensions

Downscale extensions involve extending the company's product line by adding an offering that delivers a lower level of benefits at a lower price. Downscale extensions are driven by a company's desire to increase its customer base by attracting less affluent customers that are currently not served by its offerings. Examples of downscale extensions include Armani's launch of Armani Exchange, Mercedes' introduction of the A-class, and Gap's introduction of Old Navy stores.

The main appeal of downscale extensions is the high volume of sales resulting from serving customers in lower socioeconomic tiers. Downscale extensions are especially beneficial to companies operating in industries requiring high fixed-cost investments in which economies of scale may be achieved, such as the airline, hotel, and automotive industries. For example, many upscale car manufacturers—including Mercedes, BMW, and Porsche—have opted to use their design and manufacturing resources to develop downscale product offerings.

Downscale extensions also enable companies to gain access to customers early in their life cycle by providing a lower entry point for a company's offerings. For example, Audi's "1" series cars provide access to younger customers, who despite current constrained resources are likely to evolve into a lucrative customer segment in the future. Downscale extensions are very popular among managers seeking to achieve quick results because they build on the company's existing resources and, unlike upscale extensions, are relatively easy to implement.

Despite their numerous advantages, downscale extensions have a number of significant drawbacks. A key concern is the threat of cannibalization of higher end offerings by the downscale extension (discussed in more detail later in this chapter). In cases when the extension uses the same brand name as the upscale offering, the downscale offering can also weaken the brand by creating undesirable associations with a low-quality/low-price offering. Another area of concern is that downscale extensions yield lower margins compared to higher end offerings and, as a result, they need to generate substantial sales volume to be profitable. Furthermore, serving price-conscious customers can be challenging because these customers tend to be less brand loyal than customers served by higher end offerings.

Managing Horizontal Extensions

Offerings in a horizontally differentiated product line typically belong to the same price tier and differ primarily in the type of benefits they offer (Figure 2). Unlike vertical extensions, in which the different levels of offering benefits can be clearly ordered in terms of their attractiveness (e.g., Ritz-Carlton is likely to be regarded as more attractive than Marriott), horizontal extensions do not imply such universal preference ordering. Instead, horizontal extensions are differentiated on benefits that are idiosyncratic and are likely to vary in their attractiveness across customers. For example, different designs, styles, colors, and flavors are likely to appeal to different tastes without necessarily implying differential pricing. Thus, even though prices may vary across horizontally differentiated offerings, they are not the key differentiating factor.

Figure 2. Horizontal Extensions

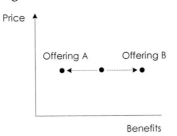

Horizontal extensions create value by providing customers with offerings that better match their preferences. Unlike vertical extensions, which provide a better preference match at different price–quality tiers, horizontal extensions aim to accommodate customers' tastes within a given price–quality tier. By providing an assortment of diverse options, horizontal extensions help companies fulfill the needs of customers with different tastes while at the same time satisfying the variety-seeking behavior of these customers. For example, Colgate-Palmolive, Procter & Gamble, and Unilever have introduced more than one hundred varieties of toothpaste aimed to appeal to consumers' diverse tastes while providing individual customers with a greater variety of options to choose from over time.

Because they draw on a company's existing core competencies and strategic assets, horizontal extensions are often easier to implement than upscale extensions. Moreover, because they are sold at similar price points and have a similar cost structure, horizontal extensions have profit margins comparable to the existing offerings, thus eliminating any cannibalization concerns—a key advantage over downscale extensions.

Despite their multiple advantages, horizontal extensions have several important drawbacks. A key concern is the cost efficiency of offering horizontal extensions. Indeed, because it is difficult to identify customers who share a particular taste, companies need to make their entire product line available to consumers so that they can self-select the options that fit their taste. The problem with this approach is that making the entire product line available to all customers can be resource intensive and ultimately cost inefficient. In addition to increasing the company's costs, extensive assortments of similar options can lead to customer confusion and choice deferral, especially in cases when customers are unable to readily ascertain which of the available options best matches their preferences.

Managing Product-Line Cannibalization

Companies typically extend product lines to grow profitability, usually by increasing sales revenues. When launching a new offering, a company expects that the new offering will generate additional sales by stealing share from its competitors. In the ideal case, all of the sales generated by the new offering will come from competitors' offerings or from growing the overall category. In reality, however, this rarely happens. A common side effect of launching a new offering is that, in addition to stealing share from competitors, it takes away share from a company's current offerings, a process commonly referred to as cannibalization (Figure 3).

Figure 3: Product-Line Cannibalization

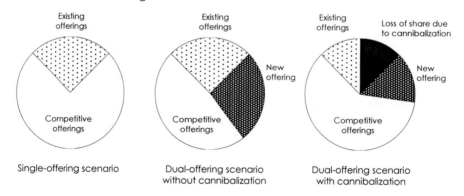

Cannibalization is a primary concern in the case of downscale extensions. This is because downscale extensions typically have lower profit margins compared to the offerings they are likely to cannibalize. Thus, every time a customer buys the new, lower margin offering instead of the higher margin one, the company generates less revenue. A key question, therefore, is how much cannibalization a company can afford before the new offering produces a net loss. The maximum amount of cannibalization of an existing offering by a new one is given by a metric commonly referred to as the break-even rate of cannibalization. Specifically, the break-even rate of cannibalization indicates the maximum proportion of the new offering's sales volume that could come from the existing offering(s) without the company incurring a loss. Calculating break-even cannibalization rates is discussed in more detail at the end of this chapter.

To deal with the threat of cannibalization, a company needs to ensure that the downscale extension is substantially differentiated from the existing offerings. When the downscale extension provides the same benefits as the original offering at a lower price, customers have no reason to prefer the higher priced offering and will ultimately gravitate toward the lower priced extension. Therefore, a key to sidestepping cannibalization is to meaningfully differentiate the downscale extensions from the original offering.

When differentiating its downscale extension, a company walks the fine line between curbing potential cannibalization—a strategy that calls for making the downscale extension less attractive than the existing offerings—and ensuring the competitive advantage of the downscale extension—a strategy that calls for bolstering the appeal of the downscale extension by making it superior to its low-priced competitors. In this context, a company can make one of two types of mistakes: "under-differentiating" and "over-differentiating" its downscale extension.

Under-differentiation involves a scenario in which the downscale extension provides similar benefits to those of the existing offering but at a lower price. Under-differentiation is typically caused by a company's desire to ensure the market success of its downscale offering by making it more attractive relative to the offerings of its direct competitors. The downside of this approach is that it also increases the attractiveness of the downscale extension vis-à-vis the company's existing offerings, thus fostering cannibalization.

Over-differentiation, on the other hand, involves a scenario in which a company, in its desire to minimize cannibalization, stretches its downscale extension so far that it becomes inferior not only to the company's existing offerings but also to the competitive offerings in the lower price tier. For example, in an effort to avoid cannibalization, Intel overstretched its downscale extension, Celeron, making it vastly inferior to its low-priced competitors. Over-differentiation can also result from over-pricing the lower end offering. For example, Gap Warehouse, the forerunner of Old Navy, failed because in an effort to avoid cannibalizing sales in Gap's core stores it set relatively high prices, which put it at a disadvantage relative to its direct competitors.

Managing Product Lines to Gain and Defend Market Position

In addition to creating value for target customers, product-line extensions can help companies gain and sustain market position. Three of the most popular competitive product-line strategies—the fighting brand strategy, the sandwich strategy, and the good-better-best strategy—are outlined in more detail below.

The Fighting Brand Strategy

A popular strategy to compete with low-priced rivals involves launching a fighting brand—an offering that matches or undercuts the competitor's price (Figure 4). For example, to compete with low-price rivals while preserving the market position of its flagship Marlboro brand, Philip Morris aggressively priced its Basic cigarette label, effectively making it a fighting brand. Similarly, Procter & Gamble launched the low-priced Oxydol laundry detergent to complement its flagship brand Tide.

Figure 4. The Fighting-Brand Strategy

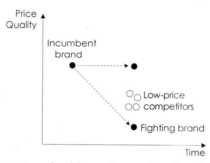

The fighting brand strategy builds on the notion that the offering's buyers have diverse (heterogeneous) preferences that cannot be successfully addressed by simply repositioning the existing offering (e.g., by lowering price). Specifically, this strategy assumes a two-tiered market in which some buyers are quality focused and others are willing to sacrifice quality for price.

The Sandwich Strategy

The sandwich strategy involves introducing a two-tier product line comprising a high-quality and a low-price offering, effectively sandwiching low-price competitors. This strategy is typically achieved by launching a downscale extension while simultaneously moving the existing offering upscale (Figure 5). For example, in anticipation of an inflow of cut-price competitors following the patent expiration of its blockbuster prescription drug Prilosec, AstraZeneca introduced a low-priced, over-the-counter version (Prilosec OTC) and at the same time replaced Prilosec with Nexium—a premium-priced and slightly more effective version of the drug.

Figure 5. The Sandwich Strategy

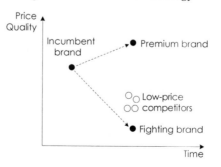

The sandwich strategy resembles the fighting brand strategy in that in both cases the incumbent brand introduces its own low-priced offering. Despite their similarities, the sandwich strategy differs from the fighting brand strategy in that, in addition to introducing a downscale offering, it also involves repositioning the core offering by moving it upscale. The upscale repositioning of the incumbent offering in the sandwich strategy reflects the change in the target market following the introduction of low-price offerings by competitors. After the incumbent brand loses some of its price-sensitive customers to low-price rivals, the remaining customers are, on average, less price sensitive and more quality oriented. As a result, the incumbent brand is no longer optimally positioned to meet the needs of its target customers, and can benefit from moving upscale. Thus, because it takes into account the changes in its customer base, the sandwich strategy can be viewed as a more comprehensive version of the fighting-brand strategy.

The Good-Better-Best Strategy

The good-better-best strategy involves introducing a downscale offering (fighting brand) as well as an upscale offering (premium brand) while preserving the core brand. Thus, the good-better-best strategy is similar to the sandwich strategy in that it involves the introduction of a low-priced offering. However, instead of a two-tier product line (moving its core brand upscale), the good-better-best strategy calls for launching a new premium offering that yields a three-tier product line (Figure 6).

Figure 6. The Good-Better-Best Strategy

The good-better-best strategy can be illustrated with Apple's response to low-price competitors of its iPod music player. Instead of directly competing with lower priced offerings, Apple extended its product line downscale by first introducing the iPod Nano and then the iPod Shuffle. iPod's good-better-best product line reflects Apple's view of the market as comprising three key segments: a segment seeking a fully functional player (iPod), a segment seeking basic functionality (iPod Nano), and a segment seeking a low-priced offering with limited functionality (iPod Shuffle). The good-better-best strategy also has been successfully employed by a number of other companies such as Microsoft (Works, Office Home Edition, and Office Professional),

Dell (Mini, Inspiron, and Studio laptops), and Gap (Old Navy, Gap, and Banana Republic).

The good-better-best strategy works well in tiered markets comprising three key segments: a quality-focused segment, a price-focused segment, and a segment seeking a compromise between high quality and low price. In such three-tiered markets, the two-pronged sandwich strategy would not work because moving the core offering upscale without having a mid-tier option leaves the company vulnerable to competitive offerings of mid-point quality and price.

In addition to being an effective tool to fence off cut-price competitors in three-tiered markets, the good-better-best strategy can be used in markets in which buyers have uncertain preferences. In such markets, buyers tend to prefer options that offer a compromise among the extreme alternatives. To illustrate, when choosing from a set composed of a high-priced/high-quality brand, a low-priced/low-quality brand, and an average-priced/average-quality brand, buyers often select the middle option because it allows them to avoid trading off price and quality. Buyers' tendency to choose the middle option in the absence of articulated preferences has important implications for choosing a strategy to compete with low-priced rivals. In this case, trying to "sandwich" the low-priced brand by simply launching a fighting brand and moving the core brand upscale without offering a mid-priced/mid-quality option might backfire because the "sandwiched" competitor might benefit from becoming the compromise option.

SUMMARY

Product-line management aims to optimize the value delivered by the individual offerings in a company's product line. The development of offerings that are part of a company's product line is similar to the development of freestanding offerings, with the main difference being that in addition to developing a strategy to manage each individual offering, the company needs to develop a product-line strategy that delineates the relationship between the individual offerings in the company's product line.

Depending on the relationship between the individual offerings in a company's product line, there are two types of extensions: vertical and horizontal. Vertical extensions involve adding new offerings that are in different price tiers. Because higher price is typically associated with better performance, vertically differentiated offerings differ in benefits such that more attractive offerings come at a higher price. Depending on the price tier of the newly added offering, there are two basic types of vertical extensions: upscale extensions in which the newly added offering is in a higher price tier and downscale extensions in which the new offering is in a lower price tier.

Horizontally differentiated offerings typically belong to the same price tier and differ primarily in the type of benefits they offer. Horizontal extensions create value by providing customers with offerings that better match their preferences. Unlike vertical extensions, which provide a better preference match at different price–quality tiers, horizontal extensions aim to accommodate customers' tastes within a given price–quality tier.

Cannibalization is a primary concern in the case of downscale extensions. The maximum amount of cannibalization of an existing offering by a new one is given by a metric commonly referred to as the break-even rate of cannibalization, which indicates the maximum proportion of the new offering's sales volume that could come from the existing offering(s) without the company incurring a loss.

In addition to creating value for target customers, product-line extensions can help companies gain and sustain market position. Three of the most popular competitive product-line strategies are the fighting brand strategy, sandwich strategy, and good-better-best strategy.

RELEVANT CONCEPTS: BREAK-EVEN ANALYSIS OF CANNIBALIZATION

The break-even rate of cannibalization indicates the maximum proportion of the sales volume of the new offering that could come from the company's existing offering(s) without incurring a loss. The break-even rate of cannibalization is calculated as the ratio of the cannibalized sales volume of the existing offering to the sales volume generated by the new offering at which a company neither makes a profit nor incurs a loss.[1]

$$BER_C = \frac{Margin_{NewOffering}}{Margin_{OldOffering}}$$

For example, consider a company launching a new product priced at $70 with variable costs of $60, which may cannibalize the sales of an existing product priced at $100 that also has variable costs of $60. In this case, $Margin_{NewOffering}$ = $70 – $60 = $10 and $Margin_{OldOffering}$ = $100 – $60 = $40. Therefore, the break-even rate of cannibalization can be calculated as follows:

$$BER_C = \frac{Margin_{NewOffering}}{Margin_{OldOffering}} = \frac{\$10}{\$40} = 0.25$$

The break-even rate of cannibalization in this case is 0.25 or 25%, which means that to be profitable to the company, no more than 25% of the sales volume of the new offering should come from the current offering, which in turn implies that at least 75% of the sales volume should come from competitors' offerings and/or from increasing the overall size of the market.

ADDITIONAL READINGS

Cooper, Robert G., Scott J. Edgett, and Elko J. Kleinschmidt (2002), *Portfolio Management for New Products* (2nd ed.). Oxford: Perseus.

Kotler, Philip and Kevin Lane Keller (2011), *Marketing Management* (14th ed.). Upper Saddle River, NJ: Prentice Hall.

Lehmann, Donald R. and Russell S. Winer (2005), *Product Management* (4th ed.). Boston, MA: McGraw-Hill/Irwin.

Jain, Dipak C. (2010), "The Sandwich Strategy: Managing New Products and Services for Value Creation and Value Capture," in *Kellogg on Marketing* (2nd ed.), Alice Tybout and Bobby Calder, Eds. New York, NY: John Wiley & Sons.

NOTE

[1] The break-even rate of cannibalization can be derived as follows. To avoid loss of profit across all offerings, profit from the new product must be equal to or greater than the lost profits from cannibalization.

$$Profit_{NewOffering} \geq LostProfit_{OldOffering}$$

Because profit is a function of unit volume and unit margin, the above equation can be modified as follows:

$$Volume_{NewOffering} \cdot Margin_{NewOffering} \geq LostVolume_{OldOffering} \cdot Margin_{OldOffering}$$

The above equation can be restructured as follows:

$$\frac{LostVolume_{OldOffering}}{Volume_{NewOffering}} = \frac{Margin_{NewOffering}}{Margin_{OldOffering}}$$

The left part of the equation is the ratio of sales volume of the old offering that was lost because of cannibalization of the sales volume of the new offering, which is exactly the definition of the break-even rate of cannibalization (BER_C). Hence:

$$BER_C = \frac{Margin_{NewOffering}}{Margin_{OldOffering}}$$

PART FIVE

THE MANAGER'S TOOLBOX

INTRODUCTION

There is nothing so useless as doing efficiently something that should not be done at all.

Peter Drucker

The first four parts of this book focused on presenting the key aspects of marketing theory, outlining a framework for applying this theory to marketing management. The application of this conceptual knowledge can be facilitated with a set of tools that help managers accomplish commonly encountered business tasks, such as solving marketing problems, developing positioning statements, and writing marketing plans. These three activities are briefly summarized below and discussed in more detail in the following chapters.

- **Solving marketing problems** involves evaluating the changes in the environment in which the company operates, identifying opportunities and threats, pinpointing the causes of performance gaps, and formulating effective action plans. The most common types of marketing problems and common strategies to use in solving them are discussed in Chapter 19.

- **Writing a positioning statement** involves developing a succinct description of an offering's targeting and positioning strategy to ensure a common understanding of the proposed course of action. The key aspects of developing a positioning statement are the focus of Chapter 20.

- **Writing a marketing plan** calls for the development of a written document that identifies a specific goal and details a course of action aimed at achieving this goal. The key principles of writing a marketing plan are the focus of Chapter 21.

A key strength of the theory presented in this book—in addition to its streamlined, logical, and value-focused approach—is that it can be readily applied to help managers solve practical problems in a way that enables them to achieve their strategic goals. In this context, the three topics discussed in Part Five help bridge the marketing theory outlined earlier in this book with managerial practice.

CHAPTER NINETEEN

SOLVING MARKETING PROBLEMS

A problem well stated is a problem half solved.

Charles Kettering, American inventor, engineer, and businessman

A n important aspect of a manager's job involves identifying and evaluating opportunities and threats facing the company, assessing the changes in the environment in which the company operates, determining the causes of performance gaps, and formulating meaningful action plans. The common types of marketing problems and strategies for solving them are the focus of this chapter.

Common Types of Marketing Problems

Depending on the type of problem facing the company, most marketing problems fall into one of the following three categories:

- **Opportunity-analysis problems** deal with identifying market opportunities, such as evaluating the viability of a new product launch and identifying growth areas for a company's existing offerings.

- **Market-response problems** deal with changes in the environment in which the company operates, including a new competitive entry, a competitive action, changes in customer demand, and changes in technology, legal regulations, and government policies.

- **Performance-gap problems** deal with discrepancies between a company's desired and actual performance on a key criterion, such as net income, profit margins, unit volume, and sales revenues.

Strategies for analyzing each of these three types of problems are outlined in more detail in the following sections.

Opportunity-Analysis Problems

Opportunity-analysis problems deal with finding growth opportunities, and typically focus on identifying customers whose needs the company can fulfill better than the competition. Common opportunity-analysis problems involve evaluating the viability of entering new markets and identifying growth opportunities in existing markets.

Solving opportunity-analysis problems typically involves three steps: identifying market opportunities, evaluating the viability of the identified opportunities, and developing an action plan to take advantage of each viable opportunity (Figure 1).

Figure 1. Solving Opportunity-Analysis Problems

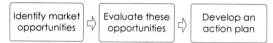

Identify Market Opportunities

Recognizing potential market opportunities is an essential aspect of ensuring a company's long-term growth. Market opportunities usually stem from changes in different aspects of the market environment—potential customers, competitors, collaborators, and context. For example, a market opportunity might result from a shift in customer needs, an exit of a key competitor, a change in the collaborator network (e.g., the emergence of new communication and distribution channels), and changes in the economic, technological, and regulatory context in which the company operates.

Identifying market opportunities involves discovering customers with needs that have not been fully met by the existing market offerings and that the company can fulfill better than the competition.

Evaluate the Viability of the Identified Opportunity

Not all market opportunities are viable options for a particular company. The viability of a market opportunity is determined by two key factors: (1) *company resources*—factors that enable the company to create superior value for target customers, and (2) *market potential*—the ability of these customers to create value (e.g., generate profits) for the company and its collaborators.

- **Company resources**. A key criterion for validating a market opportunity is the company's ability to fulfill customers' needs better than the competition. The company's ability to achieve sustainable competitive advantage in delivering customer value is determined by its core competencies and strategic assets (see Chapter 7 for more detail).

- **Market potential**. The viability of a particular market opportunity is also defined by the value it can create for the company, which in most cases is determined by its profit potential—that is, the revenue stream derived from the target customers, adjusted for the cost of reaching and serving these customers. Here, the revenue potential of target customers is determined by factors such as the size of the market, its growth potential, buying power, competitive intensity, and customer loyalty. The cost of reaching and serving target customers is a function of factors such as the company's ability to effectively and efficiently communicate and deliver the offering to these customers.

Propose a Course of Action

Analysis of the identified opportunity is usually followed by the development of a course of action designed to take advantage of it. When several opportunities are deemed viable, a separate action plan is developed for each one.

Most action plans follow the G-STIC framework, which involves defining the *goal* to be achieved by the proposed action; articulating the *strategy* — namely, identifying the target market and developing a value proposition for this market; detailing the marketing mix variables (product, service, brand, price, incentives, communication, and distribution) that define the offering's *tactics*; developing an *implementation* plan (e.g., the organizational infrastructure and scheduling); and defining the *control* aspect (e.g., performance metrics) of the offering.

The proposed course of action might involve either launching a new offering or optimizing an existing offering. The corresponding action plans are very similar, the key difference being that launching a new offering calls for developing a new action plan, whereas optimizing an existing offering calls for modifying a company's existing action plan.

Solving Market-Response Problems

Market-response problems depict a potentially important change in the environment in which the company operates that is likely to materially impact the company's business activities. Common market-response problems include factors such as a change in customer preferences, a competitive action, new government regulations, and the development of new technologies.

Solving market-response problems typically involves three steps: identifying the specifics of the market change, evaluating its impact, and developing an action plan to respond to the change (Figure 2). These three steps are discussed in more detail in the following sections.

Figure 2. Solving Market-Response Problems

Identify the Market Change

Market changes typically involve one or more of the following four factors:

- Changes in **target customers,** such as changes in customer demographics, buying power, needs, and preferences

- Changes in the **competitive environment,** such as a new competitive entry, price cuts, launch of an aggressive advertising campaign, and/or expanded distribution

- Changes in the **collaborator environment,** such as a threat of backward integration from the distribution channel, increased trade margins, and consolidation among retailers

- Changes in the social, technological, economic, political, legal, and physical **context,** such as an economic recession, the development of a new technology, and new legal regulations

Identifying the market change calls for pinpointing its primary cause. Identifying the drivers of change is important because it helps avoid misinterpreting the market dynamics and facilitates the development of an adequate response. For example, a competitive price cut can be caused not only by the desire to "steal" a company's customers but also by a variety of other factors such as inventory management issues (e.g., reducing the on-hand inventory) and product-line management issues (e.g., minimizing cannibalization of a company's other products). A competitive price cut motivated by an aggressive repositioning of the competitor's offering aimed at "stealing" the company's customers will typically require a very different response than a price cut driven by a competitor's inventory clearance or product-line optimization activities.

Evaluate the Impact

Depending on their potential impact on the company, most market changes can be viewed as either opportunities or threats.

- **Opportunities** are factors likely to have a favorable impact on the company. Factors typically considered opportunities include the introduction of favorable government regulations, a decrease in competition, or an increase in consumer demand. Evaluating opportunities follows the same logic as the opportunity-analysis problems discussed earlier.

- **Threats** are factors likely to have an unfavorable impact on the company. Factors typically considered threats involve the introduction of unfavorable government regulations, an increase in competition, or a decline in consumer demand. Evaluating threats follows the same logic as analyzing opportunities, with the key difference that instead of focusing on the positive factors, the focus is on negatives.

Note that most market changes can be framed as either an opportunity or a threat. To illustrate, a change in consumer preferences (e.g., a trend toward healthy food) can be viewed as a threat by fast-food restaurants because it is likely to reduce the demand for their services. It can also be viewed as an opportunity because it affords a chance to take advantage of this market change in a way that preempts the competition. Whether the market change is viewed as an opportunity or a threat depends to a large degree on the company's resources (core competencies and strategic assets) as well as its strategic goals and aspirations.

Propose a Course of Action

Analysis of the potential impact of the market change is followed by an action plan delineating the company's response. The key principle in developing an action plan is that the selected course of action should directly address the identified market change to take advantage of the opportunity or neutralize the potential threat.

The development of an action plan to respond to relevant market changes follows the G-STIC framework. In cases when the market change has been determined to have no bearing on the company's business (i.e., neither an opportunity nor a threat), no action is necessary and the company can carry out its existing action plan.

Performance-Gap Problems

Performance-gap problems involve a discrepancy between a company's desired and actual performance on a key metric, such as net income, profit margins, and sales revenues.

Solving performance-gap problems typically involves three steps: defining the problem, identifying its primary cause, and developing an action plan (Figure 3). These three steps are discussed in more detail in the following sections.

Figure 3. Solving Performance-Gap Problems

Identify the Performance Gap

Identifying the specifics of the performance gap typically involves evaluating the *magnitude* of the gap (e.g., whether it involves a minor shortfall or a fairly large discrepancy), as well as determining the *time frame* for closing this gap (e.g., whether the gap has to be closed quickly or over time). Knowing the specifics of the performance gap is important because they determine the scope and the type of company response needed. For example, large and time-sensitive performance gaps typically require more aggressive measures than those that are smaller in magnitude and/or allow a longer time horizon to close.

Evaluate the Cause

Understanding the primary cause of the performance gap is the key to solving it. Because profitability is the ultimate goal for most companies, performance gaps typically are either directly or indirectly related to profitability. In general, profitability gaps stem from three key factors: (1) decline in sales volume, (2) change in the per-unit price, and (3) increase in costs. These three factors are discussed in more detail below.

Declining Sales Volume

A decline in sales volume is typically caused by a decrease in the value of the company's offering to its customers. This decrease in value can be attributed to one or more of the following factors: (1) a decline in the attractiveness of the company's offering, (2) an increase in the attractiveness of the competitive offerings, (3) a change in customer needs and preferences, and (4) a decrease in the availability of the company's offering.

- **A decline in the attractiveness of the company's offering** stems from factors such as a reduction in product functionality (e.g., due to a decline in the quality of the raw materials and/or a technological change); deteriorating service quality (e.g., as a result of outsourcing); weakening brand power (e.g., due to poor brand management); and an increase in price (e.g., resulting from the company's desire to increase margins).

- **An increase in the attractiveness of competitors' offerings** can be caused by factors such as the introduction of a new competitive offering, functional improvements in competitors' products, increased service quality, increased brand power, a price cut, or the introduction of new incentives.

- **Changes in customer needs and preferences** can have a direct impact on the demand for the company's offerings. For example, an increased preference for a low-calorie food is likely to weaken the demand for calorie-dense meals, and increased price sensitivity (e.g., in times of an economic downturn) is likely to decrease the demand for upscale discretionary items.

- The decline in sales revenues can also stem from **a decrease in the availability of the company's offering** caused by factors such as limited manufacturing capacity, limited distribution coverage, low retailer support, and frequent stock-outs.

Note that these factors can influence a company's market share vis-à-vis the overall market size in different ways. Thus, a decline in the attractiveness of the company's offering is likely to lead to a decline in this offering's sales volume without necessarily affecting the overall size of the market. In contrast, a change in customer preferences can affect the overall market size without necessarily influencing the relative share of the companies competing in that market.

Changes in Price

Performance gaps also can be caused by changes in price, which can impact profitability in two ways. A decline in a company's profits can stem from a price increase when the increase in margins resulting from the price increase is not large enough to offset the corresponding decline in sales volume. A decline in a company's profits also can be caused by a price decrease when the increase in sales volume resulting from the price cut is not large enough to offset the decline in margins. Therefore, to evaluate the impact of changes in price on a company's profitability, one must evaluate the corresponding changes in profit margins and market demand.

Increasing Costs

A cost increase can be largely attributed to an upswing in some or all of the following four types of expenses: cost of goods sold, research and development costs, marketing costs, and other costs.

- **An increase in costs of goods sold** typically stems from an increase in the cost of inputs and processes to transform these inputs into the final product. The cost of inputs involves factors such as the cost of the raw materials, labor, and inbound logistics used in developing the company's offering.

- **An increase in research and development costs** can stem from an increase in the length of the product development cycle, as well as an increase in raw materials, equipment, and labor costs.

- **An increase in marketing costs** reflects rising expenditures for communication, incentives, and distribution. An increase in communication costs is typically caused by an increase in advertising, public relations, and social media costs. An increase in the cost of incentives is typically caused by an upturn in consumer promotions (price reductions, coupons, rebates, contests, sweepstakes, and premiums). An increase in distribution costs is typically caused by greater sales force expenses and trade promotions (trade allowances and volume discounts). Increased marketing costs can also stem from an increase in various other marketing costs such as marketing research and marketing overhead.

- **An increase in other costs** can be attributed to nonmarketing factors such as an increase in the cost of capital, legal costs, and various general and administrative costs.

Propose a Course of Action

Analysis of the causes of the performance gap facing the company is followed by an action plan delineating a course of action aimed at closing this gap. The key principle in developing an action plan is that the selected course of action should directly address the identified primary cause of the performance gap. For example, if a decline in sales volume stems from deteriorating product quality, then the action plan should focus on improving product quality. In the same vein, if profit decline has been attributed to a decrease in the availability of the company's offering, then the action plan should focus on improving the availability of the offering (e.g., increasing manufacturing capacity, improving distribution coverage, and reducing stock-outs). As with the other types of problems, the development of an action plan to eliminate performance gaps follows the G-STIC framework.

Summary

Most marketing problems fall into one of the following three categories: opportunity-analysis problems, market-response problems, and performance-gap problems.

Opportunity-analysis problems deal with identifying market opportunities, such as evaluating the viability of a new product launch and identifying growth areas for a company's existing offerings. Solving opportunity-analysis problems typically involves three steps: identifying market opportunities; evaluating the viability of the identified opportunities; and developing an action plan to take advantage of each viable opportunity.

Market-response problems deal with changes in the environment in which the company operates, including a new competitive entry, a competitive action, changes in customer demand, and changes in technology, legal regulations, and government policies. Solving market-response problems typically involves three steps: identifying the specifics of the market change, evaluating its impact, and developing an action plan to respond to the change.

Performance-gap problems deal with discrepancies between a company's desired and actual performance on a key criterion, such as net income, profit margins, unit volume, and sales revenues. Solving performance-gap problems typically involves three steps: defining the problem, identifying its primary cause, and developing an action plan.

Additional Readings

Chernev, Alexander (2011), *Mastering the Case Interview* (8th ed.). Chicago, IL: Cerebellum Press.

Farris, Paul W., Neil T. Bendle, Phillip E. Pfeifer, and David J. Reibstein (2006), *Marketing Metrics: 50+ Metrics Every Executive Should Master*. Philadelphia, PA: Wharton School Publishing.

Hurson, Tim (2007), *Think Better: An Innovator's Guide to Productive Thinking*. New York, NY: McGraw-Hill.

Walker, Orville C., Jr., John W. Mullins, and Harper W. Boyd, Jr. (2010), *Marketing Strategy: A Decision-Focused Approach* (7th ed.). London: McGraw-Hill.

CHAPTER TWENTY

WRITING A POSITIONING STATEMENT

Perfection is achieved, not when there is nothing left to add,
but when there is nothing left to take away.

Antoine de Saint-Exupéry, French writer, author of The Little Prince

The positioning statement is an internal company document that succinctly outlines an offering's targeting and positioning strategy to guide tactical decisions. It is a key aspect of articulating and implementing an offering's strategy and an important step toward ensuring the offering's overall success. The key principles of developing a positioning statement are the focus of this chapter.

The Essence of the Positioning Statement

Despite the importance a positioning statement plays in the development and implementation of an offering's strategy, many managers are not proficient in writing meaningful and actionable positioning statements. Moreover, there is confusion in understanding the very purpose of the positioning statement. Some confuse the positioning statement with the marketing plan, others think of it as the brand slogan that summarizes the essence of an offering's brand, and yet others confuse it with the tagline that appears in an offering's communication campaign. There is also confusion about the format of the positioning statement, whereby some managers think of it as a complex document whose value is determined by its overall length and the level of detail it provides. Although popular, these views do not adequately reflect the true nature and purpose of the positioning statement.

The positioning statement is a succinct document—usually consisting of a single sentence—that outlines the two key aspects of an offering's strategy: its target customers and its key value proposition for these customers. As such, the positioning statement is much more narrow in scope than the offering's marketing plan (in fact, it is just one component of the marketing plan). At the same time the positioning statement is broader than a brand slogan or an advertising tagline in that it encapsulates an offering's entire strategy (target customers and positioning) rather than reflecting the essence of the offering's brand or a particular message used in the development of a communication campaign.

The primary purpose of the positioning statement is to guide decisions related to the product, service, brand, price, incentives, communication, and distribution aspects of the offering. As such, the positioning statement aims to communicate the essence of the offering's strategy to all stakeholders involved in the development and management of a particular offering. The importance of the positioning statement as a communication device within the company is underscored by the fact that different entities within the company — research and development, marketing, sales force, senior management, finance, operations — often do not have the same level of understanding of the offering's strategy, such as who the offering's target customers are, why they would buy the offering, and what the company's stake is in ensuring this offering's success.

In addition to making sure that different company entities are on the same page, the positioning statement plays an important role in ensuring that the company's external collaborators — including research and development and product design partners, advertising and public relations agencies, channel partners, and external sales force — correctly understand the company's strategy with respect to the particular offering. Communicating the offering's strategy to the company's collaborators is particularly important because they are often less familiar with the company's goal and strategic initiatives. In fact, many collaborator conflicts arise from the lack of clear communication regarding the strategy guiding the company's offerings.

The positioning statement is often confused with an offering's value proposition. Although directly related, these concepts reflect different aspects of the marketing management process. An offering's value proposition captures all aspects — benefits and costs — of the value created by the offering for its target customers. The offering's positioning highlights one aspect of this value proposition (typically its key benefit) that is likely to make customers choose this offering. The positioning statement captures the offering's positioning in a succinct document that communicates the essence of the offering's strategy to company stakeholders and collaborators.

Structuring the Positioning Statement

A typical positioning statement consists of three key components: target customers, frame of reference, and reason for choice. These three aspects of the positioning statement are outlined in more detail below.

- **Target customers** are buyers for whom the company will tailor its offerings. The target customers are defined by the key benefit(s) they seek to receive from the offering as well as by their demographic, geographic, psychographic, and/or behavioral profile (see Chapter 4 for more detail).

- **Frame of reference** identifies the reference point used to define the offering. The reference point can involve (1) a customer need, in which case the offering is defined as the option that can fulfill that need, (2) a product category, in which case the offering is defined as belonging to this category, and (3) a competitive offering, in which case the company's offering is defined by its (favorable) comparison to the competitive offering. Positioning statements using customer needs or a product category as a reference point are also known as *noncomparative* positioning statements, whereas those using competitive offerings as a reference point are called *comparative* positioning statements. Because comparative framing assumes that target customers are familiar with the referent offering, it is more likely to be used by smaller share offerings to compare themselves (favorably) to the market leader. Following the same logic, market leaders tend to use noncomparative framing because comparing themselves to a lesser known offering is meaningless in the eyes of target customers while creating awareness of and lending credibility to the competitive offering.

- **Reason for choice** identifies the primary reason why customers will consider, buy, and use the offering. Most positioning statements identify a single reason for choice, although in some cases multiple reasons can be a viable option as well. Positioning statements using multiple reasons for choice often select reasons that are closely related and can be grouped into a single, more abstract benefit; using unrelated reasons for choice representing distinct benefits can present challenges because they might dilute the offering's positioning in the minds of its target customers.

An offering's positioning statements can be viewed as a concise version of its strategy. Indeed, the positioning statement comprises the two key components defining an offering's strategy: a description of the offering's target customers and an outline of its positioning (defined by the frame of reference and the primary reason for choice). Because it is a summary of an offering's strategy, the positioning statement is particularly relevant in business analysis.

Positioning Statement, Brand Slogan, and Communication Tagline

Writing a positioning statement is often confused with the development of a brand slogan and communication tagline. This is because all three capture certain aspects of the offering's strategy. Despite their similarities, however, these concepts are very different on several important dimensions, including their primary focus, structure, and target audience.

Unlike the positioning statement, which summarizes the offering's overall marketing strategy, the brand slogan and communication tagline focus on specific aspects—branding and communication—of the offering's marketing strategy. Furthermore, from a structural standpoint, the positioning statement also identifies the offering's target customer—unlike the brand slogan and the communication tagline, which capture only the offering's value proposition. Accordingly, the brand slogan and communication tagline are usually short phrases, whereas the positioning statement is typically a bit longer and is expressed as a sentence.

To illustrate, consider Gillette, the leading shaving brand in the United States. Its positioning statement can be written as: *For all men who shave, Gillette provides the best shaving experience because it uses the most innovative shaving technology.*[1] Gillette's brand slogan is much more succinct and memorable: *Gillette. The Best a Man Can Get.* Finally, one of Gillette's communication taglines for its Fusion ProGlide razor highlights a particular aspect of its razor: *Less Tug and Pull.* Similarly, BMW's positioning statement can be articulated as: *BMW is the best vehicle for drivers who care about performance because it is the ultimate driving machine.* BMW's brand slogan is: *The Ultimate Driving Machine.* And its recent advertising tagline is: *BMW. We Make Only One Thing: The Ultimate Driving Machine.*

Another important distinction between an offering's positioning statement, on the one hand and the brand slogan and communication tagline on the other is that they are written for different target audiences. The positioning statement is an internal company document aimed at company employees, stakeholders, and collaborators; it is not designed to be presented to target customers. In contrast, the brand slogan and the communication tagline are explicitly written for the offering's target customers. Consequently, the brand slogan and communication tagline are written as catchy, memorable phrases designed to capture customers' attention, whereas the positioning statement is written to be strategic and logical in nature.

Collaborator-Focused and Company-Focused Positioning Statements

So far, the focus of this chapter has been on writing positioning statements outlining the value of the company's offering for target customers. Delivering value for target customers, although important, is only one aspect of ensuring an offering's success. To succeed, an offering has to create value not only for its target customers, but also for the company and its collaborators. Accordingly, in addition to developing a positioning statement outlining the offering's value for target customers, managers also need to outline the offering's value for the company and its collaborators. The corresponding positioning statements can be summarized as follows:

- The **collaborator-focused positioning statement** identifies the company's key collaborators and delineates the offering's key value proposition for these collaborators. The core question this positioning statement must answer is: *Who are the offering's key collaborators and why should they support this offering?* To illustrate, consider the following trade-focused positioning statement: *For mass-market retailers, Gillette Fusion offers a high-demand product that will drive store traffic and provide high profit margins.*

- The **company-focused positioning statement** identifies the company's strategic business unit managing the offering and outlines its key value proposition for the business unit and the company. The core question this positioning statement must answer is: *Why should the business unit and the company invest in this offering?* For example, consider the following company-focused positioning statement: *Fusion aims to assert Gillette's position as the leader in the wet-shaving market, provide it with a technological edge over the competition, and ensure higher profit margins than its predecessor, MACH3.*

Note that unlike customer-focused positioning statements, which typically highlight a single benefit, collaborator-focused and company-focused positioning statements sometimes identify multiple benefits combining unrelated (e.g., monetary and nonmonetary) benefits. This in part is due to the fact that these positioning statements target business managers who tend to be more proficient in evaluating the variety of ways in which an offering can create company value.

SUMMARY

The positioning statement is an internal company document that succinctly outlines an offering's targeting and positioning strategy to guide tactical decisions. A typical positioning statement consists of three key components: target customers, frame of reference, and reason for choice.

Target customers are buyers for whom the company will tailor its offerings. The target customers are defined by the key benefit(s) they seek to receive from the offering as well as by their demographic, geographic, psychographic, and/or behavioral profile.

Frame of reference identifies the reference point used to define the offering. The reference point can involve (1) a customer need, in which case the offering is defined as the option that can fulfill that need, (2) a product category, in which case the offering is defined as belonging to this category, and (3) a competitive offering, in which case the company's offering is defined by its (favorable) comparison to the competitive offering. Positioning statements using customer needs or a product category as a reference point are also known as *noncomparative* positioning statements, whereas those using competitive offerings as a reference point are called *comparative* positioning statements.

Reason for choice identifies the primary reason why customers will consider, buy, and use the offering. Most positioning statements identify a single reason for choice, although in some cases multiple reasons can be a viable option as well.

To succeed, an offering has to create value not only for its target customers, but also for the company and its collaborators. Accordingly, in addition to developing a positioning statement outlining the offering's value for target customers, managers also need to develop positioning statements that outline the offering's value for the company and its collaborators.

POSITIONING STATEMENT TEMPLATES AND EXAMPLES

This exhibit presents four positioning statement examples that illustrate different ways of writing a positioning statement. Each example is offered as a template and a company-specific illustration. In addition, each example is given in two formats: one reflecting a noncomparative positioning that focuses on the needs of target customers and another that reflects a comparative positioning that explicitly compares the offering to its competitors.

Positioning Statement 1

This example illustrates one of the most common positioning statement formats.

Noncomparative positioning:

[offering] is an excellent [product category] for [target customers] because [the primary reason to choose the offering].

Aquafina [offering] *is an excellent bottled water* [product category] *for health-conscious consumers* [target customers] *because it is pure* [reason for choice].

Comparative positioning:

[offering] is a better [product category] than [competitive offering] for [target customers] because [the primary reason to choose the offering].

Brita [offering] *is a better source of drinking water* [product category] *than bottled water* [competitive offering] *for price-conscious consumers* [target customers] *because it costs less* [reason for choice].

Positioning Statement 2

This example is similar to the first one, with the key difference that the product category is not explicitly mentioned since the offering is representative of the category.

Noncomparative positioning:

[offering] is an excellent choice for [target customers] because [the primary reason to choose the offering].

Gatorade [offering] *is a smart choice for athletes* [target customers] *because it rehydrates, replenishes, and refuels* [reason for choice].

Comparative positioning:

[offering] is a better choice for [target customers] than [competitive offering] because [the primary reason to choose the offering].

Gatorade [offering] *is a smart choice for athletes* [target customers] *because it rehydrates, replenishes, and refuels* [reason for choice] *in ways water* [competitive offering] *can't.*

Positioning Statement 3

This example is similar to the first two, with the difference that the key benefit of the offering is explicitly articulated.

Noncomparative positioning:

[offering] is the [product category] that gives [target customers] [key benefit] because [the primary reason to choose the offering].

Mountain Dew [offering] *is the soft drink* [product category] *that gives young, active consumers who have little time for sleep* [target customers] *the energy they need* [key benefit] *because it has a very high level of caffeine* [reason for choice].

Comparative positioning:

[offering] is the [product category] that gives [target customers] more [key benefit] than [competitive offering] because [the primary reason to choose the offering].

Mountain Dew [offering] *is the soft drink* [product category] *that gives* young, active consumers who have little time for sleep [target customers] *more energy* [key benefit] *than any other brand* [competitive offering] *because it has a very high level of caffeine* [reason for choice].

Positioning Statement 4

This example offers a slightly different version of writing the positioning statement that begins with a description of the target customers. In addition, the key reason for choice in this example is articulated in terms of specific benefits (dependability = design quality + fast repair/replacement guarantee) .

Noncomparative positioning:

For [target customers] who seek [key benefit], [offering] is an excellent [product category] because [reason for choice].

For the tradesman who uses power tools to make a living and cannot afford downtime on the job [target customers], *DeWalt* [offering] *offers dependable* [reason for choice] *professional tools* [product category] *that are engineered to the highest standards* [reason for choice] *and are backed by a guarantee for repair and replacement within 48 hours* [reason for choice].

Comparative positioning:

For [target customers] who seek [key benefit], [offering] is a better [product category] than [competitive offering] because [reason for choice].

For the tradesman who uses power tools to make a living and cannot afford downtime on the job [target customers], *DeWalt* [offering] *offers professional tools* [product category] *that are more dependable* [reason for choice] *than any other brand* [competitive offering] *because they are engineered to the highest standards* [reason for choice] *and are backed by a guarantee for repair and replacement within 48 hours* [reason for choice].

ADDITIONAL READINGS

Barwise, Patrick and Sean Meehan (2004), *Simply Better: Winning and Keeping Customers by Delivering What Matters Most.* Boston, MA: Harvard Business School Press.

Kotler, Philip (1999), *Kotler on Marketing: How to Create, Win, and Dominate Markets.* New York, NY: Free Press.

Ries, Al and Jack Trout (2001), *Positioning: The Battle for Your Mind* (20th ed.). New York, NY: McGraw-Hill.

NOTE

[1] The examples used in this chapter are for illustration purposes only and might not adequately reflect the companies' current positioning strategies.

CHAPTER TWENTY-ONE

WRITING A MARKETING PLAN

Chance favors only the prepared mind.
Louis Pasteur, French microbiologist and chemist

The marketing plan is a written document identifying a specific goal and outlining a course of action to achieve this goal. The primary purpose of a marketing plan is to effectively communicate the company's goal and the desired course of action to relevant stakeholders: company employees, collaborators, shareholders, and investors. The key principles of developing a marketing plan are the focus of this chapter.

Overview

Writing a marketing plan is often confused with strategic planning, partially because strategic planning is frequently driven by the need to generate a marketing plan. Strategic planning and writing a marketing plan, however, are two different activities. Strategic planning is the process of identifying a goal and developing a course of action to achieve this goal. A marketing plan puts into writing an already identified goal and the decided-upon course of action. The marketing plan is the tangible outcome of a company's planning process.

Because marketing covers only one aspect of a company's business activities, the marketing plan is narrower in scope than the business plan. In addition to focusing on the marketing aspect of the company's activities, the business plan addresses technological, financial, operations, and human resource aspects. The marketing plan may include a brief overview of other aspects of the company's business processes, but only to the extent they are related to the marketing plan.

In addition to developing an overall marketing plan, companies often develop more specialized plans as well. Such plans include a product development plan, service management plan, brand management plan, sales plan, promotions plan, and communication plan. Some of these plans can, in turn, encompass even more specific plans. For example, a company's communication plan often comprises a series of activity-specific plans, such as an advertising plan, public relations plan, Internet plan, and social media plan. The ultimate success of each of these individual plans depends on the degree to which they are consistent with the overall marketing plan.

Three Key Principles in Writing a Marketing Plan

To be effective, the marketing plan must outline a sound business strategy and communicate this strategy to its target audience. The marketing plan must be:

- **Actionable**. The marketing plan should include a course of action aimed at achieving a specific goal. The proposed course of action typically involves developing or modifying one or more of the seven key marketing mix variables: product, service, brand, price, incentives, communication, and distribution.

- **Clear**. The primary goal of the marketing plan is to inform the relevant stakeholders about a company's action plan and convince them of the viability of the proposed action. Therefore, the marketing plan should be very clear in delineating the essence of the proposed action and the goal it aims to achieve. Because the marketing plan contains information concerning different aspects of the proposed action—its goal, strategy, marketing mix, implementation, and metrics for evaluating its performance—it is imperative to present the information in a systematic manner that underscores the logic of the proposed course of action. A poorly structured marketing plan is unlikely to effectively inform its target audience of the specifics of the proposed action and convince it of the plan's viability. The clarity of a manager's thought process is reflected in the organization of the marketing plan: streamlined marketing plans indicate streamlined business thinking.

- **Succinct**. Most marketing plans suffer from a common problem: they are unnecessarily long. Managers developing such plans are often driven by a misguided notion that longer plans are perceived to be more thorough and, therefore, somehow superior to shorter plans. While it is true that the length of the marketing plan is often used by some managers as an indicator of quality, more and more managers have come to realize that shorter plans are often better than longer ones. Most managers lack the time and/or desire to read long documents, especially when they abound with information that is not directly related to the problem at hand. Managers are overloaded with information, and the marketing plan should help them make sense of this information rather than contribute to information clutter.

The Key Components of the Marketing Plan

The marketing plan is comprised of four key components: (1) an *executive summary* that outlines the highlights of the marketing plan, (2) a *situation analysis* that examines the environment in which the company operates and identifies the target market(s) in which it competes, (3) an *action plan* that outlines the proposed course of action to create value for its target customers, and (4) *exhibits* that provide additional information about specific aspects of the marketing plan. The core of the marketing plan is the action plan, which outlines the company's goal and the proposed course of action. Because the action plan, in turn, comprises five different components—goal, strategy, tactics, implementation, and control (the G-STIC framework) — the company's action plan is often viewed in terms of eight key elements.

The eight components of the marketing plan can be summarized as follows.

- The **executive summary** is the "elevator pitch" for the marketing plan — a streamlined and succinct overview of the company's goal and the proposed course of action. The typical executive summary is one or two pages long and offers a summary of the key problem faced by the company (e.g., a market opportunity/threat or a performance gap) and the proposed action plan.

- The **situation analysis** section of the marketing plan aims to provide an overall evaluation of the company and the environment in which it operates, as well as identify the markets in which it will compete. Consequently, the situation analysis section involves three key components: (1) company overview, which outlines the company's strategic goals and current progress toward these goals, its core competencies and strategic assets, and its portfolio of offerings, (2) market overview, which outlines markets in which the company operates and could potentially target, and (3) target customers for whom the company will tailor its offerings.

- The **goal** section of the marketing plan involves identifying the desired outcome that the company aims to achieve, as well as the specific quantitative and temporal benchmarks characterizing this outcome.

- The **strategy** section of the marketing plan outlines the blueprint for achieving the company's goal. This section involves two key components: describing the target market (target customers, competitors, collaborators, the company, and the overall context) and designing the offering's value proposition.

- The **tactics** section of the marketing plan delineates how the desired strategy is translated into a set of specific actions. This section defines seven key decisions that managers need to make with respect to each offering: product, service, brand, price, incentives, communication, and distribution.

- The **implementation** section of the marketing plan outlines the organizational infrastructure, business processes, and scheduling aspects of executing an offering's strategy and tactics.

- The **control** section of the action plan indicates the procedures employed in evaluating the company's performance and analyzing the environment in which it operates.

- **Exhibits** typically are found in the last section of the marketing plan. The exhibit section helps streamline the logic of the marketing plan by separating the less important and/or more technical aspects of the plan into a distinct section in the form of tables, charts, and appendixes.

The eight core components of the marketing plan and their key aspects can be presented in the form of a flowchart as shown in Figure 1.

Figure 1. The Key Components of the Marketing Plan

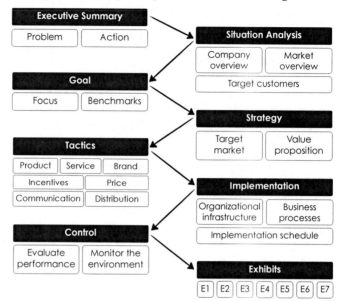

The ultimate goal of the marketing plan is to guide a company's actions. Therefore, the action plan is the focal component that ultimately determines the viability of the marketing plan. The other elements of the marketing plan—the executive summary, situation analysis, and exhibits—aim to facilitate an understanding of the logic underlying the plan and provide specifics for the proposed course of action. An outline for writing a marketing plan following the structure outlined in Figure 1 is offered at the end of this chapter.

SUMMARY

The marketing plan is a written document identifying a specific goal and outlining a course of action to achieve this goal. The primary purpose of a marketing plan is to effectively communicate the company's goal and the desired course of action to relevant stakeholders. Because it targets a broad audience with different levels of functional expertise, the marketing plan must be written in a way that is meaningful to each audience segment. To be effective, the marketing plan must be actionable, clear, and succinct.

The marketing plan is comprised of four key components: (1) an *executive summary* that outlines the highlights of the marketing plan, (2) a *situation analysis* that examines the environment in which the company operates and identifies the target market(s) in which it competes, (3) an *action plan* that outlines the proposed course of action to create value for its target customers, and (4) *exhibits* that provide additional information about specific aspects of the marketing plan.

The core of the marketing plan is the action plan, which outlines the company's goal and the proposed course of action. The action plan follows the G-STIC framework and, accordingly, comprises five key components—goal, strategy, tactics, implementation, and control.

THE MARKETING PLAN: AN OUTLINE

1. Executive Summary
Provide a brief overview of the situation, the company's goal, and the proposed course of action.

2. Situation Analysis
Provide an overview of the company and the market in which it operates, and identify its target customers.

2.1. *Company overview*. Outline the company's core competencies and strategic assets, its current product line, and market position.

2.2. *Market overview*. Provide an overview of the market (current/potential customers, competitors, collaborators, and context) in which the company operates and identify relevant opportunities and threats.

2.3. *Target customers*. Identify customers targeted by the company's offerings.

3. Goal
Identify the company's goal by defining its focus (e.g., net income) and performance benchmarks (e.g., quantify the desired net income and set the time frame for achieving it).

4. Strategy
Identify the target market and define the offering's value proposition.

4.1. *Target market*. Identify the target market—customers, collaborators, the company, competitors, and context—in which the company will launch its new offering.

- *Customers*. Define the need(s) to be fulfilled by the offering and identify the distinguishing characteristics (i.e., profile) of customers with such needs.
- *Collaborators*. Identify the key collaborators (e.g., suppliers, channel members, and communication partners) and their strategic goals.
- *Company*. Define the strategic business unit responsible for the offering, the relevant personnel, and key stakeholders.
- *Competitors*. Identify the competitive offerings that provide similar benefits to target customers and collaborators.
- *Context*. Evaluate the relevant economic, technological, sociocultural, regulatory, and physical context.

4.2. *Value proposition*. Define the offering's value proposition for target customers, collaborators, and the company.

- *Customer value*. Define the offering's value proposition, positioning strategy, and positioning statement for target customers.
- *Collaborator value*. Define the offering's value proposition, positioning strategy, and positioning statement for collaborators.
- *Company value*. Outline the offering's value proposition, positioning strategy, and positioning statement for company stakeholders and employees.

5. Tactics.
Outline the key aspects of the offering's marketing mix.

5.1. *Product*. Define relevant product characteristics (attributes, benefits, and costs).

5.2. *Service*. Identify relevant service characteristics (attributes, benefits, and costs).

5.3. *Brand.* Determine the key elements (name, logo, symbol, slogan, jingle) and the meaning of the offering's brand.

5.4. *Price.* Identify the price(s) at which the offering is provided to customers and channel members.

5.5. *Incentives.* Define the incentives offered to customers (e.g., price reductions), collaborators (e.g., trade allowances), and company personnel (e.g., bonuses).

5.6. *Communication.* Identify the manner in which the key aspects of the offering (i.e., product, service, brand, price, and incentives) are communicated to target customers, collaborators, and company personnel and stakeholders.

5.7. *Distribution.* Describe the manner in which the key aspects of the offering (i.e., product, service, brand, price, and incentives) are delivered to target customers, collaborators, and company personnel and stakeholders.

6. Implementation

Define the offering's implementation plan.

6.1. *Infrastructure.* Outline the organizational structure of the business unit managing the offering and its relationship with collaborators.

6.2. *Processes.* Outline the business processes involved in implementing the company's strategy and tactics.

6.3. *Schedule.* Delineate the implementation schedule.

7. Control

Identify the metrics used to measure the company's performance and monitor the environment in which the company operates.

7.1. *Performance evaluation.* Define the criteria for evaluating the company's performance and progress toward its goals.

7.2. *Environmental analysis.* Identify metrics for evaluating the environment in which the company operates and outline the processes for making adjustments to the plan to accommodate changes in the environment.

8. Exhibits

Provide additional information to support specific aspects of the marketing plan. This information may include target market data (e.g., industry overview, company overview, and customer analyses); financial calculations (e.g., break-even analysis, best/worst case scenario analysis, and customer value analysis); details pertaining to the marketing mix (e.g., product specifications, communication plan, and distribution structure); implementation (e.g., an overview of the infrastructure, processes, and schedules); and control (e.g., performance metrics and environmental analysis).

ADDITIONAL READINGS

Chernev, Alexander (2011), *The Marketing Plan Handbook* (3rd ed.). Chicago, IL: Cerebellum Press.

Calkins, Timothy (2008), *Breakthrough Marketing Plans: How to Stop Wasting Time and Start Driving Growth*, New York, NY: Palgrave Macmillan.

Donald R. Lehman and Russell S. Winer (2007), *Analysis for Marketing Planning* (7th ed.). New York, NY: McGraw-Hill/Irwin.

Kotler, Philip and Kevin Lane Keller (2011), *Marketing Management* (14th ed.). Upper Saddle River, NJ: Prentice Hall.

PART SIX

REFERENCES

CHAPTER TWENTY-TWO

ESSENTIAL FINANCIAL CONCEPTS IN MARKETING

Break-Even Analysis: Analysis aimed at identifying the break-even point at which the benefits and costs associated with a particular action are equal, and beyond which profit occurs. The most common types of break-even analyses include: break-even of a fixed-cost investment, break-even of a price cut, break-even of a variable-cost increase, and break-even analysis of cannibalization.

Break-Even Analysis of a Fixed-Cost Investment: Analysis aimed at identifying the sales volume at which a company neither makes a profit nor incurs a loss after making a fixed cost investment (see Appendix 2 for more details).

Break-Even Analysis of a Price Cut: Analysis aimed at identifying the increase in the sales volume needed for the price cut to have no impact on profitability (see Appendix 3 for more details).

Break-Even Analysis of a Variable-Cost Increase: Analysis aimed at identifying the increase in the sales volume needed for the increase in variable costs to have no impact on profitability (see Appendix 4 for more details).

Break-Even Analysis of Cannibalization: Analysis aimed at identifying the ratio of the cannibalized sales volume of an existing offering to the sales volume generated by a new offering at which a company neither makes a profit nor incurs a loss (see Chapter 18 for more details).

Compound Annual Growth Rate (CAGR): The year-to-year growth rate of an investment over a specified period.

Contribution Margin ($): When expressed in monetary terms ($), contribution margin typically refers to the difference between total revenue and total variable costs. Contribution margin can also be calculated on a per-unit basis as the difference between the unit selling price and the unit variable cost. The per-unit margin, expressed in monetary terms ($), is also referred to as contribution (i.e., the dollar amount that each unit sold "contributes" to the payment of fixed costs).

$$\text{Contribution margin}_{\text{Total}}(\$) = \text{Revenue}_{\text{Total}} - \text{Variable costs}_{\text{Total}}$$

$$\text{Contribution margin}_{\text{Unit}}(\$) = \text{Price}_{\text{Unit}} - \text{Variable costs}_{\text{Unit}}$$

Contribution Margin (%): When expressed in percentages (%), contribution margin typically refers to the ratio of the difference between total revenue and total variable costs to total revenue. Contribution margin can also be expressed as the ratio of unit contribution to unit selling price.

$$\text{Contribution margin (\%)} = \frac{\text{Revenue}_{\text{Total}} - \text{Variable cost}_{\text{Total}}}{\text{Revenue}_{\text{Total}}} = \frac{\text{Price}_{\text{Unit}} - \text{Variable cost}_{\text{Unit}}}{\text{Price}_{\text{Unit}}}$$

Cost of Goods Sold (COGS): Expenses directly related to creating the goods or services being sold. Cost of goods sold can have a variable (e.g., cost of raw materials, cost of turning raw materials into goods) and a fixed component (e.g., depreciation of equipment).

Economic Value Analysis: The process of translating the nonmonetary (i.e., functional and psychological) aspects of an offering's value proposition into financial terms.

Fixed Costs: Expenses that do not fluctuate with output volume within a relevant period (see Appendix 1 for more details).

Goodwill: Accounting term referring to a company's intangible assets. Goodwill is recorded on a company's books when it acquires another company and pays a premium over the listed book value of its assets. The excess paid is categorized as goodwill, added to the acquiring company's balance sheet as an asset, and then depreciated over time (usually fifteen years). The U.S. Internal Revenue Code defines goodwill as the value of a trade or business attributable to the expectancy of continued customer patronage. Such value results from several factors, including quality product lines and stable employees.

Gross (Profit) Margin: The ratio of gross (total) profit to gross (total) revenue (sometimes also used as a synonym for gross profit). Gross margin analysis is a useful tool because it implicitly includes unit selling prices of products or services, unit costs, and unit volume. Note, however, the difference between gross margin and contribution margin: Contribution margin includes all variable costs; in contrast, gross margin includes some, but often not all, variable costs, a number of which can be part of the operating margin.

$$\text{Gross margin} = \frac{\text{Gross profit}}{\text{Gross revenue}} = \frac{\text{Gross revenue} - \text{Cost of goods sold}}{\text{Gross revenue}}$$

Gross Profit: The difference between gross (total) revenue and total cost of goods sold. Gross profit can also be calculated on a per-unit basis as the difference between unit selling price and unit cost of goods sold. For example, if a company sells 100 units, each priced at $1 and each costing the company $.30 to manufacture, then the unit gross profit is $.70, the total gross profit is $70, and the unit and total gross margins are 70%.

$$\text{Gross profit}_{\text{Total}} = \text{Revenue}_{\text{Total}} - \text{Cost of goods sold}_{\text{Total}}$$

$$\text{Gross profit}_{\text{Unit}} = \text{Price}_{\text{Unit}} - \text{Cost of goods sold}_{\text{Unit}}$$

Gross Revenue: Total receipts from a company's business activities.

Income Statement: Financial document showing a company's income and expenses over a given period (see Appendix 5 for more details).

Internal Rate of Return (IRR): The annualized effective compounded return rate that can be earned on the invested capital (i.e., the yield on the investment).

Margin: The difference between two factors, typically expressed either in monetary terms or percentages. There are two types of margins: (1) contribution margins, which reflect the relationship between variable and fixed costs and (2) income margins, which reflect the relationships between a company's gross (total) profit, income, and gross (total) revenue.

Marginal Cost: The cost of producing one extra unit.

Market Share: An offering's share of the total sales of all offerings within the product category in which the brand competes. Market share is determined by dividing an offering's sales volume by the total category sales volume. Sales can be defined in terms of revenues or on a unit basis (e.g., number of items sold or number of customers served).

$$\text{Market share} = \frac{\text{An offering's sales in market X}}{\text{Total sales in market X}}$$

Market Size: Monetary value of an existing or potential market, typically measured on an annual basis. Market size is also used in reference to the number of customers comprising a particular market.

Markup: See *trade margin.*

Net Earnings: See *net income.*

Net Income: Gross revenue minus all costs and expenses (cost of goods sold, operating expenses, depreciation, interest, and taxes) during a given period of time.

$$\text{Net income} = \text{Gross revenue} - \text{Total costs}$$

Net Margin: The ratio of net income to gross (total) revenue.

$$\text{Net margin} = \frac{\text{Net income}}{\text{Gross revenue}}$$

Operating Expenses: The primary costs, other than cost of goods sold, incurred to generate revenues (e.g., sales, marketing, research and development, and general and administrative expenses).

Operating Income: Gross profit minus operating expenses. Operating income reflects the firm's profitability from current operations without regard to the interest charges accruing from the firm's capital structure.

$$\text{Operating income} = \text{Gross profit} - \text{Operating expenses}$$

Operating Margin: The ratio of operating income to gross (total) revenue.

$$\text{Operating margin} = \frac{\text{Operating income}}{\text{Gross revenue}}$$

Return on Investment (ROI): Net income as a percentage of the investment required to generate this income. Conceptually similar metrics are Return on Assets (ROA), Return on Net Assets (RONA), and Return on Capital (ROC).

$$ROI = \frac{\text{Gain from an investment} - \text{Cost of investment}}{\text{Cost of investment}}$$

Return on Marketing Investment (ROMI): A measure of the efficiency of a company's marketing expenditures. Most often calculated in terms of incremental net income, sales revenues, market share, or contribution margin. ROMI can also be calculated with respect to the overall marketing expenditures or to a specific marketing mix variable (e.g., branding, incentives, and communication).

$$ROMI = \frac{\text{Incremental net income generated by the marketing investment}}{\text{Cost of the marketing investment}}$$

Return on Sales (ROS): Net income as a percentage of sales revenues.

$$ROS = \frac{\text{Net income}}{\text{Sales revenue}}$$

Total Costs: The sum of the fixed and variable costs (see Appendix 1 for more details).

Trade Margin: The difference between unit selling price and unit cost at each level of a marketing channel (see Appendix 6 for more details). Trade margins can be expressed in monetary terms or as a percentage. Trade margins are typically determined on the basis of selling price, but practices vary among firms and industries.

Variable Costs: Expenses that fluctuate in direct proportion to the output volume of units produced (see Appendix 1 for more details).

APPENDIX 1: FIXED, VARIABLE, AND TOTAL COSTS

Cost accounting identifies three basic types of costs: fixed costs, variable costs, and total costs.

Fixed costs are expenses that do not fluctuate with output volume within a relevant period. Typical examples of fixed costs include research and development expenses, mass media advertising expenses, rent, interest on debt, insurance, plant and equipment expenses, and salary of permanent full-time workers. Even though their absolute size remains unchanged regardless of output volume, fixed costs become progressively smaller per unit of output as volume increases, a decrease that results from the larger number of output units over which fixed costs are allocated.

In contrast, *variable costs* are expenses that fluctuate in direct proportion to the output volume of units produced. For example, the cost of raw materials and expenses incurred by consumer incentives (e.g., coupons, price discounts, rebates, and premiums) are commonly viewed as variable costs. Other expenses, such as channel incentives (e.g., promotional allowances) and sales force compensation, can be classified as either fixed or variable costs depending on their structure (e.g., fixed salary vs. performance-based compensation).

Finally, the term *total costs* refers to the sum of the fixed and variable costs. The relationship between fixed, variable, and total costs is shown in Figure 1.

Figure 1: The Relationship between Fixed, Variable, and Total Costs

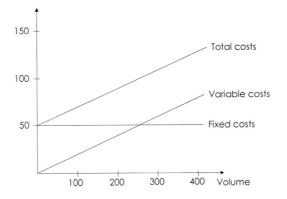

Deciding which costs are fixed and which costs are variable depends on the time horizon. For example, in the short run, the salaries of permanent full-time employees will be considered fixed costs because they do not depend on output volume. In the longer run, however, a company may adjust the number and/or salaries of permanent employees based on the demand for its products or services — a scenario in which these costs are considered variable rather than fixed. Thus, in the long run, all costs are considered variable.

APPENDIX 2: BREAK-EVEN ANALYSIS OF A FIXED-COST INVESTMENT

Break-even analysis of a fixed-cost investment identifies the unit or dollar sales volume at which the company is able to recoup a particular investment, such as research and development expenses, product improvement costs, and/or the costs of an advertising campaign. The break-even volume of a fixed-cost investment (BEV$_{FC}$) is the ratio of the size of the fixed-cost investment to the unit margin.

$$BEV_{FC} = \frac{\text{Fixed-cost investment}}{\text{Unit margin}}$$

Because the unit margin can be expressed as the difference between unit selling price and unit variable costs, break-even volume is also often given as:

$$BEV_{FC} = \frac{\text{Fixed-cost investment}}{\text{Unit selling price} - \text{Unit variable cost}}$$

The break-even analysis of a fixed-cost investment can be illustrated as shown in Figure 2.

Figure 2: Break-Even of a Fixed-Cost Investment

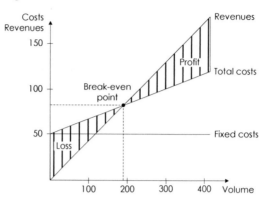

To illustrate, consider an offering priced at $100 with variable costs of $50 and fixed costs of $50M. In this case,

$$BEV_{FC} = \frac{\text{Fixed-cost investment}}{\text{Unit margin}} = \frac{\$50M}{\$100\text{-}\$50} = 1,000,000$$

This implies that for a $50M fixed-cost investment to break even, sales volume should reach 1,000,000 items.

In addition to the break-even analysis of a fixed-cost investment associated with launching a new offering, a company may need to calculate the break-even volume of a change (most often an increase) in its current fixed-cost investment. Typical problems to which this type of analysis can be applied are estimating the incremental increase in sales necessary to cover the costs of an R&D project, the costs of an advertising campaign, and even the costs of increasing the compensation package for senior executives.

To illustrate, consider the impact of an increase in fixed costs from $50M to $60M for a product priced at $100 with variable costs of $50. In this case,

$$BEV_{\Delta FC} = \frac{\text{Increase in the fixed-cost investment}}{\text{Unit margin}} = \frac{\$60M\text{-}\$50M}{\$100\text{-}\$50} = 200,000$$

This implies that for the $10M fixed-cost investment to break even, sales volume should increase by 200,000 items.

APPENDIX 3: BREAK-EVEN ANALYSIS OF A PRICE CUT

The impact of a price cut on profitability is twofold. On one hand, lowering price tends to increase the volume of units sold, thus increasing total revenues. On the other hand, lowering price decreases unit margin, thus lowering total revenues. In this context, break-even analysis estimates the increase in sales volume needed for a price cut to have a neutral impact on profitability.

To break even, lost profits resulting from a lower margin after a price cut must be equal to the additional profits generated by the incremental volume from the lower price.

Thus, to have a neutral or positive impact on the company's bottom line, the additional profits generated by the incremental volume resulting from a lower price must be equal to or greater than the lost profits that result from a lower margin.

$$\text{Profit}_{NewPrice} \geq \text{Profit}_{OldPrice}$$

Given that profit is a function of unit volume and unit margin, the above equation can be modified as follows:

$$\text{Volume}_{NewPrice} \cdot \text{Margin}_{NewPrice} \geq \text{Volume}_{OldPrice} \cdot \text{Margin}_{OldPrice}$$

Now, the above equation can be restructured as follows:

$$\text{Volume}_{NewPrice} \geq \frac{\text{Margin}_{OldPrice}}{\text{Margin}_{NewPrice}} \cdot \text{Volume}_{OldPrice}$$

Hence, the sales volume that needs to be achieved for a price cut to break even is:

$$\text{BEV}_{PC} = \frac{\text{Margin}_{OldPrice}}{\text{Margin}_{NewPrice}} \cdot \text{Volume}_{OldPrice}$$

In addition to calculating the break-even volume of a price cut, it may be useful to calculate the rate at which sales volume must increase for a price cut to be profitable. In this context, the break-even rate of a price cut (BER_{PC}) can be derived from the second equation as follows:

$$\frac{\text{Volume}_{NewPrice}}{\text{Volume}_{OldPrice}} \geq \frac{\text{Margin}_{OldPrice}}{\text{Margin}_{NewPrice}}$$

$$\frac{\text{Volume}_{NewPrice}}{\text{Volume}_{OldPrice}} - 1 \geq \frac{\text{Margin}_{OldPrice}}{\text{Margin}_{NewPrice}} - 1$$

$$\frac{\text{Volume}_{NewPrice} - \text{Volume}_{OldPrice}}{\text{Volume}_{OldPrice}} \geq \frac{\text{Margin}_{OldPrice}}{\text{Margin}_{NewPrice}} - 1$$

The left side of the equation reflects the increase in volume resulting from a price cut as a percentage of the initial volume before the price cut. Hence, the break-even rate (BER_{PC}) at which sales should increase so that a price cut has a neutral impact on profitability is:

$$\text{BER}_{PC} = \frac{\text{Margin}_{OldPrice}}{\text{Margin}_{NewPrice}} - 1$$

To illustrate, consider the impact of a price cut from \$100 to \$75 for a product with a variable cost of \$50. In this case, $\text{Margin}_{OldPrice}$ = \$100 – \$50 = \$50 and $\text{Margin}_{NewPrice}$ = \$75 – \$50 = \$25. Therefore, the break-even volume can be calculated as follows:

$$\text{BEV}_{PC} = \frac{\text{Margin}_{OldPrice}}{\text{Margin}_{NewPrice}} \cdot \text{Volume}_{OldPrice} = \frac{\$50}{\$25} \cdot \text{Volume}_{OldPrice} = 2 \cdot \text{Volume}_{OldPrice}$$

This essentially means that for the price cut to break even, sales volume should double at the lower price. It is noteworthy that relatively small changes in sales price can require what may appear to be a disproportionately greater increase in sales volume. Indeed, in the example above, a 25% decrease in price requires a doubling of sales volume.

Alternatively, one may calculate the rate at which the current volume should increase so that the price cut has a neutral impact on profitability.

$$BER_{PC} = \frac{Margin_{OldPrice}}{Margin_{NewPrice}} - 1 = \frac{\$50}{\$25} - 1 = 1$$

The above calculation means that for the price cut to break even sales volume should increase by a factor of 1, or by 100%.

APPENDIX 4: BREAK-EVEN ANALYSIS OF A VARIABLE-COST INCREASE

Break-even analysis of a variable-cost increase identifies the sales volume at which a company neither makes a profit nor incurs a loss after increasing variable costs. This type of analysis is used for estimating the incremental increase in sales necessary to cover an increase in the cost of goods sold, estimating the costs associated with increasing an item-specific level of service, and estimating the costs of item-specific promotions.

The basic principle of calculating the break-even point of an increase in an offering's variable costs is similar to that of estimating the break-even point of a price cut. The key difference in this case is that a decrease in the margin generated by the new offering is a result of an increase in the offering's costs rather than a decrease in revenues. Thus, the break-even volume of a variable-cost increase can be calculated as follows:

$$BEV_{VC} = \frac{Margin_{OldVC}}{Margin_{NewVC}} \cdot Volume_{OldVC}$$

Similarly, the break-even rate of an increase in variable costs can be calculated as follows:

$$BER_{VC} = \frac{Margin_{OldVC}}{Margin_{NewVC}} - 1$$

To illustrate, consider the impact of an increase in variable costs from $50 to $60 for a product priced at $100. In this case, $Margin_{OldVC}$ = $100 – $50 = $50 and $Margin_{NewVC}$ = $100 – $60 = $40. Therefore, the break-even volume of a variable cost increase can be calculated as follows:

$$BEV_{VC} = \frac{Margin_{OldVC}}{Margin_{NewVC}} \cdot Volume_{OldVC} = \frac{\$50}{\$40} \cdot Volume_{OldVC} = 1.25 \cdot Volume_{OldVC}$$

Thus, for the variable-cost increase to break even, sales volume should increase by a factor of 1.25, or by 125%.

Alternatively, one could calculate the rate at which the current volume should increase so that the increase in variable costs has a neutral impact on profitability.

$$BER_{VC} = \frac{Margin_{OldVC}}{Margin_{NewVC}} - 1 = \frac{\$50}{\$40} - 1 = 0.25$$

The above calculation implies that for the increase in variable costs to break even, sales volume should increase by a factor of .25, or by 25%.

APPENDIX 5: INCOME STATEMENT: AN OVERVIEW

The income statement is a financial document showing a company's income and expenses over a given period. It typically identifies revenues, costs, operating expenses, operating income, and earnings (Figure 3).

**Figure 3: An Example of Revenues, Costs, and Margins
as Shown in a Company's Income Statement**

Gross Revenues	
Product sales	$ 12,000
Services	3,000
Total (Gross) Revenues	15,000
Cost of Goods Sold	
Product costs	4,000
Services costs	1,500
Depreciation	500
Total Cost of Goods Sold	6,000
Gross Profit	9,000
Gross Margin	60%
Operating Expenses	
Sales and Marketing	5,000
General and Administrative	1,000
Research and Development	1,500
Total Operating Expenses	7,500
Operating Income	1,500
Operating Margin	10%
Interest payments on loans	500
Earnings before taxes	1,000
Provision for taxes	250
Net Income (Earnings)	750
Net (Profit) Margin	5%

APPENDIX 6: DISTRIBUTION CHANNEL MARGIN ANALYSIS

A useful approach to analyzing margins of the individual members of a distribution channel involves mapping the channel structure to identify margins for each channel member (Figure 4).

Figure 4: An Example of Distribution Channel Margins

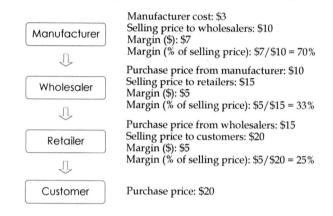

Manufacturer cost: $3
Selling price to wholesalers: $10
Margin ($): $7
Margin (% of selling price): $7/$10 = 70%

Purchase price from manufacturer: $10
Selling price to retailers: $15
Margin ($): $5
Margin (% of selling price): $5/$15 = 33%

Purchase price from wholesalers: $15
Selling price to customers: $20
Margin ($): $5
Margin (% of selling price): $5/$20 = 25%

Purchase price: $20

Margins are almost universally calculated based on sales revenue (sales price) rather than based on cost (purchase price). To illustrate, the margin for an item purchased for $10 (cost) and sold for $15 (revenue) can be calculated as follows:

$$\text{Margin} = \frac{\text{Revenue - Cost}}{\text{Revenue}} = \frac{\text{Selling price - Purchase price}}{\text{Selling price}} = \frac{\$15 - \$10}{\$15} = 33\%$$

Chapter Twenty-Three

Essential Marketing Metrics

What gets measured, gets managed.

Peter Drucker

Monitoring a company's progress toward its goals involves using performance benchmarks, commonly referred to as marketing metrics. Based on their focus, most marketing metrics can be divided into several categories: *company metrics,* which reflect a company's progress toward achieving its strategic goal(s), *customer metrics,* which capture customers' response to the company's actions, and *marketing mix metrics,* which depict an offering's performance on different marketing mix variables: *product, service, brand, price, incentives, communication,* and *distribution.* These different types of metrics are summarized in the following sections.

Company Metrics

Break-Even Point: The point at which the benefits and costs associated with a particular action are equal, and beyond which profit occurs (Chapter 22).

Compound Annual Growth Rate (CAGR): The year-to-year growth rate of an investment over a specified period of time (Chapter 22).

Contribution Margin ($): When expressed in monetary terms, contribution margin typically refers to the difference between total revenues and total variable costs. Contribution margin can also be calculated on a per-unit basis as the difference between the unit selling price and the unit variable cost (Chapter 22).

Contribution Margin (%): When expressed in percentages, contribution margin refers to the ratio of the difference between total revenues and total variable costs to total revenues. Contribution margin also can be expressed as the ratio of unit contribution to unit selling price (Chapter 22).

Goodwill: An accounting term referring to a company's intangible assets (Chapter 22).

Gross Margin: The ratio of gross profit to gross revenues (Chapter 22).

Gross Profit: The difference between total sales revenue and total cost of goods sold (Chapter 22).

Internal Rate of Return (IRR): The annualized effective compounded return rate that can be earned on the invested capital (Chapter 22).

Market Share: An offering's share of the total sales of all offerings within the product category in which the brand competes. Market share is determined by dividing an offering's sales volume by the total category sales volume. Sales can be defined in terms of revenues or on a unit basis (Chapter 22).

Market Size: The monetary value of an existing or potential market, typically measured on an annual basis (Chapter 22).

Net Income: Gross revenues minus all costs and expenses (e.g., cost of goods sold, operating expenses, depreciation, interest, and taxes) in a given period of time (Chapter 22).

Net Margin: The ratio of net income to gross revenues (Chapter 22).

Operating Expenses: The primary costs, other than cost of goods sold, incurred to generate revenues (Chapter 22).

Operating Income: Gross profit minus operating expenses. Operating income reflects the firm's profitability from current operations without regard to the interest charges accruing from the firm's capital structure (Chapter 22).

Operating Margin: The ratio of operating income to gross revenues (Chapter 22).

Return on Investment (ROI): Net income as a percentage of the investment required to generate this income. Conceptually similar metrics are Return on Assets (ROA), Return on Net Assets (RONA), and Return on Capital (ROC; Chapter 22).

Return on Marketing Investment (ROMI): A measure of the efficiency of a company's marketing expenditures. Most often calculated in terms of incremental net income, sales revenues, market share, or contribution margin. ROMI can also be calculated with respect to the overall marketing expenditures or to a specific marketing mix variable (Chapter 22).

Return on Sales (ROS): Net income as a percentage of sales revenues (Chapter 22).

CUSTOMER METRICS

Brand Development Index (BDI): A measure of the degree to which sales of a given brand have captured the total market potential in a particular geographical area based on the population of that area and average consumption per user nationally (Chapter 17).

Category Development Index (CDI): A measure of the degree to which sales in a given category have captured the total market potential in a particular geographical area based on the population of that area and average consumption per user nationally (Chapter 17).

Conversion Rate: The number of potential customers who have tried an offering relative to the total number of customers aware of the offering (Chapter 15).

Customer Attrition Rate (Churn Rate): The number of customers who discontinue using a company's offering during a specified time period relative to the average total number of customers over that same time period (Chapter 16).

Customer Equity: Monetary equivalent of the lifetime value of a particular customer to the company (Chapter 16).

Penetration Rate: The number of customers who have tried the offering at least once relative to the total number of potential customers (Chapter 15).

Retention Rate: The number of customers who have repurchased the offering during the current buying cycle (month, quarter, year) relative to the number of customers who have purchased the offering during the last cycle. Also used in reference to the number of customers who have repurchased the offering relative to the total number of customers who have tried the product at least once (Chapter 16).

PRODUCT AND SERVICE METRICS

Product and Service Preferences: A measure of the degree to which a product or a service appeals to current and potential customers. Preferences can be measured in absolute terms (independent from the other products and services in the marketplace) or relative to other offerings (the degree to which the company's products and services are better than competitors' products and services). Preferences typically comprise two dimensions: the valence of preferences (positive vs. negative) and the strength of preferences (strong vs. weak). Product and service preferences can be measured using a variety of techniques such as questionnaires, conjoint analysis, and perceptual maps.

Product/Service Satisfaction: A measure of customers' experience with a product. Unlike product-preference metrics that can be measured prior to purchase as well as post-purchase, satisfaction requires consumers to have actual experience with the product or service. Satisfaction is typically measured using a five-point scale with the following anchors: very dissatisfied, somewhat dissatisfied, neither satisfied nor dissatisfied, somewhat satisfied, and very satisfied.

BRAND METRICS

Brand Strength: A brand's ability to differentiate the offering from the competition and create customer value through meaningful associations. Unlike brand equity, which reflects the value of the brand to the company, brand strength (also referred to as brand power) reflects the value of the brand among current and potential customers (Chapter 9).

Brand Equity: The net present value of the financial benefits derived from the brand. Brand equity is a function of brand power, as well as a number of additional factors reflecting the company's utilization of the strength of its brand (Chapter 9).

PRICE AND INCENTIVES METRICS

Cross-Price Elasticity: The percentage change in quantity sold of a given offering caused by a percentage change in the price of another offering (Chapter 10).

Price Elasticity: The percentage change in quantity sold relative to the percentage change in price for a given product or service (Chapter 10).

COMMUNICATION METRICS

Advertising Awareness: The number of potential customers who are aware of the offering (Chapter 12).

Advertising Frequency: The number of times the target audience is exposed to an advertisement in a given period (Chapter 12).

Advertising Reach: The size of the audience that has been exposed to a particular advertisement at least once in a given period (Chapter 12).

Awareness Rate: The number of target customers who are aware of the offering relative to the total number of target customers (Chapter 12).

Comprehension: The degree to which the target audience understands the message embedded in the advertisement.

Cost per Point (CPP): A measure representing the cost of a communications campaign. CPP is the media cost of reaching one percent (one rating point) of a particular demographic (Chapter 12).

Cost per Thousand (CPM): A measure used to represent the cost of a communications campaign. CPM is the cost of reaching 1,000 individuals or households with an advertising message in a given medium (Chapter 12).

Exposure: The number of times a given advertisement has been seen by the target audience (Chapter 12).

Gross Rating Point (GRP): A measure of the total volume of advertising delivery to the target audience. GRP is equal to the percent of the population reached times the frequency of exposure (Chapter 12).

Net Promoter Score: A metric designed to measure customers' satisfaction based on their willingness to generate word-of-mouth recommendations for the company and its products (Chapter 12).

Recall: The degree to which the target audience remembers an advertisement (Chapter 12).

Share of Voice: A company's communication expenditures relative to those of the entire product category (Chapter 12).

Target Rating Point (TRP): A measure of the total volume of advertising delivery to the target audience. TRP is similar to GRP, but its calculation involves using only the target audience (rather than the total audience) as the base (Chapter 12).

Top-of-Mind Awareness: The first brand identified by respondents when asked to list brands in a given product category (Chapter 12).

DISTRIBUTION METRICS

All-Commodity Volume (ACV): A measure of an offering's availability, typically calculated as the total annual volume of the company's offering in a given geographic area relative to the total sales volume of the retailers in that geographic area across all product categories (hence, the term "all-commodity volume"). Also refers to the gross sales in a specific geographic area (total sales of all stores; Chapter 13).

Inventory Turnover: The number of times the inventory is replenished, typically calculated as the ratio of the annual revenues generated by a given offering to the average inventory (Chapter 13).

Same-Store Sales: A metric used in the retail industry comparing sales of stores that have been open for a year or more and have historical data to compare the current year's sales to sales during the same time frame last year (Chapter 13).

Share of Shelf Space: Shelf space allocated to a given offering relative to the total shelf space in a given geographic area (Chapter 13).

Trade Margin: The difference between unit selling price and unit cost at each level of a marketing channel (Chapter 22).

ADDITIONAL READINGS

Farris, Paul W., Neil T. Bendle, Phillip E. Pfeifer, and David J. Reibstein (2006), *Marketing Metrics: 50+ Metrics Every Executive Should Master*. Philadelphia, PA: Wharton School Publishing.

Jeffery, Mark (2010), *Data-Driven Marketing: The 15 Metrics Everyone in Marketing Should Know*. New York, NY: John Wiley & Sons.

Hubbard, Douglas W. (2007), *How to Measure Anything: Finding the Value of Intangibles in Business*. New York, NY: John Wiley & Sons.

Lenskold, James D. (2003), *Marketing ROI: The Path to Campaign, Customer, and Corporate Profitability*. New York, NY: McGraw-Hill.

Index

Terms listed in this index are grouped into four categories: (1) marketing concepts, (2) financial concepts, (3) marketing frameworks, and (4) companies, products, and brands.

Marketing Concepts

081012

CPSIA information can be obtained at www.ICGtesting.com
Printed in the USA
LVOW090937251112

308681LV00002B/14/P

9 781936 572151